Art and artists on screen

Other books by the same author:

Art since Pop, London, 1975
A Glossary of Art, Architecture and Design since 1945, London, 3rd ed. 1992
Van Gogh Studies, London, 1981
Art in the Age of Mass Media, London, 1983
Cross-overs: Art into Pop, Pop into Art, London, 1987
Design History and the History of Design, London, 1989

ART AND ARTISTS ON SCREEN

JOHN A. WALKER

Manchester University Press

Manchester and New York

distributed exclusively in the USA and Canada by St. Martin's Press

Published by Manchester University Press
Oxford Road, Manchester M13 9PL, UK
and Room 400, 175 Fifth Avenue, New York, NY 10010, USA

Distributed exclusively in the USA and Canada
by St. Martin's Press, Inc., 175 Fifth Avenue, New York, NY 10010, USA

British Library Cataloguing-in-Publication Data
A catalogue record for this book is available from the British Library

Library of Congress Cataloging-in-Publication Data
Walker, John Albert, 1938–
Art and artists on screen / John A. Walker.
p. cm.
Includes bibliographical references and index.
Contents: Cinema.
ISBN 0–7190–3780–8 – ISBN 0–7190–3781–6 (pbk.)
1. Art in motion pictures. I. Title.
PN1995.9.A73W3 1993
791.43′657 – dc20 9226877

ISBN 0 7190 3780 8 *hardback*
0 7190 3781 6 *paperback*

Photoset in Linotron Janson
by Northern Phototypesetting Co. Ltd., Bolton
Printed in Great Britain
by Bell & Bain Limited, Glasgow

Contents

List of illustrations

Acknowledgements

Thanks are due to the following people for providing information, comment and assistance: Louise d'Argencourt, Anne Baldassari, Liam Barnes, Morella Bello, Kevin Brownlow, Chris Bumstead (of the Tony Hancock Appreciation Society), Henning Carlsen, Madame Ines Clouzot, Philip Dodd, the late José Ferrer, Ray Galton, Terry Geesken, Heloise Goodman (of the Andy Warhol Foundation, New York), Peter Greenaway, Mandy Greenfield (of Aurum Press), Alistair Grant, Jack Hazan, Eliza Poklewski Koziell, Liz Reddish, Clive Phillpot, Brandon Taylor, Pierre Théberge and John Wyver.

In addition, I would like to acknowledge the following sources for information and images: Allarts, Amsterdam; Myles Aronowitz; The Art Institute of Chicago; Biblioteca Maruccelliana; The British Film Institute; Frank Buckingham; The Busch-Reisinger Museum, Harvard University; Ernst & Young Ltd, London; Peter Greenaway; Brian Hamill; Mike Laye; Middlesex University Library; Montreal Museum of Fine Arts; The Museé Picasso, Paris; Museum of Modern Art, New York; Rijksmuseum, Amsterdam; Solus Enterprises, London.

Special thanks are due to Katharine Reeve, my editor at Manchester University Press, for her unflagging enthusiasm and support.

Some sections of this book previously appeared as articles in magazines: 'The Rebel' in *AND: Journal of Art and Education*; and 'The American cinema's depiction . . .' (shortened version) in *The Times Higher Educational Supplement*; an article about 'Melancholia' and 'New York Stories' was also published in *Art Monthly*.

Program for Art on Film

The *Program for Art on Film* was established in 1984 as a joint venture between The Metropolitan Museum of Art, New York, and the J. Paul Getty Trust, Los Angeles. The goals of the program are to enhance public understanding and enjoyment of the visual arts through the media of film, video and television, and to improve the quality of film and video programs about art.

The program administers the Art on Film database and serves as an international clearinghouse for information about films on art. The Program also sponsors workshops and seminars, develops publications, and has produced a series of short films and videos involving collaborations between art scholars and film-makers. These productions were commissioned by the program's production laboratory, which functioned from 1986 through 1990 to experiment with innovative aproaches to presenting art on screen.

The Art on Film database

The Art on Film database is a critical inventory of bibliographic information about international film and video productions on the visual arts. Subjects covered include: fine arts, architecture, archaeology, photography, decorative arts, design, costume, crafts, folk arts, and related topics such as aesthetics and creativity. The database provides comprehensive coverage of English-language productions and extensive coverage of important productions from European and other countries. At present, the Art on Film database includes over 17,000 entries from seventy-one countries.

The database is maintained on computer, providing a unique central repository of information that can be accessed in a variety of ways: by title, length, date, credits, producing agency, country of production, artists' names, and so on, as well as by subject matter. New entries are added weekly, and other information (distribution sources, reviews, awards) is updated regularly.

Over one-third of the entries in this unique inventory of art on film include some critical data: citations of published reviews, festival awards and honours, comments by *Program for Art on Film* staff. Many current productions from the United States and overseas are evaluated by panels of experts in art history, education, film and television. These critical evaluations are incorproated into the database to assist film userrs in selecting the most appropriate films for their programs.

To obtain information from the Art on Film database researchers can apply directly to the *Program for Art on Film*. There is a modest service charge for searching the database and providing a printed copy of the search results.

Producers and distributors are encouraged to send information about their productions for inclusion in the database.

For more information, contact:
Program for Art on Film,
980 Madison Avenue, New York, NY 10021
Telephone: 212-988-4876
Fax: 212-628-8963

Introduction

'The historian's task is no longer to compile otherwise unknown sources and make them available to all: he must learn instead to use material that is already widely available . . . if historians today neglect audiovisual material, it will exist in spite of them as a history through pictures. Furthermore, the public will lose all interest in specialists, and the specialists themselves will be in a curiously divided position, conducting their research shut away in libraries, but turning to (film and) television when they want information on the present. Historians must take an interest in the audiovisual world, if they are not to become schizophrenics, rejected by society as the representatives of an outmoded erudition.' Pierre Sorlin.

Millions of people around the world have experienced the fine arts at second hand via feature films such as *Lust for Life* and television series like Kenneth Clark's *Civilisation.* The aim of this book is to provide a critical analysis of key English language films about art and artists from the 1930s to the present day (one French feature film – *Camille Claudel* – is also considered). A companion volume is planned which will recount the history of arts television in Britain. Among the questions this book considers are: how are the fine arts visualised by film-makers? To what extent are films about real artists of the past historically accurate? What are the dominant conceptions of art and artists conveyed by films about fictional artists and architects? What changes, if any, have taken place over the decades in the cinema's representation of art and artists? What are the main characteristics of artists' films and arts documentaries? To what extent is it possible or desirable for film-makers to resolve the tensions that exist between the values of art, education and entertainment?

In terms of cinema, *Art and Artists on Screen* is mainly concerned with a selection of mainstream, commercial, entertainment movies but some art house films, artists' films and arts documentaries are also discussed. In terms of the arts, the book concentrates upon such visual arts as painting, sculpture, architecture and avant garde film/video, rather than upon the performing arts of dance, drama, opera and music. So many different kinds of art presently exist that some limit had to be imposed. Also, my own knowledge and interest pertains to the plastic arts rather than to the performing arts.

Existing literature

Surprisingly, apart from a sprinkling of periodical articles and one anthology, no extended studies of this subject have been published. Parker Tyler, the American film critic, was probably the first writer to discuss cinematic representations of artists in his 1954 *Art News* article 'The artist portrayed and betrayed' and his later essays 'Lust for lifelikeness' and 'Megalomaniascope and *The Horse's Mouth*'. Tyler's articles were highly critical. One suspects that, given the power, he would have forbidden film-makers to tackle the subject. In Britain John Berger's 'The myth of the artist' (1959) deserves to be mentioned as a ground-breaking conference paper, while Griselda Pollock's 'Artists mythologies' (1980), published in the film journal *Screen*, was an important sustained analysis. Pollock's paper was reprinted in an anthology of articles – some new and some old – edited by Philip Hayward – *Picture This: Media Representations of Visual Art & Artists* (1988) – published to coincide with a one-day conference on the subject of 'Art and Media' held at the Riverside Studios, London, in October 1988.

How the cinema represents artists has attracted most critical attention, but one book which looked at the representation of a whole artform – architecture – was Donald Albrecht's *Designing Dreams* (1987). Albrecht examined the use Hollywood studios made of modern architecture as an inspiration for set designs during the depression era of the 1930s. He argued that these representations contributed to the public's 'acceptance' of modern architecture. It is important to realise that film images can have a feedback effect upon the very arts they represent. A case in point is the Miami Beach hotel architecture of Morris Lapidus, an architect inspired by the dynamic spaces and glamorous sets of 1930s Hollywood musicals.

It has been argued that cinematic portrayals of artists continue a centuries-old literary tradition that began with Giorgio Vasari's biographies of Renaissance artists, his famous *Lives of the Most Excellent Painters, Sculptors and Architects* (1550). Several scholarly texts trace the history of artists and architects, and the legends and myths associated with them, namely: Ernst Kris's and Otto Kurz's *Legend, Myth and Magic in the Image of the Artist* (first published in Vienna in 1934), Rudolf and Margot Wittkower's *Born under Saturn: the Character and Conduct of Artists* (1963), Spiro Kostof's *The Architect: Chapters in the History of the Profession* (1977) and Andrew Saint's *The Image of the Architect* (1983). Another relevant text is Jean Gimpel's *The Cult of Art: Against Art and Artists* (1969), a bracing critique of the quasi-religious worship of art and artists which concludes with a celebration of television as a new, more democratic artform. The contents of these books will not be summarised but certain ideas will be drawn from them.

Mass media representations of the past are forms of history-writing/visualisation. On the theme of history-writing and the cinema, Pierre Sorlin's *The Film in History: Restaging the Past* (1980) is a perceptive study. The past as conceived by Hollywood studios is described in George MacDonald Fraser's *The Hollywood History of the World* (1988). The cinema, Fraser points out, is often criticised for glamorising or distorting the past, but it is never given credit for being the greatest popular teacher of history. Moreover, its lessons are far more vivid, if not necessarily more accurate, than those supplied by academic texts.

The literature discussing cinema/fine art interactions and collaborations between film-makers and artists is not extensive but during the 1980s a number of French scholars became fascinated by the relationship between the cinema and painting: at least four books were published on the topic and in 1989 an exhibition entitled 'Peinture – Cinéma – Peinture' was mounted at the Centre de la Vielle Charité in Marseilles. Obviously, in the case of particular collaborations – such as the one between Salvador Dali, Alfred Hitchcock and David Selznick in the 1940s to be described in detail later – the published material includes monographs, exhibition catalogues, biographies, memoirs and periodical articles in specialist art and film journals.

A comprehensive history of films made by artists has yet to be written, but discussions of some of them are to be found in Roger Manvell's *Experiment in Film* (1949), Gregory Battcock's *The New American Cinema* (1967), Sheldon Renan's *The Underground Film: an Introduction to its Development in America* (1967), Parker Tyler's *Underground Film* (1969), Gene Youngblood's *Expanded Cinema* (1970),

David Curtis's *Experimental Cinema* (1971), P. Adams Sitney's *Visionary film* (1974) and Stephen Dwoskin's *Film Is: the International Free Cinema* (1975). Malcolm Le Grice's *Abstract Film and Beyond* (1977), Stan Brakhage's *Film at its Wit's End: Eight Avant Garde Film-makers* (1989) and Peter Gidal's *Materialist Film* (1989) are of special interest because they were written by leading avant-garde film-makers rather than by critics.

In addition to these books, special issues of art magazines have been devoted to the subject of avant-garde film in Europe; for instance, the 1975 November-December issue of *Studio International*. A feminist perspective on avant-garde film and video called *Indiscretions* (1990) has been provided by Patricia Mellencamp. Detailed studies exist of cinematic contributions to particular twentieth-century art movements; for instance, the 1988 anthology *Dada and Surrealist Film* edited by Rudolf Kuenzli and *The Cubist Cinema* (1975) by Standish Lawler. Studies of the films of individual artists are rare. The exception to this rule is Andy Warhol: there are several books devoted to his movie making career, namely: Peter Gidal's *Andy Warhol's Films and Paintings* (1971), Stephen Koch's *Stargazer* (1973), Michael O'Pray's *Andy Warhol: Film Factory* (1989) and Anna Abrahams' *Warhol Films* (1989).

Artists' films date from the 1920s but curatorial interest in them began in the late 1930s at the Museum of Modern Art, New York. A decade later interest in artists' films was encouraged on the East Coast when the Peggy Guggenheim Foundation began to fund them, and on the West Coast when Frank Stauffacher and Richard Foster organised a series of annual shows at the San Franciso Museum of Art entitled 'Art in Cinema'. A book with the same title was published in 1947; it included a history of avant-garde film by Hans Richter, one of its pioneers. Since then various other festivals of artists' films have been mounted in public galleries. For example, a major show entitled 'Perspectives on British Avant Garde Film' was held at the Hayward Gallery, London in 1975: the programmes consisted of films funded by the Arts Council of Great Britain. Four years later the Hayward mounted another exhibition of experimental films entitled 'Film as Film: Formal Experiments in Film 1910–75'. In 1987 the British Council supported a touring show, a retrospective of ten years of British avant-garde film, for which David Curtis edited a catalogue with the title *The Elusive Sign*.

Listings and short descriptions of artists' films are also to be found in the distribution catalogues of films and videos for hire issued by such organizations as the London Film-maker's Co-op and London Video Access.

Much has been written about documentary film but not a great deal about the sub-category of arts documentaries. However, there are some general articles about them – mainly dating from the 1950s – and reviews of individual films appear in both art and film magazines. There are also a number of reference books listing arts documentaries and some of these contain essays as part of their introductions. Catalogues of arts documentaries for hire have been published by organisations such as the Arts Council of Great Britain (which has funded the making of many arts documentaries), by broadcasting institutions and by independent, film production companies. Filmographies are extremely useful but naturally they soon become out of date. A computer database that is being constantly updated is one answer to this problem. In New York a database called 'The Critical Inventory' was established in 1984 by the Program for Art on Film; six years later it contained information on 17,000 films and videos. (A descriptive note on the Program for Art on Film is printed after the index to this book.)

A valuable source of information about artists' films, arts documentaries and television arts programmes has been the British magazine *Art Monthly* (1976–). It has published reviews on a regular basis; many of them were written by the film critic Kevin Gough-Yates.

Mediation/transformation

It is apparent from remarks made by certain individuals attending arts/mass media conferences that there are some naive viewers who assume film and television are transparent windows on the world or who believe they should act as if they were. Such viewers think it is possible to present artists and art on film and television without any 'distortion' taking place. However, works of art appearing on cinema and television screens are, in Philip Hayward's words, 'representations of representations'. Since no such re-representations can take place without some intervening medium of recording and transmission, mediation is inevitable, and this in turn means that the appearance of the original is transformed to some extent during the processes of recording and transmission. Of course, in the case of movies about fictional artists the works of art portrayed are also fictional, though paradoxically they may be 'authentic' in the sense that they may have been created by real, professional artists.

Modern cinematography certainly has the ability to record the visual appearance of an art object with a fair degree of accuracy. This explains its 'window on the world' impression. Nevertheless, the obvious physical differences between filmed images and buildings, paintings and sculptures remain. When the latter are filmed, perceptual transformations – changes of colour, scale and texture – inevitably occur. Furthermore, the medium of film has technical capabilities that far outstrip the basic mimetic function of reproducing appearances. To realise this one has only to think of time-lapse photography, the superimposition of two or more images, fast and slow motion, the distorting effects of anamorphic and telephoto lenses, the use of filters to change colour values, the later addition of sounds and music, all the alterations that are possible during the editing and printing processes, and all the special effects technicians have devised since the birth of the cinema in the 1890s.

To cite just one example of the latter: in Akira Kurosawa's movie *Dreams* (Warner Bros, 1990) there is an episode about van Gogh called 'Crows', in which a Japanese art student is enabled, courtesy of matte effects,[1] to enter some of Vincent's paintings and to meet the artist (played by the American film director Martin Scorsese). The way in which the movie oscillates between photographic naturalism and the huge, painted scenery effect of the van Gogh images is astonishing (though one's delight is somewhat vitiated by the realisation that the 'van Goghs' shown are not the genuine ones but crude imitations). As this example shows, film-makers can, if they so wish, use the fine arts as simply raw material for their own experiments.

Media differences and similarities

There are, of course, many material differences between the traditional fine arts of painting, sculpture and architecture and the mass media of film and television. Their modes of production, distribution and circulation also vary, as do their organisations and institutions. But the primary difference between the two camps is the mechanical, reproductive capacity of the mass media which enables a diffusion of culture to take place across time and space. (Obviously, this difference does not apply to the work of the minority of contemporary artists who employ film and video.)

An oil painting is a silent, still, atemporal, handmade, unique object; it can be viewed by only a few people at a time in one place; whereas the cinema's and television's images are accompanied by sounds and music; they are moving, multiple, temporal, and they can be watched by millions at the same time or at different times, in many locations. Arguably, film and television are inherently more democratic than the fine arts. True, such media restrict access on the side of production but, as John B. Thompson points out in *Ideology and Modern Culture* (1990), they are characterised by relatively unrestricted access on the side of distribution and reception, thus enabling them to reach a larger and broader audience. Also, in terms of cinema admission fees, video rental charges or purchase prices, mass-media products are much cheaper than fine art objects. (Art lovers with low incomes have to rely on public museums, free admission to private galleries and viewing new architecture from the street.)

It would be foolish and futile to regret the discrepancies between a painting directly perceived and the same work perceived on cinema or television screens, because they are inherent in the nature of the different art forms and media. One should never confuse the two experiences or assume that seeing an artwork on screen is as good as seeing it in the flesh, but neither should one overlook the tremendous benefits conferred by film and television. Through image-sound montages, space and time can be compressed, the past and the present juxtaposed; objects, people, places and events can be brought together in complex patterns and narratives. As John Berger argued in part one of the television series *Ways of Seeing* (BBC2, 1972), through the agency of reproduction the arts become a species of information, part of a second, audio-visual discourse which editors can manipulate at will. Losses certainly occur during the processes of recording and editing, but there are significant gains too.

Cinema and television

Film and television are two distinct media; nevertheless they are similar in a number of technical respects: they both depend on cameras and recorders capable of capturing images and sounds and on other machines for projecting or transmitting them. They are both temporal media in the sense that they take time to record and time to transmit. Television is capable of real-time transmission – live television – but normally in both media the phase of gathering material is followed by an editing phase. Film editors organise their raw material in a linear sequence, and this is generally employed to tell a dramatic story. Even non-fiction, television series often use a narrative structure, that is, they tell 'the story of art' in terms of a sequence of periods and styles; each style has a beginning, middle and end; and the transition from one period/style to another is presented dramatically in programmes with cliff-hanger endings.

Transfers between film and video are now commonplace and feature films are regularly shown on television without – for most viewers – unacceptable loss (in spite of the facts that films on television are reduced in terms of image size, that they are often reduced in length, and that the 'letter box' ratio of a CinemaScope film differs from the Academy ratio – nearly square – of the television screen). The images on the screens of cinemas and television sets also differ in character and quality, because in the former light is projected through strips of film on to a distant white screen, whereas in the latter a rapidly scanning beam of electrons causes phosphors on the screen to glow. In spite of several improvements in television's image resolution, 35mm film is still superior when it comes to the reproduction of the detail and colours of a painting.

Since the technologies and logistics of film and television production are so complex and expensive, they are normally compelled to appeal to the largest possible audiences. This techno-economic factor has consequences in terms of the content, level and style of movies and television programmes. The need to be popular places a limit on the intellectual difficulty that can be attempted, particularly in the cinema. Some scholars regard this 'mass' characteristic negatively, but again it has the potential of making knowledge about the visual arts available to more people than ever before in human history.

Despite the similarities listed above, film and television differ in many important respects. There are, for instance, technical, aesthetic, historical, financial and organisational differences. Dominant or mainstream, commercial cinema has traditionally set out to appeal to the widest public and therefore it has favoured fictional films rather than documentaries. Even movies based on real people and events are subject to a high degree of fictionalisation and dramatisation. Audience identification has been ensured by means of 'human interest' stories full of action or emotion, and with heroes and heroines played by charismatic actors. The presence of a particular star in a movie may be more important than its storyline. Typically, what is important in such films is the fate of one or two key individuals. This means that whereas in the discipline of art history what matter most are works of art, in mainstream cinema what count most are the individuals who made them. And those individuals need to have led dramatic lives and, preferably, to have had passionate, heterosexual affairs (the love lives of artists are of particular interest to movie makers).

Commercial cinema has given rise to a range of genres each with their special characteristics. Compared to such popular genres as the Western or the Horror movie, the artist-film is a very minor genre. There is a mismatch between élite and popular culture at this point: the appreciation of the fine arts of the past and the modern period generally requires specialist knowledge and high educational achievement which film studios aiming for the mass market cannot afford to assume, hence the drastic simplifications that occur whenever mainstream cinema does tackle the subject of art. However, this type of cinema is not all-pervasive. There are other kinds – such as documentary, art-cinema and artist's film – which aim at smaller but more sophisticated audiences.

The cinema was invented in the 1890s. By the 1930s it had become the dominant visual medium of mass communication and entertainment. Cinema's hegemony lasted until the 1950s when television became the primary mass medium in the United States and Britain. Television's chief advantage was its presence in people's homes. Going to the cinema involved a special journey and a visit to a public space, whereas television viewing took place in a private space. The communal experience of the cinema became an individual or family experience. Millions watched the same programmes but the television audience was even more geographically dispersed than cinema audiences. Television was convenient and immediate. Soon it offered consumers a continuous flow of material that could be accessed at will. The introduction of television into the home caused many changes: in the layout of rooms, in family relations and behaviour, and in society as a whole. One may presume, therefore, that it had an impact on the arts.

Compared to popular cinema, television is orientated more towards the factual: schedules feature many news programmes and documentaries (so, despite the private nature of television viewing, the public realm does enter the home). Also, its programmes and series tend to be designed with specific segments of the viewing public in mind (there is more 'narrowcasting' and 'niche marketing'). But even here dramatised biographies about artists comparable to movies like *Lust for Life* are to be found. In addition, many feature films made originally for the cinema later appear on television. For the sake of coherence, writers on the cinema and television normally treat them as separate subjects, but of course in reality they compete and interact. The wide-screen epics of the 1960s – such as *The Agony and the Ecstasy* – cannot be fully understood except in relation to cinema's attempt to defeat the competition of television by offering viewers a more spectacular visual experience. After reaching a peak in the 1940s, cinema attendances declined and for a time it seemed as if television would totally replace the cinema. Today, of course, the cinema is undergoing a revival, while at the same time there is a convergence of the two media (video-cassette distribution of films; video editing technology employed in the making of films). A thorough comparison of film and television would require a whole book. Readers seeking a more detailed account should refer to Roy Armes's paperback *On Video* (1988).

The appeal of art and artists to film-makers and movie stars

Why are some film-makers attracted to the subject of art and artists? Making profits is crucial to mainstream cinema, but this motive cannot adequately explain the interest of certain producers, directors and actors because art is by no means the most popular subject in the world. To acquire prestige by association with a form of culture generally perceived to be 'higher' is probably a more important reason. There are other, more idealistic, reasons: for many who work in the mass culture industries, the arts appeal because they represent a purer realm in which aesthetic and spiritual values count for more than crass commercialism. Also, movie directors and stars are as likely to be seduced by the romantic image of the artist as misunderstood or tragic genius as anyone else.

Many actors and directors consider themselves artists in their own fields, consequently they identify strongly with the struggles of those they are called upon to portray on screen. Some, like Alexander Korda, Charles Laughton, Vincent Price, Dennis Hopper, Kirk Douglas and John Huston, appreciated works of art and showed it by collecting them. Biographies and interviews reveal that these directors and film stars had an interest in art that went beyond its investment potential. In the case of the two British directors Derek Jarman and Peter Greenway, a commitment to the fine arts pre-dated their film careers – both initially studied painting at London art schools. Even after film became their primary medium these directors continued to paint and to demonstrate a keen interest in the history of European art.

A sceptic might describe art as 'the opium of the intelligentsia'. When the Christian religion dominated the lives of Europeans, art was its servant, but later on – as society gradually became more secular – art ceased to serve Christian propaganda functions and detached itself from the physical fabric of churches. Some works of art became portable commodities. By the nineteenth century public museums and galleries filled with works of art had become important social institutions. Intellectuals preferred to visit museums on Sundays rather than churches. In recent decades museum building and museum attendances have increased dramatically. In developed countries, the arts and 'heritage' are now essential to the leisure and tourist industries. For many millions in these countries, art has now replaced religion as the source of spiritual or transcendental experiences.

Whatever the reasons for the appeal of art, a number of feature films have been made by major directors and film stars in spite of the fact that these movies were more of a financial risk than other types. Outside the context of art cinema, no film about a visual artist has been a resounding critical and commercial success, though several have received favourable notices and done reasonably well at the box office.

It would be wrong to think that the mass media's role in respect of the arts is a purely passive one, that is, a mere reflection of the high cultural value society places on art and artists, because they actively contribute to it through their celebratory novels and films. They could be accused of double standards, therefore, if they complained about the fact that mass culture itself tends to have a lower cultural status.

Arguably, in spite of continuing mutual envy and suspicion between the fine arts and the mass media, there has been a significant narrowing of the gap between these two realms since the early 1950s when members of the Independent Group first met at the Institute of Contemporary Arts, London, to discuss the topics of art, technology and popular culture. Hard evidence is lacking but it seems likely that the marked growth in the number of people attending museums and galleries over recent decades has been due, in large measure, to the influence of film and television – particularly the latter. (Of course, the increase in printed material about the arts – books, reproductions, newspaper coverage and colour magazines – has also been significant.) The progressive 'mediasation' of art – which involves the mass media embracing art, and more and more fine artists adopting mass media forms of communication – is a process that is also fraught with danger as far as the fine arts are concerned because it threatens to obliterate whatever residual uniqueness they possess.

Our analysis will begin by considering a number of artist bio-pics, that is, films about the lives of a number of real, important artists of the past.

I

BIO-PICS OF REAL ARTISTS

1 Introduction

Feature films about real artists are premised on the existence of an anterior reality: that the artists pre-existed the cinema or, in the case of twentieth- century artists, had an existence independent of it. This means that such films pose a question of truth or realism: how accurately do they depict the artists of the past or the present? It is by no means a simple question to answer because in the case of films with historical subjects there is not a complete reality to which the cinematic representation can be compared point by point, though fragments of that reality have survived. Like all histories, such films are schematic reconstructions based upon whatever evidence – works of art, photographs, letters, memoirs, anecdotes and so forth – remains in existence. But, in addition, feature films rely on secondary sources such as histories of art and novelistic biographies of artists which are themselves reconstructions and/or interpretations of surviving fragments.

Further complications arise from the fact that the makers of feature films have few qualms about inserting completely invented material such as fictional characters, conversations and works of art. In this confusion of layers and sources, truth and invention, it becomes very difficult even for the knowledgeable viewer to disentangle fact from fiction. For instance in *Moulin Rouge* (1952), a John Huston movie about Toulouse-Lautrec, there are shots of his actual paintings and posters but also of an invented portrait which simulates Lautrec's style. This movie also includes fictional women characters. 'Faction' is an unpleasant word, but it does encapsulate the peculiar fusion of fact and fiction found in dramatised biographies whether books, films or radio or television programmes.[1]

Bio-pics of real artists

Does the issue of the relation of films to their sources and to historical fact matter? Yes, if one thinks knowing the truth – as far as one ever can – about the past is important. Yes, if one is interested in the extent to which the mass media rely upon art-historical knowledge for their information about art and artists. Yes, if one is curious about the processes of transformation and adaptation involved in making films and television programmes about arts subjects. An examination of the historical accuracy of bio-pics is also vital in view of the fact that television arts programmes about the history of the artist – such as 'The Agony and the Ecstasy' episode of *Relative Values* (BBC2, 1991) – have employed clips from them as if they were documentaries made during the lifetimes of Rembrandt and Michelangelo.

It would be naive and pedantic when considering the question of truthfulness to expect complete verisimilitude: Kirk Douglas in *Lust for Life* may look like van Gogh but the Dutch painter did not speak English with an American accent; van Gogh's career as an artist lasted ten years but the film runs for only two hours. Obviously, the very nature of images and language, the forms and conventions of films and novels, imposes an inevitable transformation on whatever is their raw material with the consequence that a perfect reproduction of the past is an impossible ideal. (In any case, at present the media of film and television offer a reduced version of reality: their images lack the third dimension; they do not cater for the senses of touch and smell.) This has not prevented some Hollywood studios from striving to achieve authenticity in their historical movies. Twentieth Century Fox, for instance, lavished millions of dollars simulating Renaissance Italian clothes, buildings and battles during the making of *The Agony and the Ecstasy*.

Other writers and directors, realising that a total reconstruction of the past is impossible, have felt free to take all kinds of liberties with history. This comment applies especially to a director like Ken Russell who regards himself as creative artist in his own right. When accused of historical errors and distortions, such directors plead 'artistic licence'. In the case of Derek Jarman, another artist-director, liberties with history during *Caravaggio* took the form of deliberate anachronisms. In Jarman's case, however, the aim was to subvert the project of total reconstruction favoured by Hollywood studios.

In judging the truthfulness of a film about a famous artist one has to consider it as a whole and to ask whether or not it corresponds to the known facts in their essentials rather than in every minor detail. (An analogy with maps may be helpful: a map is a schematic representation of a certain area, but its signs and symbols do not necessarily resemble what they represent; also, while we expect a map to be accurate, we do not expect it to depict every tiny detail of the terrain.) If several versions could be constructed from the same basic information, then one has to ask: is the interpretation in question a reasonable and plausible one?

Most scripts for commercial movies are based on successful novels because producers hope to reduce the chances of failure by capitalising on the already popular. Novels also supply ready-made narratives. We need, therefore, to pay some attention to the artist-novels that pre-dated artist-movies.

Artist-novels

Some artist-novels concern fictional characters while others are based on real historical figures. Two well-known nineteenth-century examples were Honoré de Balzac's *Le Chef d'Oeuvre Inconnu* (1837) and Emile Zola's *L'Oeuvre* (1886). Both novels were about fictional painters, but certain readers thought the artist in the latter book was based on Paul Cézanne. (Zola and Cézanne had been childhood friends.) A twentieth-century writer who achieved financial and popular success with novelistic biographies of Michelangelo, van Gogh and Camille Pissarro was the American university lecturer and historian Irving Stone (1903–89). At the end of his book about van Gogh, *Lust for Life*, Stone adds a note in which he discusses the question of the truthfulness of his account. The narrative, he acknowledges, depends primarily on van Gogh's letters and he is adamant that it is true apart from some inevitable 'technical liberties', that is, the dialogue between characters which had to be 're-imagined' and the invention of a few scenes – such as a meeting between van Gogh and Cézanne – which Stone could not document but felt probably occurred.

The difference between a fictionalised account of a real artist's life by a professional novelist and a biography written by an art historian is sometimes a matter of degree rather than kind. Normally, the chief difference between the two is that novelists invent conversations whereas art historians do not.

A detailed survey of the artist-novel genre is beyond the scope of this book, but there are some general points about it which are pertinent. In 1922 the German philosopher Herbert Marcuse wrote a doctoral dissertation on the subject of the German artist-novel. His analysis revealed that the genre presupposed a kind of golden age when art was fully integrated into society and the occupation and profession of artist as a distinct specialism did not exist. The emergence of artists as a specific profession and/or vocation different from that of artisans or craftsmen thus marks the beginning of a division between art and society: 'the artist represents a specific life-form, when the life-forms of the totality no longer correspond to his own essence . . . art is no longer immanent in life'.[2] As a result, the artist suffers a sense of alienation and longs to achieve a new kind of community which will recapture the former harmony. The goal of the artist-novel becomes, therefore, the struggle of the artist to overcome alienation or, if this is not possible, to find some other solution.

The films to be analysed here depict various aspects of the relationship of artists and society over a period of centuries. For instance, the Renaissance artist's battle to gain independence (in artistic matters) from powerful patrons is vividly portrayed in *The Agony and the Ecstasy*, while the plot of *Rembrandt* suggests that the alienation of the artist from the public began in seventeenth-century Holland. Its negative consequences for nineteenth-century artists are then made clear in *Lust for Life* and *The Wolf at the Door*.

It is the rift between artists and society which gives rise to a whole series of conceptions of artists as beings who are *different* from ordinary people: they are inspired geniuses, eccentrics, bohemians, lunatics, outsiders, rebels, iconoclasts and scourges of the bourgeoisie (upon whom, paradoxically, they usually rely for financial support).[3] Many artists, of course, welcome the idea of being different and they signal it by means of strange clothes and behaviour. Artists preserve in their practice something society in general has lost, for example control over their work, pride and pleasure in their labour. They are still in touch with unconscious desires and forces – the erotic, the perverse, the obscene and the blasphemous – which 'straight' society has outlawed or repressed. They also invoke archaic and primitive forms – pagan religions, magic, alchemy, the occult, shamanism – which rational, scientific society considers it has transcended. The artist thus becomes a repository of values which mainstream society has relinquished. So, for those undertaking the routine jobs of society

– such as the office workers depicted in *The Rebel* – it is no wonder that the mode of life of artists seems either enviable or weird.

In novels and in life there are several ways in which the conflict between artists and society can be 'resolved': artists can become successful by accommodating themselves to society, that is, by modifying their standards so that their work is accepted by major patrons; they can seek refuge in a bohemian subculture or an artists' colony, an urban or rural enclave where they can live out their ideals in permanent opposition to the rest of society (an independent income or a generous relative is helpful here); they can leave cities and 'civilisation' to make their home among native peoples in remote corners of the world (as Paul Gauguin did); they can fail to resolve the problem and so give up art altogether or commit suicide; they can decide that the alienation of the artist is due not to some personality defect on their part but to an oppressive political and economic system, and that the way to combat this is to place their art in the service of those political groups seeking reform or revolution (for example, John Heartfield). On a purely psychological plane, artists can escape from a sense of social isolation by losing themselves in their work or by constructing within it dream or fantasy worlds such as the idealised visions of medieval England retailed by the Pre-Raphaelites.

What the history of modern art reveals is yet another 'resolution' none of the above quite describe. This is the incorporation and celebration of the artist as rebel, outsider, iconoclast and anti-bourgeois. Picasso, for instance, remained a committed modern artist all his life. His restless formal experimentation proved in the end no barrier to his achieving immense fame and success – indeed, quite the opposite. Nor did his radical political allegiances – first anarchist and then communist – prevent him from becoming a multi-millionaire or discourage wealthy collectors from acquiring his work. This particular story does not seem to have appealed to feature-film-makers very much (because radical artists are supposed to be neglected while they are alive, to die young and to achieve glory posthumously), though in *The Fountainhead* the fictional Howard Roark, an extreme modern architect, finally compels the world to accept him on his own terms. Amusingly, in *The Fountainhead* it is the architect's chief patron who commits suicide.

Just as radical modern artists have been celebrated and contained by private wealth and by the cultural institutions of the state, so their image has been celebrated and contained by the mass media. The 'outsider's' struggle has been packaged for consumption, for enjoyment. Vicariously, the artist's life is experienced by the audience, who then resume their everyday routines as if nothing had happened. The unconventional values espoused by artists and implicitly endorsed by the film-makers may evoke the audience's sympathy for the duration of the film but there is little doubt that most viewers are content to leave starvation, suffering and sacrifice to artists. However, as more recent movies have made clear, the image of the artist as a financial failure and social outcast is now out of date.

Feminists will not be surprised to learn that the gender bias of the cinema reflects that of the discipline of art history: the vast majority of the artists featured are male. This is what makes the French film *Camille Claudel* so exceptional and worthy of discussion (see ch. 8).[4] The male artists tend to be white Europeans too. The chances of a feature film being made in the West about an African or Asian artist are virtually nil. British cinema has even been slow to pay homage to its own leading artists – where are the bio-pics of William Blake, J. M. W. Turner, John Constable, Christopher Wren or Henry Moore? – and the American cinema likewise. In the latter case, Jackson Pollock is the obvious omission. Given that this abstract expressionist painter fulfilled so many of the standard requirements of a Hollywood artist-hero – innovative, powerful art, rugged appearance, long years of struggle, mental instability, alcoholism, eccentric social behaviour, a violent death – it seems odd that it has taken them so long to make a feature film about his life (at the time of writing one is reported to be in production).

The seven examples to be considered in detail span a period of forty years and comprise films from four countries: Britain, Denmark, France and the United States. Some of the films are international rather than national in character. For example, *The Agony and the Ecstasy* can be regarded as a trans-Atlantic production because it was financed by an Hollywood studio, shot in Italy, directed by a Britisher, and has two stars, one American and one British. *The Wolf at the door*, a Danish-French co-production with an American star, also involved the skills of people from several countries. The artists chosen by the film-makers comprise two Dutch, two Italian and three French. Only one of the seven is female. Four of the films count as examples of popular cinema while the other three count as art cinema. Apart from the pre-Second World War film *Rembrandt*, all the films are in colour.

In general, bio-pics focus upon the artist not the art – a curious inversion of priorities, since it is the art which makes the artist famous in the first place. It is not only the artist's work that is marginalised: history, social context and the infrastructure of the art world also tend to receive short shrift. Even when art is featured, it tends to be presented as an aspect of the artist's personality and biography: a limited conception of art as subjective expression, diary or autobiography. Nevertheless, all the variables cited above generate many differences and contrasts. In order to do justice to their particular characteristics and to describe their disparate origins, the films deserve individual examination.

2 *Rembrandt* (1936)

Rembrandt Harmensz van Rijn (1606–69) belongs to that select group of artists commonly characterised as 'one of the greatest painters who ever lived', so it is no surprise to find that a major feature film has been made about him. *Rembrandt*, premiered in The Hague and London in 1936, was the result of a combination of continental film production skills and British acting talent: the director was Alexander Korda and the star was Charles Laughton. The script of this prestigious costume drama was written by Carl Zuckmayer and its elaborate sets were designed by Vincent Korda, the director's brother. Rembrandt's last mistress Hendrikje Stoffels was played by Elsa Lanchester who was, in real life, Mrs Laughton, and the part of the artist's first mistress, the vulgar housekeeper Geertge Dircx, was taken by the extrovert actress Gertrude Lawrence (whose loudness on the set irritated Laughton).

Rembrandt was a painter to whom chiaroscuro was vital, consequently a film shot in black-and-white was not inappropriate. (Since almost no actual paintings appear in the film, the absence of the red and gold hues of Rembrandt's palette hardly matters.) Lighting was clearly more crucial than usual to the look of this film. George Perinal was the chief cameraman and his style of lighting was intended to evoke the north-lit studio of the Dutch painter. The whole film was shot in film studios: it was the first movie made at Korda's expensive new production complex at Denham.

Alexander Korda, who came from a Jewish-Hungarian peasant background, arrived in England in 1931 at the age of thirty-eight and proceeded to galvanise the British film industry. He was a highly cultured, flamboyant, lavish-spending film director and entrepreneur. To establish himself in England Korda needed a successful, nationalistic film. This was provided by *The Private Life of Henry VIII* (1933) with Charles Laughton as the monstrous monarch. This film was a hit

1 **Charles Laughton as Rembrandt.** ***Rembrandt*****, 1936**

in the United States and in the world market generally. Korda wanted to repeat his success, consequently *Rembrandt* was primarily intended as a follow-up and as another vehicle for Laughton. The Dutch artist was chosen as a subject because Laughton resembled him. However, there were other reasons: as a child Korda had been fascinated by history and by the biographies of great men. For some time he had wanted to make a movie about a notable artist. He had a taste for art too: as a penniless youth in Paris he had learnt to appreciate painting in the Louvre while sheltering from the winter cold. Also, his brother

2 Rembrandt, 'Self Portrait as the Apostle Paul', 1661

Vincent was a trained painter. Vincent was persuaded to become Korda's art director, though he gave up a fine-art career with reluctance. In later years Korda acquired an extensive art collection: Vincent selected and Alexander paid. Eventually he owned works by Cézanne, van Gogh, Monet, Vuillard, Renoir, Pissarro, Gauguin, Toulouse-Lautrec and Soutine.

Korda was not a trained film-maker. He had learnt his directing skills through practice in Budapest and Hollywood. When he made a film the story and acting interested him more than the camerawork. However, in the 1930s he sought to make films in which 'every frame was a picture'. In the case of *Rembrandt*, therefore, his approach to film-making was sympathetic to the subject.

Charles Laughton (1899–1962) was a rotund, Yorkshire-born actor and movie-star who has since been described as 'half genius, half ham'. He was certainly a powerful and gifted performer and speaker, but he was also a self-loathing homosexual who felt ill at ease in a society he considered stuffy and class-ridden. Eventually he left Britain and made his home in California. In 1950 he and his wife became American citizens.

Laughton was enthusiastic about playing the part of Rembrandt because he identified with Korda's proposed interpretation of the artist as a victim of the pomposity and stupidity of the Dutch bourgeoisie. (This interpretation will be challenged later.) He threw himself into research, reading everything in print about the artist and visiting museums to study his paintings; he even took painting lessons from Vincent in order to gain insight into the mysteries of the craft.

Another reason Laughton felt close to Rembrandt was his own self-doubt as a person and as an artist: he worried about the ugliness of his fat body and his abilities as an actor. As he learnt more about the Dutchman, he became convinced that Rembrandt viewed his artistic gift as a burden and life as a cage, and that the painter too was tortured by self-doubt and hate. After the film's release, Laughton was to claim that Korda could have been franker about the tribulations of Rembrandt's existence. Korda, for his part, wanted another commercial success and so was keen to lighten Rembrandt's story.

A third reason for Laughton's interest in the role of Rembrandt was his own love of paintings. He was a keen, discriminating collector who one day would own canvases by Renoir, Rouault, Siqueiros, Manessier, Matthew Smith and Pierre Soulages. A favourite artist of his was to be the American West Coast painter Morris Graves.

Rembrandt opens optimistically with a cheerful artist greeting the sunshine. Street scenes reveal an affluent, bustling, mercantile society. We see the artist spending lavishly in a colour shop and his house is shown to be large and well appointed. Rembrandt, the film makes clear, is a highly successful artist who works in the midst of society. A consequence of beginning the narrative at this point – 1642 – is, of course, the omission of the whole of Rembrandt's childhood and his three-year apprenticeship with Jacob van Swanenberg in Leiden. The film ends in 1669 – the year of Rembrandt's death – so the narrative jumps forwards decades at a time in places.

To fund his extravagant lifestyle, Rembrandt has to fulfil commissions such as the group portrait of the officers of the night watch. Reluctantly he paints *The Night Watch* – though Korda shows him only signing it – but the huge canvas is received by its patrons with derision because its originality confounds their expectations. Angrily, Rembrandt denounces them, saying, in effect, that he was true to his personal vision – the tragedy of Saskia's (his first wife) death having induced a profounder outlook – and that was why he refused to flatter them or to obey the conventions of the group portrait. At this point, therefore, a rift has opened between the needs and desires of the artist, the demands of truth and art, and the requirements of the patrons who represent society as a whole. In short, the antagonism between art and society which was to become endemic in later centuries is seen as having its origins in seventeenth-century Holland. Today, Rembrandt scholars deny the legend that *The Night Watch* was badly received; they claim there is nothing in the historical record to support the story.

In an attempt to repeat the success of *The Private life of Henry VIII*, Korda foregrounds Rembrandt's love affairs: first Geertge, the housekeeper, becomes his mistress and then Hendrickje, the maid. Rembrandt plans to marry Hendrickje but before he can do so she dies. The complications and tragedies of the artist's emotional life are compounded by financial and legal problems. Rembrandt's debts mount until he is forced into bankruptcy. Paradoxically, all his attempts to follow an independent path result only in his becoming more and more entangled in society's rules and regulations.

By the end of the film, Rembrandt's features have aged and he is shown wearing the turban and coat familiar from his late self-portraits. During a tavern scene, the artist reminds a group of young people of King Solomon's words that all human life is vanity. One of his ex-students seeks him out and gives him money for food but the artist prefers to spend it on paint. We take our leave of him as he scrutinises his face in the mirror next to his easel and reiterates the message: 'All is vanity.' Evidently, this is one film-maker's conception of the essence of Rembrandt's vision.

For the art lover the most disappointing aspect of *Rembrandt* is the almost total absence of the artist's works. Apart from *The Night Watch*, hardly any other painting is shown, certainly no drawings or etchings. Korda seems to assume that the audience is already familiar with Rembrandt's pictures and that therefore they can be taken as read. Whenever we see Rembrandt at work in his studio painting a portrait, the camera is invariably placed behind the easel so that we are prevented from seeing either the canvas or the artist's painting technique. The lack of the works somewhat contradicts the film's relentless propaganda on behalf of Rembrandt and his art: if it is so wonderful why is it not shown? It seems Korda and Laughton decided not to include Rembrandt's paintings because they thought their presence would remind the audience that Laughton was not really the painter. The high cost of insuring borrowed masterpieces was another factor.

Instead of showing us Rembrandt's actual paintings, Korda presents us with tableaux based upon them. For instance, there is a sequence that purports to show how a certain picture came into being: symbolically, it is winter; Rembrandt wanders the snow-covered streets seeking a beggar with a fine head to serve as the model for an Old Testament figure. He finds one whom he dresses up as King Saul. (The presence of a beggar implies that the artist too is dependent on handouts from the rich. To reinforce this point, the real beggar offers to teach the painter 'the art of begging'.) As the man poses on a throne with Rembrandt's son Titus beside him as a harp player, the painter recounts the Biblical story of Saul and David to such effect that he brings tears to the beggar's eyes. The beggar then wipes his eyes on a curtain as in the painting *David playing the harp before Saul* (1655) in the Mauritshuis, The Hague.

Viewers who are familiar with this canvas will obviously gain more from this scene than those who are not. The device of recreating for the camera scenes depicted in paintings was to become typical of films about artists, whether the actual works of art were shown or not.

Artists transform motifs into pictures, film-makers reverse the process by turning pictures into motifs. The resulting screen image is a more illusionistic version of the painting; the painting stripped, as it were, of the medium of oil painting.

The work of another famous artist – Pieter Bruegel the elder – is also evoked at one point. Rembrandt tries to escape his problems by fleeing to his father's mill near Leiden. A boisterous festivity then takes place in an enormous barn. The scene effectively animates Bruegel's peasant wedding pictures. Rembrandt's flirtation with a local lass results in his becoming embroiled in a brawl with her menfolk. Here the film touches upon the age-old antagonism between the country and the city, the peasantry and middle-class urban intellectuals, which Rembrandt has foolishly ignored. He realizes that he must return to where he belongs – Amsterdam.

Perhaps the most questionable assumption of the film is its clichéd idea that great art cannot please patrons. There are thousands of instances which prove that this can indeed happen. Pleasing a patron or a public does not necessarily mean any loss of artistic integrity. Rembrandt is shown as an artist at odds with society and we are meant to take his part, but if all artists adopted this attitude how would they live? (Private visions require private incomes.) And if all artists followed their own paths regardless of others, what social role would be left for art?

Appropriately, the premiere of *Rembrandt* took place in the artist's homeland. Korda and his main stars attended the opening in The Hague and were greeted by cheering crowds. Mixed notices greeted the film when it was released in Britain in November 1936. At that time Graham Greene was film critic of *The Spectator*. In his opinion 'reverence and a good cameraman' were not enough to prevent the film from being 'a series of unrelated tableaux'; it had no story, continuity or drive; and it was 'pompous'.[1]

Rembrandt also failed to excite the cinema-going public and so was a commercial flop. (The film's production costs were £138,945, whereas receipts by April 1937 were only £36,141.) Korda's plan for a series of films about great artists including van Gogh was abandoned forthwith. In 1936 (the year of the Jarrow marches) Britain was in the midst of an economic depression with one and a half million unemployed. *Rembrandt* – a serious film – lacked the escapist, entertainment value of gangster movies and musicals which might have guaranteed box-office success. The combination of worldly troubles and Biblical messages also made for a somewhat gloomy film. A self-contradictory one too – if all human life is vanity, then so too is painting and film-making. Nevertheless, *Rembrandt* remains an eminently watchable, finely crafted film. Today it can be purchased cheaply on video.

Simon Callow is a British actor with an immense respect for Laughton's acting abilities. In his 1987 biography of Laughton, Callow quotes the verdict of the critic C. A. Lejeune about *Rembrandt*: 'probably the finest acting performance ever recorded on celluloid'. Callow argues that the performance was a rare one in Laughton's career because it was 'naturalistic'. Laughton's purpose, according to Callow, was 'to celebrate his own love of beauty, his creative aspirations, his sense of humanity'. He concludes: 'His Rembrandt, I believe, is an idealised self-portrait . . . it is one of the very few filmed representations of an artist that actually convince.' Nevertheless, Laughton's performance aside, Callow judges the film an artistic failure: 'it's poorly shaped, the rhythms are dull, and there's a flatness about the whole thing.' He blames Korda for the film's deficiencies and observes: 'the film should have been titled *The Private Life of Rembrandt* . . . structurally it is simply an account of the painter's relationship with his various women, through which certain other episodes are woven. By the end of it one feels cheated of a full explanation of the central character.'[2]

As we have seen, the film is not exclusively about Rembrandt's domestic life; it also contains information about the artist's career and his troubled relation with Dutch society. Indeed, one could argue that the dominant theme of the film is the question of value: what counts as success in life and in art? What relation is there between art and commerce? There is a relentless preoccupation with money in the film which may well reflect Korda's own problems in raising finance in order to make the movies he wanted.

How accurate was Korda's and Laughton's portrait of Rembrandt? There is a persistent, naive assumption amongst writers of artist-novels and directors of artist-films that because an artist's work is great the person responsible for them must be a great and good human being. Arguably, in the case of *Rembrandt*, this leads to a systematic misrepresentation of the artist's life and character. The film is constructed entirely from his point of view and he is glorified and romanticised. An enormous amount is known about Rembrandt's work, his domestic affairs and his patrons – witness the immensely detailed and scholarly text *Rembrandt: His Life, His Paintings* (1985) by Gary Schwartz. If we compare the account of Rembrandt given by Schwartz with that presented in the film, then an entirely different picture of the artist emerges.

Crucial to Korda's thesis is the idea that as his art developed, Rembrandt became too advanced and independent for his patrons and that his financial problems stemmed from this situation. Schwartz's account, on the other hand, reveals Rembrandt's almost total dependence on particular circles of patrons within the wealthy and influential ruling strata of Amsterdam. Rembrandt's fortunes fluctuated not because he was too original but because the fortunes of his patrons fluctuated. (When they were in power and affluent Rembrandt received commissions, when they were out of office and short of money he did not.) A few landscapes by Rembrandt are known but he discontinued making such works when they did not sell. This example seems to show that he did not paint purely for the sake of art when it was unprofitable to do so.

Is this argument contradicted by his large number (over fifty) of self-portraits? Were there buyers for them? Why did he paint so many images of himself? The usual explanation is a quest for self-understanding but perhaps there are other explanations such as vanity. If this is the case then the artist's final remark about all being vanity takes on a new, ironic twist. Schwartz acknowledges that Rembrandt's self-portraits were his most original contribution to the art of painting but he argues that most of them sold and he also suggests that they served a useful function for the artist as a form of self publicity. Schwartz cannot resist the temptation to psychologise in response to the late self-portraits even though he criticises the art historian's habit of reading an artist's character from his works and claims the idea seventeenth-century painters chose their subjects in order to express inner convictions is without foundation.

Geertge, Rembrandt's housekeeper-mistress, is represented in the film as a money-obsessed shrew but what was she really like? Has she been misrepresented because everyone takes Rembrandt's side? Having served the artist for several years and promised marriage, she was cast aside for a younger woman. Her attempt to obtain some financial compensation – she was sick and had no means of support –

led to a bitter legal dispute. Rembrandt and others conspired against her and vilified her character to such effect that she was sent to a house of correction in Gouda for five years. A feminist film of Rembrandt's life from Geertge's perspective would, one suspects, generate a very different impression of the artist's character.

What were the reasons for Rembrandt's financial difficulties? Korda shows he enjoyed a high standard of living early in his career and that he was profligate with money but the film is not honest about the extent to which Rembrandt's complex financial affairs and money problems were self-induced. From Schwartz's account it appears the artist lived beyond his means. When Rembrandt married Saskia he acquired a considerable dowry; in 1639 he moved into a fine house which he never in fact completely paid for. He speculated in the art market and borrowed large sums which he often failed to repay. Some of the sales of his property were instituted by himself in order to forestall his creditors. It would appear that he manipulated all those around him in order to preserve his life-style. Today, of course, no one sympathesises with Rembrandt's creditors but some may well have suffered hardship on his account.

The late self-portraits show a wise and humane individual but does this necessarily mean that the real person was like that? Would we normally accept a person's own self-evaluation? Schwartz uses terms like 'arrogant', 'bitter', 'vindictive' to describe the artist and bluntly sums him up: 'a nasty disposition and an untrustworthy character'.[3] If Schwartz's scholarship is to be trusted, then Korda's adulatory representation of Rembrandt should be viewed with extreme scepticism. If the real Rembrandt was indeed a less than perfect human being this does not detract, of course, from his artistic achievement though it may result in changes in the interpretation of its meaning.

Schwartz explains the reverence with which Rembrandt has generally been presented in the centuries since his death as follows: 'By keeping the image of the profound Rembrandt alive. art historians lay claim to a share in his superior spiritual status. . . . By feeding the notion that the objects artists create are not only beautiful and interesting but also filled with wisdom, art historians elevate their own importance as well'.[4] Korda and Laughton too, it is clear, identified closely with Rembrandt and their uncritical portrayal of him can, perhaps, be explained on similar grounds.

3 *Moulin Rouge* (1952)

A screenplay about a fictional French aristocrat who is badly crippled as a child, who then becomes a radical modern artist, who frequents brothels and depicts the nightlife of Paris during its period of decadence at the end of the nineteenth century, and who ruins his health with drink to die at the early age of thirty-seven, might well have been rejected by a Hollywood film studio for being too far fetched. But, of course, such was the true story of Henri de Toulouse-Lautrec (1864–1901) the son of Comte Alphonse de Toulouse-Lautrec. In 1951 his life story was published in the form of a novel – *Moulin Rouge* – by the French writer Pierre La Mure, and this text in turn was made into a feature film, released in 1953, by the distinguished American director John Huston.[1]

Huston (1906–87), the son of the actor Walter Huston, was a prolific and successful director. He will be remembered for such outstanding movies as *The Maltese Falcon*, *The Asphalt Jungle*, *Key Largo*, *The Treasure of the Sierra Madre*, *The African Queen* and *The Misfits* but not, in all probability, for *Moulin Rouge*. In his youth Huston was interested in physical activities such as boxing and horse riding but he also developed a fascination for the visual arts. At the age of seventeen he discovered modern art and studied at art school in Los Angeles for a time; he was taught by Stanton MacDonald-Wright, an abstract painter obsessed with colour and co-founder of synchromism. Later on, when Huston could afford to buy works of art, he built up a collection which included Japanese and Pre-Columbian artefacts as well as paintings by Klee, Soutine, Gris and Toulouse-Lautrec. When Huston first thought of converting La Mure's novel into a film, the actor he had in mind for the major role was José Ferrer. By a lucky coincidence, when he came to inquire about the book's film rights he discovered they had been obtained by Ferrer.

Location shooting for *Moulin Rouge* took place in Paris in 1951 during a heat wave; Picasso was one of the curious onlookers. Studio work was undertaken in London. The film was very much a personal project of Huston's: he produced as well as directed it, and he co-

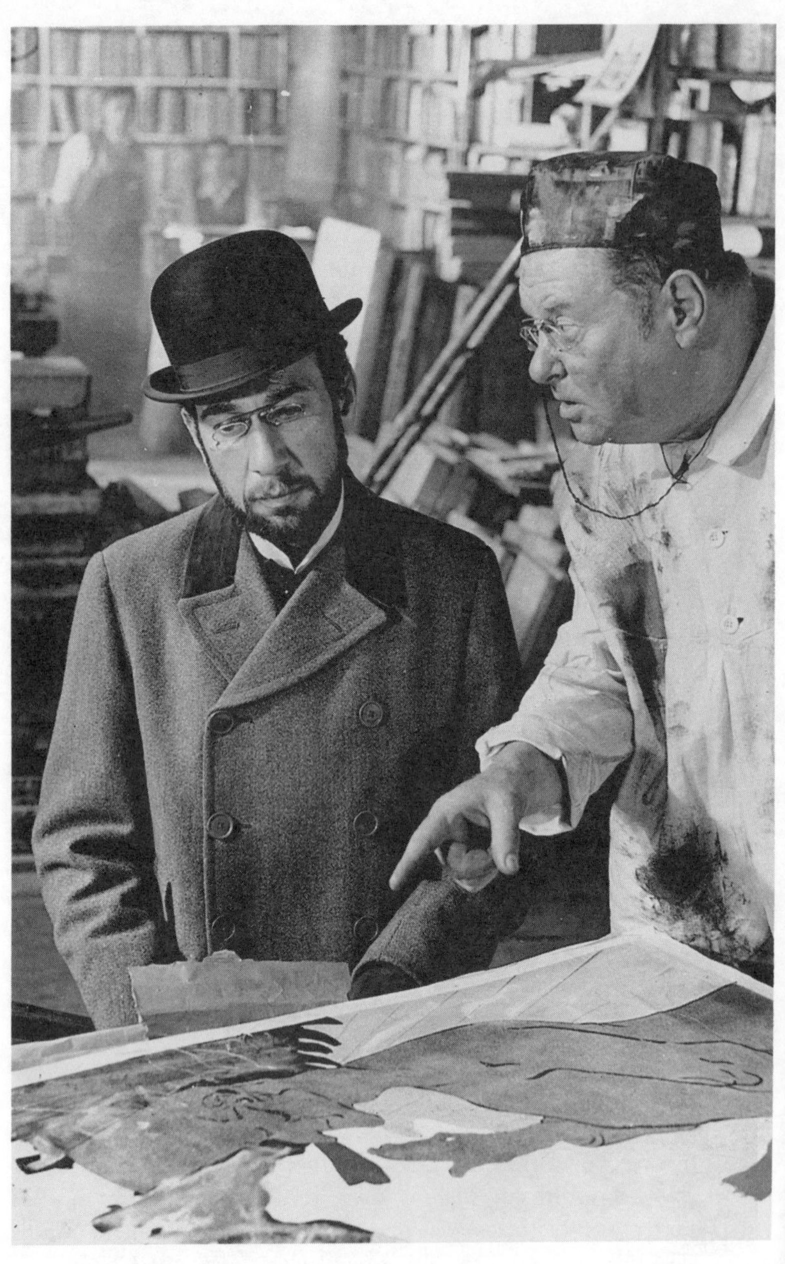

3 José Ferrer as Henri de Toulouse-Lautrec. *Moulin Rouge*, 1952

4 Toulouse-Lautrec in 1892

authored the script with Anthony Veiller. Huston recognised that the novel was a somewhat romanticised and sentimentalised account of Lautrec's life but, given the restricted moral and political climate of 1950s America – in particular the power of censorship vested in the Hollywood Production Code and the pernicious power of McCarthyism – he felt that the full truth could not be told. So, an infatuation for a single streetwalker was substituted for extended scenes inside Parisian whorehouses.

Paul Sherriff was engaged as art director to design the sets while the decor and costumes were by Marcel Vertes (apart, that is, from Zsa Zsa Gabor's dresses which were the work of the noted Italian fashion designer Elsa Schiaparelli). The exhilarating dance numbers in the film were directed by William Chappell and the music was composed by Georges Auric.

Given that this was a film about a painter, Huston considered its colour scheme to be crucial. He wanted to emulate the kind of hues Lautrec had achieved, hence some modification of the basic Technicolor process was needed. 'Our idea', he said, 'was to flatten the colour, render it in planes of solid hues, do away with highlights and the illusion of the third dimension. I hired *Life* photographer Eliot Elisofon to experiment with the use of this sort of colour in still photography and he and Oswald Morris, the cameraman, attempted to obtain with the motion picture camera the effects we had in the stills.'[2] Elisofon argued that since films were 'fictional', their colours could also be 'fictional', that is, they need not be naturalistic. He also considered that filters were to the photographer what glazes were to the oil painter. This experimental approach to colour alarmed the Technicolor Company and their objections had to be overcome. A fog filter was used on the camera and gelatin filters placed in front of the lights. The effects achieved by these means were not so much flat areas of colour (such as we find in Lautrec's posters) as misty, pastel tints which evoked an impressionist rather than a post-impressionist palette.

Huston and Morris also experimented with camerawork. A handheld camera was used in certain dance sequences. Huston later claimed it was the first time this technique had been used in a feature film.

José Ferrer (born 1912, Puerto Rico, died 1992) was chosen for the part of Lautrec because he was an accomplished stage actor, because he facially resembled the painter, and because he had a melancholy and acerbic manner. It was a physically demanding role because he appeared in virtually every scene and had to act on his knees with his calves strapped back to simulate Lautrec's dwarf-like stature (he was about five feet tall). In long shots a real dwarf was used. Ferrer portrayed Lautrec as an emotionally bruised, self-mocking and bitter individual. It was a plausible characterisation and Ferrer received a Best Actor Academy nomination for it. However, it was probably an excessively gloomy picture of Lautrec who, according to the testimonies of his intimates, was a charming and amusing companion, a man who bore his affliction with remarkable fortitude and who had a tremendous gift for friendship. At times though he was extremely nasty, especially to women who were his social inferiors. What the film does not show at all was the pleasure Lautrec took in outdoor physical activities such as sailing, swimming and travel.

After the title credits, a text informs us that Lautrec was 'a genius' and that the movie will enable 'his time to live again'. It is clear from the outset, therefore, that Huston had no intention of questioning the artist-as-genius stereotype nor of making problematic the idea that the past can be faithfully reconstructed. The opening scenes, set in Paris in 1890, introduce us to the dance and music hall located in Montmartre which gives the film its title. At night, the public arrive to partake of an evening of entertainment. Inside the brightly-lit hall, in an extended sequence, we encounter the various professional dancers and singers of the Moulin Rouge as they perform their routines with verve and energy: the insolent white female dancer called La Goulue (which means 'glutton' in Montmartre slang), her black rival – these two are soon fighting like wildcats – the male dancer Valentin (known as 'the boneless wonder') whose face resembles that of Punch, the female singing star Jane Avril – played by Zsa Zsa Gabor – whose many love affairs never last for long, the black male circus performer and dancer nicknamed Chocolat, and the famous chahut and can-can dancers with their erotic, zestful high kicks and splits.

Eventually, the camera reaches the smartly dressed figure of Lautrec who sits at a table adjoining the dance-floor consuming glass after glass of cognac while sketching the entertainers with remarkable speed and facility. Thankfully, these drawings are skilfully executed. In fact, they were the work of Vertes who, it is reported, was previously a forger of Lautrecs. (Forgers were attracted to the work of Lautrec as soon as it became well known. Some were prosecuted during his lifetime.) Henri is greeted affectionately by the entertainers and so we gain the impression of a man who is respected and at home in this social milieu. We also meet Charles Zidler, the manager of the Moulin Rouge, who promises free drinks in exchange for a poster. Maurice Joyant, an ever-optimistic art dealer – played by the British actor Lee Montague – also drops in. The real Maurice met Lautrec at school; they remained life-long friends. Finally, the fun and games over, Lautrec remains in the darkened space while cleaners mop the floor. Only when he rises from the table to depart do we discover how small he is, that his legs are stunted, and that he walks with difficulty. It is an effectively contrived moment.

Those familiar with Lautrec's oeuvre will already know the entertainers of the Moulin Rouge. The film animates the characters depicted in his drawings, posters and illustrations; it reverses the artist's original process by turning his two-dimensional images back into their three-dimensional models. This device, so typical of films about artists, often generates a sense of the uncanny.

As Lautrec walks slowly home through the dark streets, he recalls in flashback his childhood and we learn the causes of his disability: his father, a French nobleman who owns a large chateau at Albi, and his mother are first cousins, hence there is a genetic deficiency which means that when the boy falls down stairs and breaks his legs, the bones do not mend properly and cease to grow. (In fact Lautrec only fell off a low chair and, on a second occasion, he fell into a ditch.) As a child Henri delighted in horse riding but once disabled he has to develop another of his childhood skills, that of drawing and caricature. Art was not in fact alien to his aristocratic family: Henri's father and some of his other male relatives were amateur artists.

According to the plot of *Moulin Rouge*, the young Lautrec is spurned by a woman to whom he proposes. He then has to face up to the fact that he is lame and grotesque and that he will be unable to live a normal life. His father is distant and unsympathetic but his mother supports his desire to seek the consolation of becoming a professional artist in Paris. Given this information, we now understand why Ferrer's Lautrec is isolated, haughty, cynical and a heavy drinker. In his letters the real Lautrec refers to his father as 'sweet Papa', so their relationship does not appear to have been as cool as the film makes out.

Artists are commonly thought of as exceptional beings, people who are different from the mass of humanity. In the sense that they have specialised skills, artists are different, but the popular conception of difference goes far beyond divisions of labour. Artists are different because of their 'abnormal' emotions, personalities and behaviour. Many artists, of course, deliberately adopt marks of difference (for example, a unique set of clothes which they always wear). In Lautrec's case this was unnecessary because difference was inscribed on his body at birth (his noble but inbred family) and during his adolescence (the two accidents). Of course he might well have become an artist if his constitution and growth had been normal, but this will always remain a matter for conjecture.

Most of the content of *Moulin Rouge* concerns Lautrec's doomed search for the love of a good woman. He pursues two females, Marie who is from the lumpen proletariat and Myriamme who is from the petty bourgeoisie. (In both cases, therefore, Lautrec's objects of desire belong to social classes lower than his own. Class as well as deformity stands in the way of romantic bliss.) On his way home from the Moulin Rouge, Henri saves Marie, a vulgar and grasping young prostitute – played by Colette Marchand – from arrest and takes her back to his studio/apartment. Lautrec is fascinated by her despite her tactless inquires about his legs. Next morning Henri paints while Marie sings. The film is coy at this point: there are no sexual scenes in bed though these do occur in La Mure's novel.

Since most of the film is about Lautrec's private life, scenes that concern the production and distribution of art are few and far between. In one, set in a café, Lautrec encounters his painter friends Georges Seurat and Louis Anquetin. They invite him to join the Société des Artistes Indépendants, but Henri is sceptical of the value of such artist-run exhibition societies. In actual fact the real Lautrec did show work at the Salon des Indépendants. Henri is in a quarrelsome mood and he provokes an argument about dealers, critics and the *Mona Lisa*. Lautrec indicates his commitment to modernism and his contempt for tradition by calling the Louvre 'a graveyard'. Later on in the film, however, he takes Myriamme to 'the graveyard', praises the beauty of the Venus de Milo statue and remarks, fatuously, 'great art is not simple'.

The café scene is one of the few which places the painter in the art-world of the period and considers his relation to his contemporaries and to the past of art. Because the narrative begins in 1890, we do not see the many years of training Lautrec underwent in the painting schools of the academic artists Bonnat and Cormon. Also, there is little indication in the film of Lautrec's many contacts with the intellectual circles of Parisian society. One of the most intriguing aspects of his life was his ability to move between the various social classes and to bridge the divide between high culture and popular culture.

There are some scenes which show Lautrec at work. In one he paints a half-length portrait of Marie. She is too restless to make a good model and, naturally, she wants to be paid for posing. At this point there is an all-too-brief discussion of the relative values of the work of art and the work of the model. Henri offers Marie the canvas as a gift but she is indifferent to the aesthetic value of art. What she wants is an immediate cash payment for her modelling, not an object to hang on a wall, an object that might or might not prove a profitable investment in the long term. It soon becomes clear that Marie will never return Henri's affection. After yet another painful rejection, Henri attempts to commit suicide by turning on the gas. As he waits for it to take effect, the camera pans across his half-finished canvases. Henri's interest in painting revives and he turns the gas off in order to resume work. His love of art has saved his life. In reality, art did not save Lautrec from the slow suicide of alcoholism.

Lautrec was one of the first modern artists to cross the divide between fine and commercial art by designing posters for the Moulin Rouge and the café-concerts of Montmartre. There is a scene in which Lautrec takes one of his daring designs to a lithographic printer. We see him experimenting with inks and supervising the printing process. The real Lautrec employed several printers. One of his technical innovations was a gun filled with ink fired at the stone to give a splatter effect. Lautrec's poster receives a mixed reception: it excites considerable public interest, but it enrages his father who calls it 'pornographic trash'. Henri responds by describing his father as a fossil of a bygone age and saying that at least he works for his living as an artist. Elsewhere, the film presents Henri as a republican, as a man who considered aristocratic titles outmoded. Yet, the real Lautrec never renounced the wealth that came with his noble birth and his family's ownership of vineyards. Like that of so many of the major French artists of the nineteenth century, Lautrec's artistic independence was secured by an independent income.

The real Lautrec received regular sums of money and casks of wine from his parents. He was affluent enough to employ a maid and to travel to Spain, Belgium, Holland and Britain (he visited London several times). As an artist he was also far more successful – financially speaking – than his friend van Gogh: he sold pictures and prints, and received commissions for posters, book and magazine illustrations.

As a result of the poster campaign, business at the Moulin Rouge booms. However, the manager notes with regret that this causes a change in the clientele: high society begins to visit the dance hall. We are then shown a series of stills of Lautrec's Moulin images animated by means of details and fast intercutting. Later on, it emerges that the original stars of the Moulin Rouge have been dismissed. La Goulue is shown reduced to a drunken wreck. Seeing her, Lautrec observes fatalistically: 'One always destroys the thing one loves.' His posters made the dance hall famous but they also ruined it by making it fashionable and respectable.

Another scene set in the art world concerns a one-man show of Lautrec's paintings at Maurice's gallery. Henri arrives drunk in time to hear a scandalised matron condemning one of his brothel scenes in which a male client watches a whore undressing. Henri defends his realistic vision with heavy sarcasm. Meanwhile, the discerning King of Serbia is buying a painting for a high price. Lautrec then passes out in his dealer's office. Maurice later berates him for his excessive drinking but Henri sardonically observes that the value of his work will increase if he dies young. Afterwards Lautrec visits a brothel. It is shown briefly via another set of still images of his studies of brothel interiors. The film-makers exercised self-censorship at this point. They did not think it possible to show Lautrec living and working in a brothel for an extended period as was his wont (at least according to some reports). Nor, at the end of the film, is there any acknowledgement that it wasn't just drink that killed him but the sexually transmitted disease of syphilis.

Ten years elapse. 1900 finds the artist in a carriage near the newly constructed Eiffel tower. He leaves the cab to speak to a woman on a bridge over the Seine who he thinks is going to drown herself. This character, played by Suzanne Flon, is called Myriamme. We learn later that she works as a model in a dress shop, that she is a dignified single woman who lost the love of her life five years before, and that she is throwing away the key to an apartment given to her by a rich man who wanted her to become his mistress. Myriamme appears to be a representative of a new female type: an emancipated, independent woman capable of living alone and supporting herself through work.

Lautrec's courtship of Myriamme provides the film-makers with the opportunity to show more of the subjects that inspired him as an artist. In one scene Henri and Myriamme visit a racecourse where Lautrec makes rapid sketches of the horses and jockeys. Lautrec's passion for horses was shared by Huston who was a regular visitor to the Paris racetrack. In another scene they visit the circus. The real Lautrec delighted in the popular culture represented by the Cirque Fernando in Montmartre.

Myriamme receives an offer of marriage from the man who desires her. She accepts despite the fact it is Lautrec she really cares about. Henri's cynical attitude has made him blind to her affection and fear of another rejection has prevented him from revealing his true feelings. The result is he has spoiled his final chance of happiness. A year elapses: Lautrec is now an alcoholic. The film thus omits altogether the three months Lautrec spent in 1899 as a prisoner in a sanatorium where he had been placed by his family in a last attempt to cure his addiction to drink. Patou, a policeman friend, finds him fighting drunk in a rough bistro and takes him back to the studio and leaves him on the couch to sleep. But as Patou leaves the house Lautrec awakes delirious and then falls downstairs.

Berthe Sarrazin was a housekeeper appointed by Henri's mother to keep an eye on her son. Sarrazin's reports reveal that the final phase of his life was pathetic, squalid and tragic. Lautrec became aggressive, suffered memory lapses, virtually ceased to work, behaved strangely and experienced a variety of delusions. Many of his old friends deserted him and he became a prey to hangers on. A truthful cinematic portrayal of Lautrec's final years would serve as a health warning to painters who like to drink.

Finally, we see Henri on his deathbed at home in the family chateau. His father – a role also played by Ferrer – reads a letter from Maurice saying that Henri's paintings are to hang in the Louvre. The Comte apologises to his son, admitting he had not grasped the importance of his art. There is a touching last scene: as Henri dies he is visited by the spirits of the entertainers of the Moulin Rouge immortalised in his work, and so the narrative of the film comes full circle.

There is a much historical truth in Huston's film and it plausibly evokes the time and place, yet the film's mix of fact and fiction could mislead uniformed viewers. For instance, while the majority of the people represented in *Moulin Rouge* were real historical figures, a minority were inventions, most notably Marie and Myriamme. This means that the portrait of Marie which appears in the film is the work of Vertes not Lautrec. The painting is indeed too pretty to be a genuine Lautrec. It also means that doubt is thrown upon the psychological motivations attributed to Lautrec by the film-makers. Huston admitted in later interviews that the portrayal of Lautrec was too sentimental, that it would have been more faithful to his vision if it had matched the painter's 'clinical detachment'.

As we have seen, Lautrec's painting and the subjects which inspired it were featured in the film to a certain extent, nevertheless the movie's emphasis is on Henri's private, emotional life rather than his art. His failure to gain the love of a woman becomes the explanation for his bitterness and his increasing dependence on drink. From the art-historical point of view, the film would have been of greater value if it had reversed its order of priority and paid more attention to Lautrec's art than to his love life. Even if one accepts the film-maker's preference for the life rather than the work, it is possible to criticise the film for sanitising his life story. Arguably, an explicit, historically precise film of Lautrec's personal life would have much more engrossing than that supplied by *Moulin Rouge*.[3]

The film was premiered in Los Angeles in 1952. The opening was marred by the presence outside the cinema of a picket of McCarthy-inspired protesters accusing Ferrer and Huston of being communists. Ferrer, it seems, had the reputation of being politically on the far left. Apart from Lautrec's love of popular entertainers, his dislike of noble titles, and a short discussion of the issue of work and value, there was nothing overtly left-wing in the content of the film to which the protesters could object. There was little in the film to upset moralists either, because any potentially shocking aspects of Lautrec's life had been edited out at the scriptwriting stage. No doubt Henri would have been amused by the longevity of bourgeois prudery.

When the film was released in 1953 it received mixed reviews but, somewhat unexpectedly, it succeeded at the box office. Lautrec was undoubtedly a famous and popular painter but the general public may well have been enticed to the cinema by titillating trailers featuring the can-can dancers of the Moulin Rouge. British viewers in the early 1950s lived in a somewhat repressed society; for them, Paris was a city with a reputation for 'naughtiness'. The movie was later awarded Oscars for its art direction and costume design. Subsequently, the reputation of *Moulin Rouge* declined. One of Huston's obituaries described it as 'alarmingly trite'.[4] Despite the film's seriousness and genuine qualities, it was certainly not in the same class as some of Huston's other movies, particularly the thrillers and adventure stories starring Humphrey Bogart.

4 *Lust for Life* (1956)

Vincent van Gogh's life story has all the ingredients likely to appeal to popular novelists and film-makers: an idealistic, passionate man who searched for a long time before he discovered his true vocation; a brief, ten-year career as an artist packed with incident and changes of locale; an oeuvre which included memorable, brightly-coloured images with the power to move millions; a struggle to live, to learn his craft, to overcome the opposition of his parents and to cope with isolation and commercial failure; friendships with famous post-impressionist painters such as Bernard, Gauguin and Toulouse-Lautrec; a transition from northern gloom to southern radiance; bizarre behaviour, fits of 'madness' climaxing in suicide; an artist who, from near total obscurity at his death, became one of the most famous and revered in the whole history of art; canvases unsaleable in his lifetime being auctioned a hundred years later for tens of millions of pounds.

It was inevitable, therefore, that sooner or later someone would make a movie about him. The film, vulgarly entitled *Lust for Life*, finally appeared in 1956. It was shot in CinemaScope, directed by Vincente Minnelli and starred Kirk Douglas as van Gogh and Anthony Quinn – the all-purpose foreigner of Hollywood – as Gauguin. The screenplay, adapted from Irving Stone's novel *Lust for Life*, was written by Norman Corwin. Any film about van Gogh had to be in colour; in this case the process was called 'MetroColor'. Although *Lust for Life* was to be criticised by intellectuals on various grounds, many admirers of van Gogh's art were relieved that the film was not as dreadful as they had feared. In fact, given the inherent limitations of the bio-pic genre, it was a sincere, serious effort.

Minnelli was born in 1910 into a family of entertainers. In his youth he demonstrated a flair for the visual arts by undertaking billboard painting, photographic studio work, set and costume design. His directing career dates from the mid 1930s. Before *Lust for Life*, he was noted for a series of musicals though he also made comedies and melodramas. Minnelli is generally respected by film historians as an impeccable craftsman with a lavish visual style, but he is also viewed as a middlebrow director with a penchant for taking art to the people.

Kirk Douglas (born 1916), his main star, was an actor famous for his egocentric, virile persona and athleticism in boxing films, Westerns, crime stories and costume dramas. The actor admired van Gogh's art and wanted his own production company Bryna to make a film about the painter but it transpired that MGM already owned the movie rights to the novel. He was very keen to play the role and once a new script had been written by Corwin (Stone's script was judged unsuitable), Douglas and MGM came to an agreement. There is a certain irony in the fact that Douglas (originally named Issur Danielovitch Demsky), the son of poor immigrants – Russian Jews of peasant stock – wanted to play the part of a painter who had honoured the labour of poor peasants. Douglas had fought hard to escape the poverty of his childhood and so he empathised with van Gogh's struggle to make a living through art.

When Douglas achieved stardom he decorated his home with paintings by Chagall, Picasso, Rouault, and Vlaminck, but none by van Gogh. While preparing for his role, Douglas read van Gogh's letters, studied his work in museums and took painting lessons so that he could be filmed applying paint to canvas. This he mainly does in the famous penultimate scene (actually the first to be shot) where van Gogh depicts crows in a cornfield. It seems Douglas practised painting the birds hundreds of times until he could render them with some degree of conviction. For this scene, six hundred crows were bought and tethered by lengths of monofilament. Men hiding in the cornfield made noises to make them fly and then pulled them down again.

With his hair cut short and his beard dyed ginger, Douglas closely resembled van Gogh. The actor recalls that when they were filming on location with him in period attire, old peasants who had known the real van Gogh crossed themselves and remarked: 'He has returned.' In his memoirs Douglas says that playing van Gogh was a painful experience because he was unable to maintain the normal distance and illusionism of acting. The part took him over: 'I felt myself going over the line, into the skin of van Gogh. Not only did I look like him, I was the same age he had been when he committed suicide.'[1] Douglas

5 **Kirk Douglas as van Gogh.** ***Lust for Life*****, 1956**

certainly brought to the part a fierce intensity which conveyed the highly charged emotion of the painter's personality, but this left little room for the portrayal of the rational intellectual: the real van Gogh was fluent in three languages, extremely well read, knowledgeable about the history of art, and fascinated by colour theory. Some questions of aesthetics were dramatised in the electric scenes in which Vincent and Gauguin argue about their favourite artists and disagree about their respective methods and techniques. Such arguments did indeed take place.

Since Douglas normally played tough-guys there was a certain risk in acting the part of a man who was vulnerable, self-destructive and, in his lifetime, a failure. Douglas's fellow actor and tough guy John Wayne saw the movie at a special preview and was astonished that Douglas was willing to undermine his screen image by playing the part of someone Wayne considered 'a weakling'.[2]

The film was generously financed by MGM. Location shooting took place in Europe during the summer of 1955. Minnelli wanted the settings to be as authentic as possible and so he filmed in several of the places where van Gogh had lived including the asylum at St Rémy in Provence. The realistic effect of the film was reinforced by period clothes and by the construction of sets from the visual information supplied by the artist's paintings. A team of art directors headed by Cedric Gibbons worked on the picture. Despite their efforts, some supposedly outdoor scenes were clearly shot in studios.

When van Gogh's paintings – in fact colour photos of them – were introduced into these scenes, the correspondence between set and painted image was, naturally enough, exact. (Colour photographs had been made earlier by F. A. Young and Russell Harlan, the cameramen, from two hundred original van Goghs in various museums and galleries.) As in *Rembrandt*, the motifs of some of Vincent's masterpieces were recreated for the camera. For instance, the evening meal of a poor Dutch peasant family – *The Potato Eaters* – was uncannily brought to life in the studio. Vincent's nephew, who owned the largest number of van Goghs in Holland, refused to co-operate with the film-makers because he disliked the script, so some photos needed for copying purposes had to be taken secretly.

The half-completed paintings on which Douglas is shown working were produced by a young high-school art teacher called Robert Parker (though his name does not appear on the credits). Parker, a graduate of the Chicago Art Institute, was hired via John Rewald, the famous authority on impressionism and post-impressionism, who seems to have been the film's art-historical consultant. The hands of van Gogh were to have been those of Parker, but in fact the hands shown belonged to Douglas. Parker came to detest Minnelli and the producer John Houseman because they behaved in the old Roman town of Arles like Roman emperors. In his opinion, 'neither man had any feeling for the country, the light, or anything else that interested van Gogh, and I think the movie shows it'.[3]

Lust for Life concentrates on van Gogh's struggle to become an artist, consequently it ignores his childhood and his years in London working as an art dealer and as a teacher. It also omits the time he spent in Antwerp seeking an artschool education. The film begins in 1878 as van Gogh, dressed formally in a dark suit, awaits the decision of a Church committee as to his suitability to become a missionary. He is rejected out of hand because he cannot deliver sermons properly. In the opening scenes, therefore, van Gogh is established as a failure in the eyes of conventional society. This theme is reiterated throughout the movie.

Vincent, his voice tremulous with emotion, pleads with one of the committee: 'Use me, use me.' Douglas, by speaking all through the movie as if he is about to break down or weep, conveys an impression of suppressed, violent emotion. It works in terms of the aims of the film-makers but results in a one-note performance. Another acting device Douglas uses is that of rubbing his face and head with his hands. He employs this mannerism increasingly as the plot progresses in order to indicate the growing inner desperation of van Gogh as he approaches mental breakdown. A sense of emotional tension pervades the whole film and much of this is due to the strained, plunging chords of the music, composed by Miklos Rozsa.

Theo, Vincent's art-dealer brother, is played by the British actor James Donald. He gives a low-key performance and is convincing as the gentle, long-suffering financial supporter of van Gogh. Theo reads Vincent's letters aloud so that the painter's words function as a voice-over commentary to scenes in which Douglas acts out the content of the letters. By this means and a series of dissolves, Minnelli is able to convey a great deal of information economically and to drive the narrative forward. He uses these techniques repeatedly.

There are times though when the film resembles a crash course in art history. The film-makers obviously felt there were certain basic facts about van Gogh's life and work that had to be communicated. But at other times they assume the audience is familiar with what happened. Several times, for instance, they prefigure future events. To cite one example: in a brothel scene in Arles the whore Rachel anticipates Vincent's act of self-mutilation by placing her bangle over one of his ears.

Condensing a decade of a man's life into two hours necessarily plays havoc with the historical record. A clear-cut example of the film-makers' poetic licence occurs when Vincent, having travelled from Paris to Arles by the night train, awakens and throws open the shutters of his hotel window to reveal scenes of brilliance and colour. Shots of natural beauty and fertility – the blossoming trees of springtime – are accompanied by loud, stirring music. It is an effective way of portraying the transition from the predominantly dark tonality of the Northern scenes to the vivid sunlight and intense hues of the South. But in reality when van Gogh arrived in Arles in February 1888 it was still winter and there was snow on the ground.

To a certain extent, van Gogh was a symbolist painter. Minnelli follows his subject's example by making the opening of a window the symbol of a new beginning. It is a device used again later on when van Gogh is a patient in the mental asylum at St Rémy: a nun opens the shutters to reveal a golden cornfield. We see Vincent adding the figure of a reaper to one of his pictures of this field. He tells the nun it is an image of death, but not a sad death. Again the film heavy-handedly signposts future developments: Vincent is shortly to shoot himself in a cornfield. Art historians can object at this point to the purely personal and psychological 'reading' being given of the reaper painting. The film gives no indication that this death-metaphor is an ancient one which, as van Gogh well knew, occurs in the Bible. It is especially unconvincing that the nun seems to be ignorant of the Biblical reference.

In the final scenes we see Vincent painting the landscape at Auvers which, according to popular legend, was the last picture he painted before he committed suicide. Since the canvas used was a long oblong, this painting is one of the few which matches the elongated shape of the CinemaScope screen. At the beginning of the scene we hear the harsh sound of black crows. Van Gogh is attacked by these harbingers of death and it is then that he adds them to the grey clouds of his canvas. To the accompaniment of straining music, he says 'It's impossible', scribbles a farewell note, and takes out a pistol. We next see him lying mortally wounded in bed with his pipe. As he dies, Vincent tells his loyal brother: 'I'd like to go home.' In the final shot the camera pulls back to reveal a solid wall of Vincent's radiant canvases. In a voice-over we hear van Gogh repeating his remarks to the nun about the reaper, that it is not a sad death, that it takes place in 'a light of pure gold'.

When the film was released in 1956 some reviewers praised it and Douglas was nominated for an Oscar. However, the film was not a box-office success. Reaction to the movie from art-world intellectuals was, predictably, negative. Parker Tyler, for instance, described the film as 'flat' and Douglas's performance as 'dull'. The sound of Douglas's voice particularly incensed him: 'a creepy, undignified whine'. He also questioned the value of recording paintings via the media of photography and film: 'the idea that colour photography can do anything but remotely suggest the true optical impact of van Gogh's oil paintings is fraudulent'. His main complaint was that as Hollywood thrived on heroes and champions it felt a compulsion to present van Gogh as a champion of art even if he only became one posthumously.[4]

Lust for Life has been subjected to more critiques by left-wing art critics and art historians than any other film about an artist. van Gogh's fame as a person depends ultimately upon the high quality of his paintings, drawings and letters. Without them his personal tragedy would be unknown to posterity. In *Lust for Life* this relationship is reversed: the person has priority over the paintings and drawings. This is because mainstream cinema is interested above all in people, mainly exceptional people, and in their life stories. It takes note of works of art, therefore, only in so far as they relate to the life or express the hero's feelings. The idea that art might be a *construction* (based upon pre-existing materials and skills, and upon objective observations of reality) rather than an *expression*, or that it might be the consequence of a host of social factors, is alien to the ethos of Hollywood. It is unthinkable, therefore, that any Hollywood studio would make a film about the life and work of a non-expressionist, abstract artist such as Piet Mondrian.

The film's inevitable compressions are compounded by the film-makers' predilection for melodramatic rather than mundane incidents. In 1959 John Berger said of *Lust for Life*: 'fundamentally this film was a perversion of the truth. The last thing I want to do is to talk from the snobbish point of view of a scholar who minds that a few facts have been mistaken. This doesn't matter. The essential thing is that in this film van Gogh was presented as a kind of problem-child-come-gangster. . . .'[5]

Berger was critical of the 'cult of the disorientated personality' because in his view van Gogh's suicide was a *rational* act: he killed himself in order to avoid succumbing to the illness which was threatening his sanity and his work. His achievement as an artist was overwhelmingly that of a lucid, intelligent, educated individual, not that of a madman, yet the mass-culture preference for the artist-as-madman stereotype negates the rationality of his art and the rationality of his decision to kill himself: 'and so one has the colossal irony of a man who destroyed himself because of the disability he suffered under, now being worshipped because of that disability'.[6]

Berger also stressed the social and historical factors governing the modern artist's sense of alienation, that is, the indifference or hostility of the bourgeoisie. Antonin Artaud went even further when he claimed van Gogh was 'suicided by society'.[7] In short, the aim of the left-wing critique is to shift the responsibility for alienation and suffering away from the supposed defective psyche of the artist to the external circumstances associated with the capitalist mode of production and social order. Of course, the validity of this thesis has to be argued for, but *Lust for Life's* reproduction of the myth of the artist as tortured genius and madman precludes its even being considered.

Griselda Pollock's long, complex article 'Artists mythologies.' (1980) also takes *Lust for Life* as its prime example, partly because Pollock, a socialist-feminist art historian, has made several significant contributions to van Gogh scholarship. Like Berger, Pollock emphasises the socio-historical character of art. She also argues that the mass media's focus on the individual is simply a repetition of what happens in most art-history texts: 'The preoccupation with the individual artist is symptomatic of the work accomplished in art history – the production of an *artistic subject for works of art*. The subject constructed from the artwork is then posited as the exclusive source of meaning – i.e. of "art", and the effect of this is to remove "art" from historical or textual analysis by representing it solely as the "expression" of the creative personality of the artist. Art is therefore neither public, nor social, nor a product of work.'[8]

Pollock then considers the vexed question of the relationship between artistic ability or genius and madness. The idea that there is a connection between creativity and mania, Pollock contends, is an ancient one. In the case of the myth of van Gogh, his mysterious illness is taken as a sign of his genius and this in turn confirms his status as an artist. Pollock in fact has no sympathy with the view that van Gogh was mad, nor with the notion that madness is some kind of prerequisite for being a good artist. In her opinion, the cause of van Gogh's fits was a form of epilepsy. She stresses that the attacks were sporadic and claims they had no influence on his painting.

Finally, Pollock turns her attention to *Crows over Wheatfields*, the painting the van Gogh myth and *Lust for Life* endow with climactic significance as 'the last painting he produced before he killed himself'. She argues that an accurate dating of the paintings of the Auvers' period shows that this work was not in fact van Gogh's last canvas, and also that the iconography and style of the picture can be explained in terms other than symptoms of a deranged personality about to destroy itself. Again, Pollock cites evidence to show that *Lust for Life's* interpretation of the painting corresponds to the way most critics and art historians have written about it. In the light of this conclusion, one cannot assign too much blame to Hollywood for its uncritical reproduction of the van Gogh myth.

5 *The Agony and the Ecstasy* (1965)

Two years after its publication in 1961 Irving Stone's book *The Agony and the Ecstasy* had sold over fifty million copies. The book is not, as its absurd title might suggest, about sado-masochism, but about the Italian Renaissance sculptor, painter, architect and poet Michelangelo Buonarroti (1475–1564). Seeking to capitalise on the commercial success of Stone's fictionalised biography, Twentieth Century Fox financed a cinematic version. The movie, a CinemaScope spectacular, starred the American actor Charlton Heston as the artist and the British actor Sir Rex Harrison (1908–90) as Pope Julius II, one of the artist's patrons; it was directed by Sir Carol Reed (1906–76).

For a time, Reed and Alfred Hitchcock were the two most celebrated film directors in Britain. Reed's career began on the British stage – he acted in plays and he also directed them. For these reasons he was later thought of as a film director skilled in casting and managing screen actors. Unlike Hitchcock, who specialised in thrillers, Reed tackled a range of subjects and he gradually gained the reputation of being 'a cool professional', 'a brilliant technician', someone capable of working to time and to budget. What his films tended to lack was a personal style, passion and intellectual rigour. This was partly because Reed considered film-making to be a craft not an art; to him it was above all a commercial medium whose purpose was mass entertainment.

During the 1940s and 1950s, with black-and-white films like *Odd Man Out*, *The Fallen Idol*, *Outcast of the Islands* and *The Third Man*, it seemed as though Reed would transcend his own modest ambitions and develop an authentic vision. But everything he subsequently directed – including *The Agony and the Ecstasy* – has been considered part of a decline.

Michelangelo had a long life (eighty-nine years) and a long career as an artist; altogether he worked for seven Popes. The film focuses on just a short period – 1508–12 – and just one Pope. It virtually ignores Michelangelo's achievements as a sculptor in order to concentrate on his achievements as a fresco painter, in particular the execution of his most famous mural, the ceiling of the Sistine Chapel in the Vatican, Rome. A film of someone painstakingly painting metres of damp plaster month after month would prove tedious viewing, hence the initial problem: how to make the decoration of a chapel dramatic? The solution adopted by Philip Dunne, the scriptwriter, was to make the commission the occasion of a clash between two powerful male egos. The theme of the film, therefore, is not so much the fresco as the stormy relationship between the two men. There was some historical basis for this solution because the artist and the Pope did fall out, mainly over money.

In order for the clash between the two protagonists to appear convincing, they had to be played by actors with strong screen presences. This Heston and Harrison provided. Biographies of the two men record that the battle of wills was not all simulated: it seems there was considerable rivalry between them on the set as each tried to upstage the other. Heston was used to playing the roles of important historical figures in costume dramas. 'Michelangelo', he remarked, 'was the first genius I ever played who was also a great artist.'[1] The actor prepared the part conscientiously by reading up on the artist and learning to carve marble and to paint fresco.

Filming took place in Rome and other Italian locations during the summer of 1964. Heston visited the Sistine Chapel and was tremendously impressed by the ceiling; he resolved to make the role the best of his career. He was optimistic about the film's prospects because he thought Dunne's script was the finest ever submitted to him. Facially Heston closely resembled Michelangelo (especially when he grew a beard and Ben Nye, the make-up expert, endowed him with a broken nose) but not in stature: Heston is well over six feet tall whereas the sculptor was, it seems, of medium height. Even Rex Harrison, a tall man himself, had to resort to built-up shoes in an attempt to get on level terms with his co-star. Heston gave a low-key performance. For once he was not required to leap around with sword or gun in hand. Reed's objective was to show an artist 'tormented by self-criticism . . . a man who thought of his art as an act of self-confession'.[2] As result, Michelangelo comes across as a gloomy workaholic, a person with no sense of humour nor any joy in his life apart from the satisfactions of art.

Since the subject matter concerned Italy and costs were less there than in Hollywood, filming took place at the Dino de Laurentiis Studios near Rome. The real Sistine Chapel could not be used because the fresco's colours had darkened and there were large cracks in the plaster. A full-size replica was therefore built at a cost of nine million dollars. It was constructed in interlocking sections in such a way that each section could be removed to facilitate different camera angles. Regarding the Sistine's images, Jeff Rovin reports: 'over sixty technicians were employed to recreate these paintings in the same vivid colours that were present when the original was rendered over four hundred years earlier . . . special colour photographic processes were used in transferring the basic images from the Chapel to the set'.[3]

Pope Julius II was a powerful man because he was Christ's representative on Earth, the head of a rich, ideologically influential religious institution. There is some shock-value in the fact that when the film opens we discover that this 'man of God' is also a warrior dressed in armour on horseback, the head of an army fighting a war against France and Germany, the enemies of Rome. Michelangelo is beholden to the Pope because he is the spiritual leader of the faith in which the artist believes, and because he is a wealthy patron. But the artist too is powerful because he enjoys the reputation of being the finest in all Italy and because the Pope relies on his unique skills to construct a tomb and to embellish Church property. Michelangelo can always withdraw his labour and the Pope knows that such a person is virtually irreplaceable. It is a situation of mutual dependence but also of friction.

When we first see Michelangelo he is helping to manhandle a huge block of marble, so the first impression is of a sculptor, an artisan, a manual worker, rather than an intellectual. This echoes Leonardo's view of sculpture as a sweaty and dirty occupation which compares unfavourably with the elegant art of painting.

A long scene follows in an audience chamber in which the Pope chastises Michelangelo for leaving Rome without his permission. Julius impresses on him the Papal authority and his power to dispense commissions and money to artists. The clear import of this exchange is that there were no free, independent artists during the Renaissance, that there was no art outside the main systems of patronage and that those who paid had control over content and cost. In most bio-pics about artists the emphasis on the individual creator precludes consideration of the institutional and infrastructural aspects of artistic production, so *The Agony and the Ecstasy* is unusual in giving equal weight to patronage (although, of course, the patronage of the Church is personified via one individual – Pope Julius).

Since Michelangelo has to obey orders he doesn't like, it might seem that the film is not about two equals, but the very fact that it centres on the relationship between the two men implies that they were of comparable status. Historically, exceptional artists did achieve a new social position and celebrity during the Renaissance, symbolised by the anecdote in which one pope picked up a brush Michelangelo had dropped. By undertaking work directly commissioned by the rulers of society – popes, princes, bankers, merchants – these artists escaped the control of the medieval guilds and were spared the necessity of opening a shop and plying for trade. In one of his letters, Michelangelo haughtily dismisses those who did the latter in order to make a living.

Ernst Kris writes: 'the special social position granted by most societies to those who exercise certain arts rests upon two grounds:

6 **Charlton Heston as Michelangelo.** ***The Agony and the Ecstasy*****, 1965**

7 Etching of Michelangelo, c 1560

upon admiration of the artist's *skill* and upon awe of his *inspiration*. The artist appears either as a master of his craft or as a genius'.[4] Michelangelo's contemporaries admired him on both counts. Vasari, his biographer, described him as 'divine', a special gift from God to Italy. Artists were viewed as God-like because they, like the Almighty, had the capacity to create. Not only did they serve the Church, like priests they acted as mediators between humanity and God. Vasari's views, as we shall see shortly, were faithfully reflected in the movie.

Moving to the adjoining Sistine chapel, the Pope instructs Michelangelo to decorate the ceiling and overrides the artist's protest that he is a sculptor not a painter. Meanwhile Bramante, the Pope's chief architect – played by the British actor Harry Andrews – smirks in the background. This character introduces a sub-theme of the film, namely the rivalries and jealousies among Renaissance artists. We glimpse the existence of an art-world in which full-time professionals compete against one another for the plum jobs and strive to outdo one another in terms of artistic excellence. However, this competition was not yet as fierce as it became in later centuries when artists produced work speculatively for the open market. Again, this suspicion of other artists was based on fact: Michelangelo certainly thought his rivals schemed against him.

Michelangelo builds a scaffold, hires assistants and starts painting the ceiling (in passing we learn something about the techniques Renaissance artists employed), but his heart isn't in it. He destroys the parts already completed and flees to Florence where he seeks the advice of an old friend, Contessina de Medici, played by Diane Cilento. We see her several times during the course of the film. This is Michelangelo's only relationship with a woman and it is fraught with embarrassment – as far as the film-makers are concerned – because there is no love interest to pursue. The reason why – the artist's homosexuality – cannot be broached, therefore his indifference to the Contessina's advances, his lack of friends and his emotional coldness are explained in terms of his dedication to art.

Julius's soldiers search for the artist and discover him toiling in the famous marble quarries of Carrara. He escapes into the mountains and at night falls asleep. There then follows a kitsch scene highly reminiscent of the Hollywood biblical epics in which Heston has also starred: to the accompaniment of stirring music, alone among the mountain peaks, the small figure of the artist witnesses the dawn and sees in the formation of the clouds the image of God as it later appears on the Sistine ceiling in the panel where God creates Adam with a pointing finger. Nicholas Wapshott, Reed's biographer, judges this scene 'a serious lapse of taste'.[5]

At this point, the movie implies an affinity between the artist and Christ: both have to go into exile, into the wilderness, in order to find inspiration. It also purveys the idea that artistic creation is a divine gift, literally God-given. As we have already seen, this idea had a basis in Renaissance aesthetic discourse. There is another correspondence too: when seeking ways to compose pictures, Renaissance artists were advised to study clouds or stains on walls. Obviously, the basis for this practice is the human ability – not exclusive to artists – to *project* images on ambiguous or indeterminate shapes.

Having found a solution to the ceiling commission that satisfies his own sense of artistic integrity, Michelangelo seeks out the Pope (while the latter is busy laying siege to an enemy town) and asks his permission to resume work and to implement his new scheme. The implication here is that although artists remain dependent upon patrons they are beginning to assert themselves, to gain more control over content. Art is now no longer simply a question of satisfying a client, it must also satisfy its maker and meet its own internal criteria or aesthetic standards. Furthermore, the suggestion is that art now involves invention – the addition of something new – not merely repetition of standard formulae. As the artist takes on more responsibility, he enlarges his freedom but at the same time there is a greater risk of conflict with the patron because if the artist departs too far from existing tastes and conventions the patron may well be upset and society scandalised. In Michelangelo's case, the nudity of his figures in the Sistine's *Last Judgement* mural he executed in later years proved disturbing and unacceptable; drapery was added by other artists to conceal the figures' genitals.

Lying on his back, high above the floor of the Chapel, Michelangelo, paint dripping on his face, labours to complete his mammoth task. (Modern scholars think that the artist stood up to paint the ceiling. Heston has remarked that he tried it both ways and it was painful either way.) Apparently, chocolate pudding was used instead of paint so that if it fell into Heston's mouth it wouldn't taste so bad! Below, the curious, impatient Pontiff keeps asking when he will make an end. The rest of the movie continues in the same vein, charting the ups and downs in the relation of the two protagonists.

A great deal is known about Michelangelo and the Sistine ceiling commission from his letters, Vatican archives, contemporary biographies and examination of the fresco itself, but art historians still argue over the details: exactly how long did it take him? How much in total was he paid and in what instalments? What kind of scaffold did he construct? Did assistants paint part of the ceiling? If so, which bits? It follows that estimating the accuracy of Reed's film is not a question of comparing the film directly with the past, but comparing it to the most authoritative, recent art-historical accounts. As explained earlier, there is little point in worrying about small details. Of more importance are questions of emphasis and interpretation, but these occur in scholarly texts too. Allowing for the adaptation into film factor, *The Agony and the Ecstasy* seems to stay close to what art historians know of the event. Certainly the costume and set designers went to great lengths to produce authentic-looking clothes and settings.

As the summary of the movie's content has shown, it is quite informative from the art-historical point of view: it is strong on the topic of patronage; it shows some of the methods used in fresco painting; it indicates the disturbed socio-political situation in which Michelangelo had to work; it also touches on the new social status of the artist, the condition of the artworld and several issues of Renaissance aesthetics.

However, in spite of the two bankable principals with trans-Atlantic audience appeal, four thousand extras, expensive decor, seriousness, high ambitions and positive qualities, the film did poorly at the box office following its release in New York and London in October 1965 (domestic gross was only four million dollars). In London the film was given a Royal send-off, while in New York the premiere served as a benefit for the Metropolitan Museum. The film ran for 139 minutes and was shown with an interval.

Critics complained of boredom, describing the film as 'dull, dull, dull'. Bosley Crowther, the *New York Times* reviewer, said it was 'an illustrated lecture of a slow artist at work'. In his judgement, Dunne's script was too wordy. His sympathies, he added, were entirely with the Pope and when the latter demanded of Michelangelo: 'When will you make an end?', Crowther thought: 'That is the question the viewers feel like shouting at the makers of the film.'[6]

Reed's career was blighted by the movie's poor reception: for three years after its release he was without work. Reed directed in a self-effacing way in order to privilege the acting of his two stars and so, in spite of the odd battle scene and the large-screen Todd A-O image and De Luxe colour, the film resembled a recording of a rather static stage play. Robert Moss, author of a study of Reed's work, claims the director made a major error in agreeing to the commission because the material he had to work with was 'intractably mediocre'. Moss also blames Heston, saying he was 'stolid, a lump of marble'.[7]

Heston, for his part, was disappointed because he felt he had delivered a fine performance and because sneak preview responses had been the best for any of his films. In retrospect it seems clear that the artist-Pope exchanges were over-extended. Since both parties were, in fact, committed to the same objective, after the initial skirmishes the battle of wills seemed forced and tedious. In the end the screenplay was not sufficiently gripping to attract and hold the interest of mass audiences. The making of a major work of art is not a subject likely to appeal to such audiences and, since we in the West now live in a predominantly secular society, the religious content no longer seemed as crucial as it did during the Renaissance. Art historians would have found the film more rewarding if it had concentrated less on the artist-Pope squabble and more on the painting, whereas more of the general public might have been enticed to the cinema if the film had been bold enough to explore the reasons for Michelangelo's life-long obsession with the male body.

In the case of *The Agony and the Ecstasy* all the resources of a major studio were deployed to produce a naturalistic simulation of a Renaissance artist's world. It was as if the film-makers had said to the gaping tourists in the Sistine Chapel, 'let us take you back to the moment of this monument's creation; Michelangelo and Pope Julius will come alive before your very eyes. . . .' Such a film claims to tell the truth, to show 'what really happened' but, as we have seen, in the matter of Michelangelo's sexual orientation it was less than honest. It was precisely this kind of cinematic tourism that Derek Jarman, a gay artist and independent film-maker, set out to oppose in his 1986 film about another famous Italian artist – *Caravaggio*.

6 *Caravaggio* (1986)

Derek Jarman (born 1942), the scriptwriter and director of *Caravaggio*, is an artist/film-maker whose work, like that of his former employer Ken Russell, tends to provoke controversy. His film career is undoubtedly unusual: he has graduated from the amateur to the professional, from the avant-garde fringes to the mainstream of art cinema if not popular cinema. Budgets increase each time he makes a film but they are still minuscule compared to those normally spent on feature films.

Jarman studied painting at the Slade School, London, during the 1960s. Loyal to his fine-art training and the aesthetic principles of modern art, he is experimental in all that he undertakes. His films and paintings are original in both form and content, though uneven in quality. Since his first Super-8mm films of 1970, Jarman has made movies about St Sebastian (*Sebastiane* (1976), with dialogue all in Latin), the punk scene in Britain in the mid-1970s (*Jubilee* (1978)), a Shakespearean play (*The Tempest* (1979)), and the decay of British society in the years since 1945 (*The Last of England* (1987)). *Caravaggio* was the first film in which Jarman developed acting parts for professional actors and in which a narrative in the traditional sense was employed. It was also his first 35mm film.

In addition to his direct knowledge of painting and film-making, Jarman also has considerable experience of set-designing for both stage and screen. Proud of his freedom as an independent film-maker, Jarman is highly critical of the British arts establishment, mainstream cinema, and what he calls 'consumer-vision'. Difference is often forced upon him because of a lack of conventional resources and support, but it is also a value he cultivates.

It was Nicholas Ward-Jackson, a picture-dealer and friend, who first suggested the idea of a film about Caravaggio to Jarman in the mid 1970s. Years were to elapse before the idea was realised. A film about a famous artist made by a contemporary artist is obviously of exceptional interest because it enables us to discover if there are ways of representing art and artists that are significantly different and more insightful than those typical of Hollywood movies. Jarman's cross-media experience made him ideally qualified to undertake such a task.

Jarman's subject – Michelangelo Merisi Da Caravaggio (1573–1610) – was an Italian artist who became famous not only because of his powerful, innovative religious paintings, but also because of his quarrelsome behaviour. Police reports of his day reveal an unstable, violent man who enjoyed the company of roughs and who was frequently involved in street brawls. In 1606 he had to flee Rome after stabbing a man to death in a duel.

Caravaggio took his name from a village near Bergamo in northern Italy. His family origins appear to have been lower middle class: his father was a builder to the local Marchese. From 1584–88 Caravaggio was apprenticed to Simone Peterzano, an ex-pupil of Titian, who had a workshop in Milan. He also learnt his trade by studying the painters of the Venetian school, particularly their habit of painting in oil direct on canvas from life. (Jarman's film ignores Caravaggio's years of training.) He has often been characterised as a 'realist' or 'naturalist' because of this method and his practice of depicting peasants, labourers, whores and street urchins 'honestly' (with dirty feet, wrinkles and so forth) rather than the bland, idealised types of the classical tradition. He startled his contemporaries by allocating the roles of saints to sinners and depicting scenes of violence with what Jarman calls 'passionate detachment'. Despite the various challenges he mounted to sexual and social conventions in art, Caravaggio received support from important individual and institutional patrons. The Catholic Church employed him because it needed, at the time of the Counter-Reformation, a visual propagandist with the ability to communicate with the common people.

Establishing himself in Rome in 1592, Caravaggio produced a series of small, secular/mythological pictures with half-length figures and still lives. These were brightly illuminated and precisely rendered. A second phase of work involved larger, more dramatic religious paintings commissioned by the Church. These were much darker in tone and featured the theatrical lighting for which he was to become famous. Forced into exile by the killing of 1606, he spent the last four years of his life in Naples, Malta and Sicily. He died at Porto Ercole, on the western coast of Italy north of Rome, on his way back to seek a pardon.

Sensual male nudes are a prominent feature of Caravaggio's art. His sexual leanings have prompted much speculation: some think he was a homosexual, others that he was a bisexual. If an artist's personality can be deduced from the works he or she produces – and there are some art historians who take this view and others who do not – then Caravaggio's images of Cupid and St John the Baptist make it highly likely that he was a homosexual. If he was not, then he was adept at producing titillating homo-erotic images. According to Margaret Walters, Caravaggio 'was catering to an openly homosexual sub-culture in Rome; sophisticated, confident and wealthy enough to indulge its fantasies and to develop its own codes and ironies. The tone of Caravaggio's work for this group is distinctive. It is, for the first time, recognisably camp, in its ironical and theatrical subversion of sexual stereotypes.'[1]

Since Jarman is a practising homosexual and supporter of gay rights, there is little doubt that Caravaggio appealed to him as a subject as much for his sexual leanings and tempestuous character as for his paintings. In the person of Caravaggio creativity and violence were combined; Jarman seems convinced the two are interlinked. Caravaggio died at the age of thirty-nine (from malarial fever) and so he falls into the category of artists who appeal because they died tragically young. The life style of gay artists, Jarman believes, particularly exposes them to the risk of an early death.

Caravaggio's innovations of form and content sometimes led to his paintings being rejected by the ecclesiastical authorities who had commissioned them on the grounds of theological inaccuracy and a lack of decorum. He has been viewed, therefore, as perhaps the first avant-garde artist. Since Jarman has encountered similar problems with the authorities of our own day, this is another reason for his identification with Caravaggio.

Reports of Caravaggio's restless life-style in Rome also suggest he was one of the first bohemians. Jarman's circumstances are not identical, but he too has participated in an urban, bohemian-artistic subculture and in the gay nightlife of the streets and clubs with its chance sexual encounters and danger of violence. It is characteristic of the male homosexual, Jarman has argued, citing the instances of Caravaggio and Pasolini, to invite self-destruction by placing himself in perilous situations.

Jarman's journal entries – published as *Dancing Ledge* (1984) – reveal an obsession with the person of Caravaggio. A second prime source of information about the film is another text – *Derek Jarman's Caravaggio* (1986) – which reproduces the film script. This book was issued when the film was released and is notable for a series of evocative photographs taken during shooting by Gerald Incandela.

From 1978 onwards, for a period of seven years, Jarman travelled back and forth to Italy undertaking research and negotiating the finance to make the film. It was eventually funded by the British Film Institute (BFI) to the tune of £475,000 plus some support from Jarman's patron Ward-Jackson. The producer was Sarah Radclyffe, head of Working Title and Aldabra (independent drama and video companies). During this time Jarman also struggled to perfect a script. Altogether seventeen versions were produced. The large number of scripts suggests he was uncertain about what he wanted to say about Caravaggio. Whether to be objective or subjective was one problem. That Jarman identified strongly with the Italian painter is indicated by the fact that he described one version of the script as a self-portrait told through the life of Caravaggio. He has also remarked: 'This story, as it grew, allowed me to recreate many details of my life and, bridging the gap of centuries and cultures, to exchange a camera with a brush.'[2] Since the film is about two artists, one living and one long dead, it cannot be regarded as just the 'truth' about Caravaggio. Indeed, Jarman believes there is no truth as such, only points of view.

There were other reasons for the numerous scripts. One was the fragmentary nature of the information about Caravaggio which makes it difficult to reconstruct his life. Faced with this problem, the art historian Walter Friedlander resorted to the paintings as evidence of the artist's personality and state of mind at various periods.[3] Jarman felt compelled to follow suit. He writes: 'The narrative of the film is constructed from the paintings. If it is fiction, it is the fiction of the paintings.'[4] The question arises: can the character and milieu of an artist be deduced unproblematically from pictures with Christian or mythological subjects? Perhaps one can argue that someone with a violent disposition might well be attracted to biblical subjects concerning flagellation, beheading, and so forth. Even so, in the case of commissioned works, the decision as to subject matter would not be the artist's alone.

A second reason was Jarman's desire to achieve something different from English historical costume drama which he despised as 'ersatz historicism'. Unlike most makers of historical films and television series, Jarman was aware of the problem of the relation of the past to the present. He understood that a recreation of the past through the use of authentic settings, costumes, etc., was ultimately impossible, and indeed undesirable if one wanted to demonstrate the contemporaneity of the past. 'I am obsessed', he remarks at one point, 'by the interpretation of the past. How to present the present past.'[5]

Caravaggio's extant paintings are simultaneously historical and contemporary objects. If we find his works moving and meaningful, then they are contemporary statements. This is certainly how Jarman regarded them. His solution to the problem was to scramble past and present by making references to both the sixteenth century and the twentieth century. Besides the ambiance of Caravaggio, Jarman evokes that of the immediate post-1945 period in Italy before its consumer boom. For this reason he watched a number of Italian neo-realist films, including *Bicycle Thieves* and *Rome, Open City*, while making his preparations. Some characters speak with modern slang, smoke cigarettes and use electric light. Modern machines also appear: a lorry, a motorbike, a typewriter, and a pocket calculator. When these prop 'jokes' occur the effect is to undermine the historical illusionism of the film, to make the viewer abruptly conscious of the present age. Such devices provoke the viewer into a consideration of the differences but also the similarities between past and present; they heighten awareness of continuities and discontinuities. Disrupting period, Jarman has argued, is beneficial in two ways: it ensures a continuing contemporaneity and it helps to prevent a film from dating.

Caravaggio is set in Italy but it was not filmed there because the budget was not sufficient. However, many of the sounds heard in the film were recorded in Italy. The film was shot in six weeks in a warehouse in London's Docklands. Every scene takes place indoors in austerely furnished rooms. The hot Mediterranean sun is suggested by the use of strong lighting through windows or muslin drapes; some scenes take place by candlelight. Props and clothes were made by either Jarman's production designer Christopher Hobbs or his costume designer Sandy Powell, or bought cheaply at flea markets.

Jarman was determined to turn every constraint into a virtue. Confinement to sets meant that nothing extraneous disturbed Jarman's vision. The sets' hermeticism also echoed the dim interiors of Caravaggio's paintings. Furthermore, what could not be presented directly because of a shortage of money, could always be suggested in other ways; for example, a patron's private collection of art treasures was implied by means of a room full of objects covered with dust sheets.

Since Jarman approached his subject with a painter's eye, the design and 'visual grammar' of the film were of particular importance to him. Different colour combinations, for instance, were used to characterise the various phases of Caravaggio's life, and overall there was a progression from light to dark in order to emulate the Italian painter's own journey towards the deepest shadows. Jarman sought a concentrated, severe style of filming. Besides colour, light was a crucial factor. One of Caravaggio's pictorial innovations had been his dark interiors with bodies partially illuminated by shafts of sunlight or beams of artificial light from sources placed high up, penetrating the depicted space from beyond the framing edge. Caravaggio is thus noted for his mastery of chiaroscuro. Jarman considered this mode of lighting 'cinematic' and he worked with his Mexican cameraman and lighting expert Gabriel Beristain to achieve comparable results.

In many scenes the camera hardly moves. Jarman sought to compose the screen image like an oil painting by Caravaggio: scenes are carefully framed, figures and objects lovingly lit and photographed. Several scenes set in the artist's studio consist of models posing for a Caravaggio composition like a tableau of waxworks at Madame Tussaud's. At the beginning of the film, scenes tend to be short and to lack dialogue and development, as if the characters cannot communicate or converse with one another. The camera frequently lingers on the handsome features of Caravaggio – played by Nigel Terry, an actor who resembles the artist's only known self-portrait drawing – whose thoughts and motivations remain opaque despite interior monologue voice-overs.

Jarman's writings reveal that the enigmatic character of Caravaggio was deliberate (he thinks films should be mysterious rather than explicit). He says he selected Terry for the role partly because he had the ability to be absent-minded, as if thinking of more important matters. Jarman wanted to present the artist as a secretive and withdrawn person, but also as someone who had the inner resources to transfigure his life through his art. Somewhat surprisingly, Jarman observes: 'the world which surrounds an artist is always more interesting than the life of the artist, which is introspective and often static.'[6] This may explain why Caravaggio, supposedly the central figure, often seems no more than a void around which other, more vivacious, characters revolve.

Seeking a contrast in the rhythm of the scenes, Jarman alternates

8 **Nigel Terry as Caravaggio *Caravaggio*, 1986**

9 **'Portrait of Caravaggio' after a drawing by Ottavio Leoni**

calm ones in which the artist works from models, with others which are energetic and violent. The latter include fist and knife fights, a celebration with a horse and a red flag, a fancy-dress party, and a killing. The scenes featuring violence are gripping without being exploitative. As Jarman acknowledges, he could have made more sensational use of this material, but his aim he says 'was not to shock but to reveal, as Caravaggio did, the old myths as living reality'.[7] The painter had taken the stale stories of the Bible and given them a new, contemporary relevance by using ordinary people as models and by presenting Biblical tales as dramatic events. This is what Jarman in turn attempted to do with the life and work of Caravaggio.

To avoid the standard chronology of the bio-pic, Jarman begins with Caravaggio on his deathbed and then uses flashbacks to portray highly selected episodes from the painter's life as these relate to his paintings. There are fifty-eight scenes altogether and since most are fairly short, the story proceeds by fits and starts. The plot interweaves the public and the private aspects of the painter's life, but it is so convoluted that it is hard to follow. Caravaggio lusts after Ranuccio, a young workman and model, but he is involved with Lena, a whore. So, despite its avant-garde elements, the nucleus of the film seems to be the eternal triangle. And when Ranuccio murders Lena to be with Caravaggio, who then slits Ranuccio's throat for killing Lena, the plot almost degenerates into the cheap melodrama of a television soap opera.

Jarman's casting is original – a mix of the professional and the amateur, the famous and the unknown. Like Caravaggio, he recruited extras from his circle of friends and the streets. The professional actors include the stalwarts Michael Gough and Nigel Davenport as two patrons, the Scottish actress Tilda Swinton as Lena, and the television and film star Robbie Coltrane as Cardinal Borghese.

At times Jarman's film becomes a vehicle for his personal hobbyhorses. For instance, at one point an art critic comes under attack. Jarman dislikes art critics; he has good reason: they have panned his exhibitions of paintings. In places voice-overs are also employed to make explicit the political functions art serves, the way wealthy patrons and powerful institutions take advantage of artistic innovation. For example, one claims that the Catholic Church used the 'pernicious poison' of Caravaggio's art as an antidote to Satan and Protestantism. A pope informs the painter: 'revolutionary gestures in art are a great help to us' (in maintaining the status quo).

Given Jarman's intention to exploit certain historical material in order to comment upon contemporary issues, one cannot really complain – as some reviewers did – that his film was a travesty of the truth about Caravaggio. Available to Jarman were biographies, scholarly studies and a set of paintings: his aim was not a filmic portrayal of the 'truth' about Caravaggio as perceived by the artist's contemporaries but rather an interpretation in the light of his own lived experience as a painter and as a homosexual. If Caravaggio was indeed a homosexual and this fact inflected the nature of his painting, then a 'reading' of his work by a living homosexual might reveal more than a 'reading' of it by a heterosexual art historian. In reality, Jarman's reading was not at odds with those of some art historians. Indeed, art-historical analyses of Caravaggio's homo-erotic imagery pre-dated Jarman's film; witness Donald Posner's 1971 article 'Caravaggio's homo-erotic early work'[8] and Margaret Walter's 1978 book *The Male Nude*.

Although Jarman is franker about sex than mainstream directors, there were bounds even he was not prepared to overstep. For instance, Caravaggio's painting *Profane Love* shows a nude twelve-year-old boy posing provocatively as Cupid. This subject – 'a homo-erotic pin up' in Jarman's words – proved too risky to film because of the difficulty of casting such a young boy. In the event, the role was taken by a female, Dawn Archibald, who kept her clothes on.

In spite of the large number of Caravaggio paintings referred to in Jarman's film, some key works were missing: the *Supper at Emmaus*, the *Calling of St Matthew* and the *Conversion of St Paul* for instance. One suspects that this was because these particular religious paintings did not lend themselves so easily to Jarman's purposes. Many of Caravaggio's religious pictures were designed for particular physical locations, consequently one really needs to view them in their architectural settings. Jarman's refusal to film actual works inside churches means that their display context is never seen.

How to present paintings on screen is always a problem for bio-pic directors and Jarman struggles to find a satisfactory solution. What is vital about Caravaggio – the real historical figure – is surely the high quality of his paintings. It seems essential to convey this fact if no other in a film about him. Yet Jarman refused to provide any shots of his actual canvases. A set of colour transparencies were made in Italy but Jarman discovered that the proportions of the paintings were at odds with those of the film image. Also, when magnified on screen, the photos of the paintings revealed unacceptable cracks and other signs of decay. For these reasons, it was decided to represent Caravaggio's paintings by recreating what the artist saw in his studio and by contemporary paraphrases of them executed by Hobbs.

Unfortunately, Hobbs is not Caravaggio and although Jarman was happy with the results and thought they connected with 1980s vogue for neo-expressionism, the half-finished paintings in the film totally lack conviction; they are like comic-book versions of the originals. Caravaggio may have painted direct from life but his figures are carefully modelled. The gestures of his figures are expressive but there is nothing expressionist, in the modern sense, about his drawing and brushwork. This destroys much of the film's credibility: how can we respect this violent man or understand why others respected him unless we are convinced he was an exceptional artist?

Jarman's supporters would no doubt argue that *Caravaggio* is more poetry than prose ('poetic' is an overworked adjective in relation to Jarman's work), a subjective response in the medium of film to the painter's life and work. At one point in the movie Jarman makes Caravaggio say: 'Outside the garden the wilderness lies waiting.' Jarman seems to interpret the blackness from which Caravaggio's characters emerge as the sign of an existentialist crisis, an awareness – which Jarman shares – of the vanity and transitoriness of life, youth and love. The real Caravaggio painted religious pictures. One would imagine that having faith in Christ and an afterlife would dispel doubt and pessimism, but apparently not. How devout the painter actually was is hard to determine: he certainly didn't behave like a true Christian in his private life. In the film we never see him observing the rituals of the Church and when he dies he prefers to grip his knife rather than a crucifix. Indeed, a Christian might well find Jarman's film blasphemous in places – in a living tableau of the deposition, for instance, Christ's corpse is that of the dead Caravaggio – consequently it cannot be regarded as a film with a religious message.

Given the reaction of a leading art critic to *Caravaggio*, it is ironic that Jarman should have written: 'films about painters end up pleasing nobody; there is a visionary tug-of-war from which neither artist nor film-maker emerges victorious.'[9] Waldemar Januszczak attacked the historical accuracy of the film in an article entitled 'The assassination of Caravaggio'.[10] He accused Jarman of presenting the artist as the

James Dean of the Italian Baroque. While he praised the movie as 'an example of tense, atmospheric, inventive film-making', he also deemed it 'a true successor to *Lust for Life*'. Hence, in the opinion of one critic at least, Jarman failed to transcend the norms of Hollywood artist-films.

In contrast, Derek Paget, the left-wing author of a study of drama-documentaries, has cited *Caravaggio* as an exemplary, transgressive film.[11] He described it as 'a kind of "magic realistic" discourse' and claimed that 'Jarman challenges his audience to meet him within a defined debate about, history, art and sexuality.' Paget welcomed the deliberate anachronisms because they 'disclose the culturally determined nature of representations of historical reality'. What 'the political gay film-maker' achieved, according to Paget, was 'a radical re-thinking of the process of representation'. Paget is in favour of a 'melding of the discourses of factuality and fictionality in documentary drama' because this 'subverts *both* discourses'.

Caravaggio transcends some of the norms of Hollywood but not all. Jarman certainly subverts historical illusionism and, in relation to homosexuality, he is franker than most Hollywood productions. But what the director shares with Hollywood is a psychologistic approach to works of art, that is, they are seen as expressions of the character, emotions, etc., of the artist rather than constructions made from existing ideological and pictorial material which become independent of the artist and may in fact reflect not his particular subjectivity but the world view of the patrons and public for whom the work was made.

To expect, as Januszczak seemed to do, *Caravaggio* to be a scholarly essay in the history of art, is to misunderstand its character and objectives. The viewing conventions of cinema preclude an exploration of the complexities of Caravaggio's life and work such as a lengthy monograph by an art historian can provide unless, that is, we envisage movies with much longer running times (a week, a month?).

On the whole film critics were kinder to the film than art critics. *Caravaggio* was widely reviewed, received an award at the 1986 Berlin Film Festival, and was fairly successful on the art-cinema circuit (in Britain it was shown also on Channel 4 television). If the film is regarded as a modest, idiosyncratic statement about art and sexual desire with a narrative which is only loosely based on the life and work of a famous Italian painter, then it will be seen in its true colours.

7 *The Wolf at the Door* (1986)

Paul Gauguin (1848–1903) achieved fame not only because of the opulent colour, decorative beauty and enigmatic symbolism of his post-impressionist canvases but also because of his late start as an painter, his financial and marital problems, his egotistical and virile personality, and his supposed rejection of European civilisation in favour of the exotic, 'primitive' society of Oceania. In fact, the name 'Gauguin' immediately conjures up a whole cluster of legends and myths, many of which the artist himself originated or endorsed. Gauguin is famous also for his friendship with van Gogh, a relationship that ended so disastrously. As we saw earlier, this friendship was depicted in *Lust for Life*, a film in which the part of Gauguin was played by Anthony Quinn.

In 1919 Somerset Maugham's, *The Moon and Sixpence*, a novel loosely based on Gauguin's life story, was published and it was made into a film with the same title by United Artists in 1943. It was directed by Albert Lewin and starred George Sanders as Charles Strickland, the Gauguin-like character. This movie was notable for its transition from black-and-white to Technicolor when the action moved from Europe to Polynesia.

Gauguin's wife Mette was Danish, so the Danes have a special reason to be interested in him. Henning Carlsen, the Danish producer-director of a 1986 film about Gauguin – *The Wolf at the Door* – has explained that Gauguin had a poor reputation in his country because he was remembered for having abandoned his wife and five children in order to fulfil his artistic calling. Carlsen's motivation for making a movie about Gauguin seems to have been, therefore, a desire to present a more rounded portrait of the man; he realised Gauguin was no saint, but he wanted to explain the reasons for his unconventional behaviour. However, *The Wolf at the Door* is not likely to rehabilitate Gauguin in the eyes of the Danes because the artist is permitted to describe Denmark as 'that abominable little country'.

The Wolf at the Door, an Eastmancolor feature film that lasts 102 minutes, was the result of an international effort. A team of European film-makers collaborated with a leading American star – Donald Sutherland – and a major Swedish star – Max von Sydow. Sutherland is based in Paris; he was so committed to the film that he co-produced it. Christopher Hampton, a British theatre and television dramatist, wrote the English-language screenplay; it was based on a scenario by Carlsen and Jean-Claude Carrière which in turn made full use of the detailed biographies and vast quantity of art-historical literature about Gauguin.[1]

Music was supplied by the noted Danish composer Ole Schmidt and the Odense Symphony Orchestra. The expert cinematographer was Mikael Salomon. The film, a Danish-French co-production, was made by Dagmar Film Production ApS, Copenhagen, and shot in Denmark at the Nordisk Films Studio and the Danish Film Studio. Finance was provided by the Danish Film Institute, Danish Radio and Television and the French Ministry of Culture.

Carlsen (born Aalborg, 1927) is a film-maker little known outside Denmark. For many years he directed and produced Danish-language films of various kinds – documentaries, travelogues and commercials. *Dilemma*, his first long film made in 1962, was a drama-documentary set in South Africa. Several of his films have been adapted from novels and he has made a historical drama as well as a comedy and a thriller. Carlsen was prompted to become a film-maker by the writings of Eisenstein and Pudovkin and he was also influenced by the French film-makers Jean Rouch and Claude Chabrol. The subjects he has tackled range from politics, unemployment and middle-class sexual behaviour to life in a commune. His work is noted for its commitment to realism and its sympathetic portrayal of ordinary people and struggling artists. Of his earlier films, the most relevant to *The Wolf at the Door* is *Sult* or *Hunger* (1966). The script was based on an 1890 semi-autobiographical novel by Knut Hamsun and tells the story of Pontus, a failed writer – brilliantly acted by Per Oscarsson – on the verge of starvation in Kristiania, the capital of Norway. This bleak film is the most relentless and harrowing depiction of an artist's sufferings and struggle to survive that the cinema has yet produced.

Perhaps because of his own long battle to win recognition, Carlsen is fascinated by the plight of the radical modern artist in capitalist bourgeois society. He evidently agrees with Gauguin that bourgeois existence and values are hostile to art. However, while Carlsen, as Peter Cowie puts it, 'champions the rights of the individual' he is also aware of 'the collective responsibilities from which nobody can escape'.[2] At first Carlsen responded to Gauguin's writings rather than to his paintings, but what eventually captivated him was the artist's disrespect for authority, his rebellion against the social conventions of his time.

Donald Sutherland (born Canada, 1934), the 6' 4" star of the film, is a stage and screen actor who has appeared in over fifty movies. He is an intelligent and versatile performer who has chosen to work for the finest directors and played a great variety of roles. Two of his memorable performances were the character of Hawkeye Peirce in *M.A.S.H* (1970) and the caring detective in *Klute* (1971). With a moustache, hooked nose and period clothes Sutherland looks like Gauguin and he convincingly evokes the man's swagger and confidence in his artistic talent.

During the title sequence we are shown a number of Gauguin's famous paintings, otherwise the film contains the usual mixture of real works and mediocre copies and half-completed works created by 'special effects', that is, François Marçepoil and Karl-Otto Hedal. The sets and costumes based on old photographs and contemporary descriptions are more successful reproductions.

Carlsen's film focuses on one short period of Gauguin's life, namely, the two years from August 1893 to July 1895 which he spent in Paris and Brittany. He had been to Tahiti and arrived back in France penniless but with a pile of canvases and woodcarvings. Some of the first scenes of the film – dramatic ones – concern the exhibition Gauguin held at the Durand-Ruel Galleries in Paris in November 1893. Gauguin had hoped this show would mark a triumphant return to Europe. There is a hostile public response and the critical reception is mixed. Only a quarter of the paintings are sold, though one is bought by Edgar Degas. 'Gauguin', Degas remarks, 'paints like a wolf.' At the end of the film, having held an auction of his work which raises even less money, Gauguin departs again for the tropics never to return. So a central theme of the film is Gauguin's settling of accounts with European society, his last attempt to make a living there.

Gauguin – the ex-stockbroker – came to believe that Europe was a decadent civilisation, a corrupt, materialistic society obsessed with gold. He may have identified with native peoples and tried to imitate their life style, but he too was a European and since he needed cash to work and live he too was obsessed with money. Throughout the film we see him talking and arguing about it, seeking it from dealers and collectors, and spending it when an uncle dies and leaves him a small inheritance. Carlsen makes it clear that although Gauguin travelled far from Europe, he could not escape it. His writer friend August Strindberg – the part played by Max von Sydow – twice tells him so.

There is one scene designed to make clear Gauguin's critical attitude towards French colonialism: he visits an official of the French Government to denounce the cruelty and corruption of the colonists. Gauguin fled Europe to escape it but of course he took it with him, and since some of the South Sea islands were French possessions, European 'civilisation' awaited him at the end of the voyage. Even if he had found an unspoilt native culture and painted it, the market for 'primitivism' was in Paris not Tahiti. The film shows that Gauguin was highly critical of the colonising process and that he blamed it for ruining the Eden-like paradise, the simplicity and innocence he had gone in search of in order to rejuvenate himself and art, but it doesn't quite bring out the extent to which he too was part of the same process of exploitation, domination and destruction. Gauguin made sexual use of the young women of the islands just like any other lusty male colonist. He appreciated and valued the ancient pagan culture of the islanders but he also appropriated it for his own purposes.

Another major theme of the film is Gauguin's relationships with the opposite sex. Scenes set in Denmark introduce us to his estranged wife Mette, played by Merete Voldstedlund. Meanwhile, in Paris, Gauguin resumes sexual relations with his mistress Juliette Huet – played by Fanny Bastien – who works as a seamstress to support his bastard child. Gauguin also has a flirtatious, erotic relationship with a fourteen-year-old Swedish girl, Judith Molard, who is the daughter of a composer and sculptress who live in the studio below Gauguin's. (It is through the Molards that Gauguin meets Strindberg.) Sofie Gråbøl gives an assured, sensual performance as Judith. This character also functions as a kind of narrator since at times we hear her thoughts about Gauguin in voice-over. After learning that Gauguin's 'wife' in Tahiti was only thirteen years old, Judith develops a crush on Gauguin and poses for him in the nude. She wants him to make love to her but in the end Gauguin refrains because the girl reminds him too much of his favourite daughter Aline.[3] Their relationship, therefore, has overtones of paedophilia and incest.

Gauguin acquires from the art dealer Vollard a thirteen-year-old half-caste from Java called Annah – played by Valerie Moréa – whom he sleeps with and employs as a model. She has to suffer the indignity of being called 'nigger' by the French, but eventually she adopts European ways and deserts Gauguin after slashing one of his paintings and stealing his money. The wittiest moment in the film occurs while Gauguin is painting the well-known study of Annah sitting naked in a blue chair with a red monkey at her feet: as the artist stares at her brown flesh the film cuts to a close up of a tube of pigment being squeezed out on to a palette; painting is thus equated with ejaculation. In this picture – *Annah the Javanese* (1893–94, private collection, Switzerland) – there is a partly obscured inscription in pidgin Tahitian which translated means 'The child-woman Judith is not yet breached'.

Finally, we see Gauguin picking up a street prostitute. The film is less than frank at this point: it does not explain that Gauguin acquired syphilis at this time, the disease that eventually contributed to his death.

Sutherland presents Gauguin as an attractive, skilled lover. He enjoys women and wants to please them but he cannot bear them to become possessive or dependent on him financially. The real

10 **Donald Sutherland as Paul Gauguin. *Wolf at the Door*, 1986**

Gauguin, an ex-sailor, was undoubtedly a womaniser. He had affairs with many women and fathered many children whom he didn't support properly. He was the archetypal irresponsible, absent father. However, he never divorced his wife Mette and for years he dreamt of a reunion, of earning enough to support his official family.

Gauguin has a perennial appeal because he fulfilled the daydream of freedom shared by millions of men tied down by routine jobs and family responsibilities, the dream of escape to a sunlight world of easy living and free love. At one point in the film Gauguin compares himself to a wolf who prefers to starve to death rather than submit to wearing a collar like a dog (the source is one of La Fontaine's fables). This absurd, romantic notion is not questioned by the film (an artist who starves to death will cease to make art, an artist totally divorced from society has no public or patrons), but it does imply that the ideology of freedom without responsibility has negative consequences for the freedoms of others: the women left to bring up children alone, the children left without a father. As in Korda's *Rembrandt*, bourgeois society is seen by Gauguin as a cage or prison that restricts the artist's freedom rather than as the very thing that makes art possible in the

11 **Photograph of Gauguin, Paris, 1891**

first place. (Yes, Gauguin experienced poverty and struggled to make a living but then, so do many workers, inventors and small businessmen and women.) Paradoxically, the radical modern artists of the nineteenth century wanted to rebel against the conventions of art and society and at the same time to be celebrated and financially rewarded by that society. The career of Picasso, another notorious womaniser, demonstrated that this was perfectly possible in the twentieth century.

The Wolf at the Door does not present a feminist critique of Gauguin's sexual behaviour – a film made from Mette's point of view would be enlightening[4] – but at least the women in the film are not depicted as pathetic victims: Mette is bitter but she obtains as much money as she can from the sale of the Gauguins in her possession. Juliette, his ex-mistress, tries to be independent but in order to to satisfy her own sexual needs she tolerates his fecklessness. Annah becomes disillusioned with Gauguin but she exacts her revenge by stealing from him. Judith pursues Gauguin of her own volition.

Max von Sydow gives an effective performance as the strange, misogynist Swedish writer Strindberg and there are some fascinating, if appallingly reactionary, exchanges between the painter and the writer. At one point Gauguin asks Strindberg to write a catalogue introduction. Strindberg is reluctant because he finds Gauguin's work unintelligible and because he regards the native women in Gauguin's pictures as inferior to European women, who in turn are inferior to men. Gauguin has seen Strindberg's play *The Father* (performed in Paris in December 1894). It showed him, he says, 'that the ordinary bourgeois household is more dangerous than the deepest jungle'. While in hospital with a skin rash, Strindberg informs Gauguin: 'artists suffer mentally, physically and in the very act of creation.' (Do artists, one wonders, have a monopoly of suffering?)

The film contains no footage of the tropics, though they are represented by the paintings and carvings Gauguin has brought back with him. His explanations of the meanings of their Tahitian titles and iconography are unconvincing; nor does the script acknowledge that most of Gauguin's knowledge about Tahitian mythology was derived not from the Polynesians themselves (after all, they had been Christianised) but from an ethnographic book by Jacques Moerenhout published in 1837. Also, many of Gauguin's Tahitian paintings were based on European styles and compositions (some were even based on photographs), so they were a synthesis of European and

Polynesian cultures. In fact, Gauguin borrowed from many ancient cultures. Achieving a synthesis of the world's cultures might be might be considered the central purpose of Gauguin's artistic programme.

Toulouse-Lautrec's Paris – the grand boulevards, lively dance halls and brothels – is also absent from the film. The action is set mainly in a quiet backwater of the city, the courtyard and wooden studio complex in the Rue Vercingétorix, Montparnasse. This is a bohemian enclave where artists and composers live, work and relax by holding discussions, poetry readings and parties once a week on Thursdays. Nothing is shown either of the political context: in Paris at that time anarchists were throwing bombs and the Dreyfus case was under way.

There are some outdoor scenes set in Brittany and Denmark but mostly the action takes place indoors in studios, cafés, galleries and auction houses. In the main the film consists of brief scenes that are shot and edited in a naturalistic style. Lamp-lit interior scenes resemble paintings by nineteenth-century Salon painters like Henri Fantin-Latour rather than Gauguin's flatter, more abstracted compositions. Unlike Derek Jarman, Carlsen did not question the assumption that the past can be faithfully reconstructed by the cinema. Some kind of contemporary commentary or cinematic meta-discourse was needed to disrupt the historical, costume-drama flavour of the film.

How accurate is *The Wolf at the Door*? It stays close to what is known about Gauguin's last sojourn in Europe though naturally it omits many details and incidents. For instance, Gauguin paid a visit to Brussels to see an exhibition in which some of his paintings were included. The time he spent in Brittany is not as fully treated as the time he spent in Paris. There is a scene in which Gauguin says goodbye to Mette and his daughter Aline, but this seems to be an example of poetic licence because, according to Gauguin's biographers, he did not travel to Copenhagen on his last visit to Europe. (Nor was Mette willing to bring the children to see him in Paris.) Carlsen's use of dark interiors and bursts of doom-laden music gives the film a brooding, melancholy atmosphere. Gauguin works sporadically and takes steps to further his career but luck seems to be against him: he fractures his leg in a fight with sailors in Brittany (however, the time- and money-consuming legal proceedings that followed are not depicted); the final auction sale raises far less money than he needs; the dealer Vollard will not agree to send him a regular monthly allowance in exchange for all Gauguin's work; at the last minute his male friends renege on their agreement to come with him to the tropics to found an artists' colony; in short, his fate seems determined by malevolent forces beyond his control. He decides to return to Oceania because he 'might as well starve in the tropics as in France' and because he has to keep up the image of the artist who has renounced civilisation for barbarism. As Vollard observes, people are confused to find Gauguin in Paris; his presence there undermines the legend he has created.

The Wolf at the Door has been distributed in some territories with the title *Oviri*, a Tahitian term for 'the wild or savage one'. Gauguin used it as a title for a self-portrait and as the title of a stoneware female figure. (Gauguin surely intended the word to mean 'savage' as opposed to 'civilised', rather than someone who is violent and out of control.) The film was screened at the 1986 Venice Film Festival. One critic judged the script 'tame', the photography 'beautiful' and the fight and love scenes 'clumsily handled'. Jay Reiner, an American critic writing for *The Hollywood Reporter*, compared the film to 'a drab watercolour'; he suggested an alternative title – 'Lamb at the Easel – and accused the film and Sutherland of lacking the passion that drove Gauguin.[5] Carlsen's film is certainly a modest, low-key affair. Perhaps Reiner was expecting from Sutherland the kind of intense performance Kirk Douglas gave in *Lust for Life*. The critic might have considered that 'the wolf at the door' could also be taken to mean poverty.

Despite having Donald Sutherland as its principal, *The Wolf at the Door* is an obscure film: it does not seem to have been screened in British cinemas or on British television and, although it is cited in books listing films available on videotape, copies are difficult to obtain. Carlsen reports that the foreign distributor of the film went bankrupt, so it appears that even modern film-makers experience a hostile environment and are the victims of economic forces.

8 *Camille Claudel* (1988)

Feature films about women artists are rare, consequently the 1988 French bio-pic *Camille Claudel* directed by Bruno Nuytten was something of a landmark. Although ostensibly an art-house film, it managed to excite the French public's imagination and so became a popular success. Besides the cinemas, crowds visited the Rodin

Museum, where some of Claudel's sculptures are preserved, in order to see her work rather than Rodin's. In fact, the movie was the climax of a long process of art-historical rehabilitation which was in turn the result of the impact of feminism within the realms of art and art history. Claudel was one of the many women artists who were rescued from obscurity by the efforts of feminists (and some male scholars) determined to counter the 'hidden from history' syndrome.

It was during the 1980s that interest in Claudel gathered pace: in the winter of 1981–82 a play about her written by Anne Delbée and Jeanne Fayard was put on in Paris and Delbée later published a romanticised, fictionalised account of the artist's life which became a best-seller. In 1983 Anne Rivière issued a more scholarly text and in the following year a major exhibition of Claudel's work was held in Paris and Poitiers. An important biography/monograph by Reine-Marie Paris, Claudel's grandniece, appeared in the same year.[1] The film's screenplay, written by Nuytten and Marilyn Goldin, was based on the latter text.

Camille Claudel (1864–1943) was a French sculptress who before the 1980s was chiefly known as a pupil, assistant and mistress of Auguste Rodin (1840–1917). Their relationship lasted fifteen years from 1883 to 1898. She was also known as the sister of the Catholic poet and playwright Paul Claudel. Those who knew her name were probably also aware that her love life and artistic career ended tragically and that she spent the last thirty years of her life, unproductively, incarcerated in a lunatic asylum. Even these basic facts indicate why film-makers were attracted to Claudel rather than to other female artists – the parallels with van Gogh's life are obvious.

From the outset, therefore, the subject matter of the film *Camille Claudel* raises a host of questions: what were the conditions and prospects for a women artist in the French art world of the late nineteenth century? Was or is it possible for a woman to combine an artistic career with romantic love, children and family life? Was Claudel a major or a minor artist? Was she a significant artist whose work has been unfairly overshadowed by the greater fame and success of her teacher and lover Rodin? Did she achieve her own style or was her work too dependent on Rodin's? To what extent did she, as Rodin's assistant, contribute to his art? Did she, in fact, influence him? What was the nature of her mental illness? Did her unhappy love affair with Rodin really precipitate her madness or did it run in her family?

12 **Isabelle Adjani as Camille Claudel.** ***Camille Claudel*****, 1989**

13 **Camille Claudel aged twenty, 1884**

Was Claudel correct in thinking that Rodin and his friends conspired against her? Were her family justified in keeping her locked up for so many years?

No film is likely be able to answer or even explore adequately all these questions. Given that the film-makers were attracted by the romantic and sensational lifestory of Claudel, is it still possible for them to provide a convincing account of the sculpture-making process and an insight into the aesthetic merit of her pieces?

The movie begins in the 1880s in Paris. Camille Claudel is a young, talented, highly ambitious and determined sculptress who has left the Colarossi Academy in order to work independently in a studio she shares with a female English artist, Jessie Lipscomb. Both are hoping to benefit from the advice of a visiting tutor, the soon to be famous Rodin. (He was then in his forties, a heavily bearded man with a prominent nose and bandy legs.) Claudel is aware of his sexual relations with his models but she admires his art and longs to become his assistant. Claudel is played by Isabelle Adjani who, it seems, also helped to fund the project because she was so keen to see the film made. At times it is hard to accept that this exquisitely beautiful actress has the physical strength and the will to engage in the tiring and dirty work of carving and modelling. Furthermore, the make-up artists do not really succeed in persuading us that Adjani ages as the years pass. The real Camille was nineteen when she first met Rodin. At that age she was an extremely attractive woman but in photographs her features suggest more arrogance and stubborness than Adjani's.

Beginning when it does, the film omits Claudel's childhood. She grew up in the provinces and retained a country accent all her life. It seems she showed a passion and a talent for modelling figurines from clay at the age of fifteen. A sculptor called Alfred Boucher noticed the girl's skill and encouraged her. When the Claudel family moved to Paris in 1881, Boucher gave advice and introduced her to Paul Dubois of the Ecole des Beaux Arts. The latter perceived a similarity between Camille's work and that of Rodin's but this was the first time she had heard his name, so her style was developed before she met him. Two early surviving works – *Paul Claudel at thirteen* (1881) and *Old Helen* (1882) – show a portrait sculptor of great ability and technical skill. Claudel scholars argue that if any artist influenced the youthful Camille it was Boucher.

Apparently, Rodin was primarily a modeller rather than a carver of wood or marble. Camille, on the other hand, was a skilled carver. Rodin's marble sculptures were executed by technicians working from his clay or plaster models. Claudel manages to persuade Rodin to let her have a small piece of marble from which she carves a human foot which so impresses Rodin that he signs it: this is an indication that Camille is worthy to become his assistant. She treasures the foot until their relationship founders, then she dumps it in the Seine.

Rodin is played by the French movie star Gérard Depardieu who gives a serious and plausible impersonation. The part is challenging because on the one hand it calls for Depardieu to represent an artist who is a master sculptor, a sensuous lover, a public figure, the supervisor of large projects involving patrons and teams of assistants and, on the other hand, someone who in personal relations is indecisive and weak. At least this is how Camille comes to see him when he refuses to abandon Marie-Rose Beuret, his long-term partner and mother of his son. Rodin met Beuret in 1864 but he married her only two weeks before her death in 1917. In one scene Beuret defends her possession of Rodin by attacking Claudel with a red-hot implement.

A sub-plot of the film concerns Camille's relationship with her family. By all accounts it was a bad-tempered, argumentative family. She was the eldest child of three. Her sister Louise was two years younger and her brother Paul four years younger. The Claudels were a long-established, provincial bourgeois family. However, Camille's rustic youth leads some writers to describe her as virtually an untutored peasant. Her father was a registrar of mortgages. A proud man, he was surprisingly keen for his daughter to make a success as an artist and so he encouraged her and supported her financially. Her mother, on the other hand, favoured Louise and was opposed to the profession of sculpture and constantly made scenes about it. Even a visit by Rodin and his 'wife' to their house in the country – a summer scene strongly evocative of Monet's and Renoir's impressionist paintings of lunches held in gardens – fails to reassure her.

Camille's most intimate relationship within the family was with her brother Paul whom she dominated. With Rodin's help he joins the diplomatic service in order to escape the constraints of family life and so he is often abroad when Camille most needs help. Paul, a serious, tormented young man played by Laurent Grevill, eventually finds solace in the Catholic faith (Camille was an agnostic). He still loves Camille but he is shocked and upset by her sinful affair with Rodin and, like his mother, he dreads the scandal and humiliation which public exposure will bring upon the family name. Eventually, it is Paul (rather than Camille) who through his writing becomes the famous artist in the Claudel family.

When we meet Camille she is so spirited, independent and determined to be an artist that it almost comes as a disappointment when she finally succumbs to the charms of Rodin and becomes his model, lover and collaborator. Several erotic scenes testify to the intensity of their mutual sexual attraction. The film claims, as do the history books, that Rodin was 'inspired' by his love for Camille to new artistic heights – so Camille became his muse as well as his mistress. She posed for several of his works (for example, *Thought*, 1886, *La France*, *c.* 1907–08) and he also undertook portraits of her which still survive. Camille responded by executing a powerful portrait of Rodin (*Head of Rodin*, bronze, *c.* 1888). When Rodin's and Claudel's sculptures are reproduced side by side in art history texts, there seems to be no difference in quality between them. Some scholars, indeed, argue that Claudel's work is superior. At the time, male critics were amazed that a woman could sculpt as well as a man.

Becoming an assistant to a major artist has been a well-recognised stepping stone to artistic success in Europe since the Middle Ages. It enables the novice to gain experience of processes and techniques and to see how a studio is run and how a full-time professional artist operates. The association with the famous artist is also a means of becoming known in the art world itself. However, the danger of such an association, if it is carried on for too long, is that the assistant may become merely an imitator or follower. Brancusi came to Paris with the intention of offering himself as an assistant to Rodin, but he soon came to the conclusion that 'nothing new could grow in the shadow of a great tree.' In those cases where the two artists in question are male and female, perhaps a married couple, the situation is even more fraught. Lee Krasner, the wife of Jackson Pollock, was a painter in her own right but it seems likely that she will always be associated with his career and fame, and that her work will always end up being compared to his.

Camille, as Rodin's assistant, devotes herself to his work and so, over a period of time, she loses sight of her own artistic identity. (Claudel experts claim to detect figures, hands and heads by her in Rodin's unfinished project *The Gates of Hell* and in other works.) Her father perceives this; he seems more upset by the fact that she has abandoned her own work than the fact that she is living in sin. Eventually, the inevitable happens and Camille becomes pregnant. (At the time it was rumoured that she had had several children by Rodin.) She does not inform Rodin but she does beg him to marry her. Unwilling to abandon Beuret, he refuses. In anguish Camille leaves him. She has an abortion and then attempts to resume her career as an artist. This is difficult because she and her work are now indelibly associated in the public's mind with Rodin.

During the day she works hard in her studio and in the evening she flirts with the musician Claude Debussy. She makes a deliberate attempt to produce sculptures which are different from Rodin's: she gives her figures clothes and tackles subjects which are drawn more from everyday life (for example, *Dream by the fire*, marble, 1902). In reality she also tried her hand at painting but this is not shown in the film. Interest is expressed in her work by various dealers, patrons and state bodies. Her work is exhibited regularly and it has its supporters among the critics. The film suggests that Claudel's lack of tact in dealing with clients hinders her from achieving success. When her work appears in mixed exhibitions with Rodin's, she thinks there is a whispering campaign against her. Gradually she isolates herself, takes to drink, becomes paranoiac about Rodin and his supporters thinking they are spying on her, stealing her ideas and conspiring against her. In fact, most historians and biographers believe that Rodin did what he could to help Claudel after their separation.

Eventually, one winter, the dealer and bronze-founder Eugène Blot – who has faith in her art – rescues the ragged Camille and her many cats from a studio half flooded by the Seine. He then organises a one-person show which is well attended but nothing is sold. Camille appears at the opening like a mad woman in weird clothes and heavy make-up. Her brother Paul also spoils the occasion by making a speech attacking Rodin. (In 1905 he dismissed Rodin's sculpture as 'peasant work, served by a devious mind and ill-served by a naturally glum and impoverished imagination'.) Later on, in her studio, Camille in despair and rage smashes all the plaster sculptures she has so painstakingly constructed. (The destruction of a major part of her oeuvre is obviously one reason why Claudel was neglected by the artworld and art history. 122 works are known to scholars, some of which are known only via photographs.) She also persecutes Rodin by dumping garbage on the steps of his house and shouting up at the windows that he is a 'capitalist, an exploiter of the poor'.

Immediately following the death of Camille's father, her mother and brother have her removed by force from her barricaded studio to an insane asylum. They were outraged by Camille's life style: she lived alone in a condition of filth and squalor, she did not earn enough from her work and so had to be supported, and she made wild accusations. A key reason for the removal was the fact that as the eldest child she would have been first in line to inherit the family's property.

The film is frank about Camille's mental and physical deterioration and the anti-social behaviour which resulted in her committal. And while the film obviously identifies with her suffering, it does not blame Rodin for all her troubles as Camille did. The viewer is left to decide to what extent Camille's neurosis was prompted by Rodin's rejection. Due to the compression of the narrative, the film fails to make it clear that a long interval occurred between Camille's definitive break with Rodin – 1898 – and her committal to an asylum – 1913. During this fifteen-year period, Camille produced a great deal of work and was recognised by many in the Parisian artworld as a leading sculptor, and it may well have been the sheer difficulties of the medium and the market that defeated her. Sculpture is a slow and expensive art form: studios need to be rented and heated, costly materials bought, models and casters paid. The market for sculptures is also more difficult than for paintings. Leading sculptors at that time were very dependent upon official commissions. Claudel received few and her work was probably too unusual for the conservative tastes of the period.

Once in the asylum Claudel gave up art altogether. All she seems to have done with her time was to write pleading letters to be let out or asking for improvements in her conditions. Some of the letters are perfectly rational; others make the familiar denunciations. The film-makers were not prepared to depict the thirty miserable, unproductive years she spent in institutions: they simply give the basic facts of her fate over a photograph of the real Camille, in her decrepit old age.

There is nothing exceptional about the film in terms of its technique or form. It is a costume drama in the Hollywood manner photographed in a naturalistic way. In terms of the film's decor and settings – interiors, the clothes worn, the city and country scenes, the sculpture studios and workshops of nineteenth-century Paris – the film is extremely convincing. Sculptures for the film were provided by a team of artists led by Hervé Boutard. The workshops with their clay, marble, tools, platforms for models, etc., in particular communicate an authentic impression of the cold, dirty environments in which sculptors have to work. Convincing too are the rough, almost cruel methods Rodin and Claudel use to force naked models into contorted poses. Claudel's experience of sexual harassment from one of Rodin's young male assistants also has the ring of truth.

However, the film is much less convincing in terms of showing the creative process. We see materials such as clay and plaster being modelled and marble carved but only in snatches, so the drawn-out sequence of steps from concept to finished work normally involved in making a sculpture is never fully documented. Nor are the complicated procedures for making bronzes shown (quite a number of Claudel's sculptures were issued in bronze editions by Blot). Similarly, discussions of the ideas and aesthetic principles involved in Claudel's and Rodin's sculptures are few and far between. There is no indication of what was happening in the sister arts, no information about the impressionist, post-impressionist and symbolist painting being produced during the period of the film or indeed about the birth of the cinema itself. Only a somewhat corny shot of the half-built Eiffel Tower serves to remind the viewer of what else was happening in Paris at the time.

Arguably, the work of Rodin and Claudel was the final spasm of the Renaissance humanist tradition of sculpture rather than the beginning of modern sculpture. In their work the naked human body was all-important: the figure was the vehicle for all subject matter and emotions, and some critics would regard the overwrought, melodramatic statues that they produced as a sign of cultural decadence and also, perhaps, as equivalents to the overwrought emotional private lives they led. The sculptures, especially the nude figures and portrait busts, were rooted in reality in the sense that they were based on direct observation and frequently adopted a naturalistic mode of representation, but they also at times veered towards caricature, symbolism and allegory in order to convey the emotions of love, fear, etc., associated with their historical, biblical, and literary subjects. Allegories and narratives were particularly evident in large-scale sculptures in which groups of figures were employed, for instance, Rodin's *Burghers of Calais* and *The Gates of Hell*.

Both Rodin and Claudel delighted in representing movement.

Dancers appealed to them for this very reason. Claudel's *The Waltz* (plaster and bronze of 1893–94), depicts a man and woman dancing in a swirl of drapery. The drapery was added at the insistence of a government official who perceived that the dance was a metaphor for sexual intercourse. One feminist art historian has argued that while it was acceptable for a male sculptor to exhibit erotic sculptures of naked men and women in the 1890s, it was not acceptable for women sculptors to do so.[2] She concludes that such forms of censorship made it more difficult for a woman to succeed than a man.

Critics who admire Claudel's work strive mightily to distinguish it from Rodin's in order to establish an independent artistic identity for her. There is not space here to rehearse all the detailed arguments; suffice to say there are significant differences, but compared to the differences between, say, Brancusi and Rodin, or Naum Gabo and Rodin, the differences are minor. It is clear that the work of both Rodin and Claudel belonged to the same nineteenth-century aesthetic framework.

Camille Claudel is a colour film photographed by Pierre Lhomme. There are many night scenes and overall the film is very murky. To a certain extent this view of the past is justified because Europe before electric light was obviously a much dimmer place, but artistic work normally requires good, even daylight and it strains credulity at times when one sees the gloom in which Claudel and Rodin are shown working. The emphasis on darkness in the film may have been derived from Paul Claudel's characterisation of his sister's sculpture as 'interior': 'henceforth proscribed from public square and open air, sculpture, like the other arts, withdraws into that solitary room where the poet shelters his forbidden dreams. Camille Claudel is the first practitioner of this interior sculpture.'[3] Light's role in the making and appreciation of sculpture is partially indicated by scenes in which the two artists manipulate cast light in order to examine the profiles and silhouettes their models' bodies form in different positions and poses.

The film is nearly three hours long and half way through it almost degenerates into a sentimental, women's-magazine type of romance. It is rescued from bathos by a powerful scene in which the two protagonists clash for the last time. The two lovers have been separated for some time. Camille can no longer bear to be apart from Rodin and she follows him in the street at night. Tearfully they embrace and then visit her studio for what one expects to be a restoration of their former passionate relationship. However, Rodin is upset by the sculptures he encounters and accuses Camille of copying him and bringing him into disrepute by depicting him torn between a younger and an older woman. The sculpture in question was *Maturity* (plaster 1899, bronze 1902) – a group of three figures: an imploring young, naked woman on her knees appeals to an ageing naked man who turns away into the embrace of an older woman who is generally regarded as representing death.

Whatever generalised allegorical interpretations art historians and critics have given this sculpture, it is obvious why Rodin should have thought it referred to the relationship between himself, Claudel and Beuret. Camille responds angrily and defends her work. Rodin declares the affair is over and he walks out. In this scene Rodin and Camille cease to be lovers; they are transformed before our eyes into deadly artistic rivals. In spite of the misery it causes her, Camille the proud artist takes precedence over Camille the lovesick woman.

The lessons of *Camille Claudel* appear to be: female artists should not mix love and art; they should put their work before personal relationships. Indeed, the film can be considered a feminist health warning to female art students: do not sleep with your male tutors – to do so may bring short-term advantages but in the long run it will adversely affect your work and your career prospects. It is advice they would do well to heed.

II

FILMS ABOUT FICTIONAL ARTISTS AND ARCHITECTS

9 Introduction

Surprisingly, fictional films about artists date back to the very beginnings of the cinema: a poster advertising a programme of films in London in 1896 lists one with the title *The Disappointed Artist*. The earliest films were very short and the fictional ones mainly consisted of comic scenes, romantic or tragic incidents, and trick effects. One of the first British films to depict an artist was Robert William Paul's *The Artist and the Flower Girl*. This 80′ reel lasted a minute or so and is thought to date from 1898. It was made at Paul's North London studio, an establishment large enough to provide employment for a scene painter. The film recounted a romantic anecdote in which a struggling artist rescues a flower girl from the snow only to suffer social embarrassment when friends visit his studio.

Two other films judged to date from 1898 were *The Jealous Painter* in which a painter pours whitewash over a rival, and *The Artist's Model* in which a model cuts a hole in a painting and pokes her head through it. Another film with the title *The Artist's Model*, made in 1907, showed a poor artist's model being lured away by a rich patron. In 1904 Paul made *The Sculptor's Jealous Model*, a tragic drama in which a love-crazed model smashes a statue, stabs the sculptor and then kills herself. Six years later A. E. Coleby made a short entitled *The Sculptor's Dream*, a trick film in which a sculptor tries to embrace his model but every time he does so she changes shape. It is clear that the artist/model theme was a popular one, offering as it did potential for female nudity, melodrama and trick effects.

An early American film – *The Starving Artist* – was made by Vitagraph, Brooklyn, in 1907. A still from the film shows the artist – a

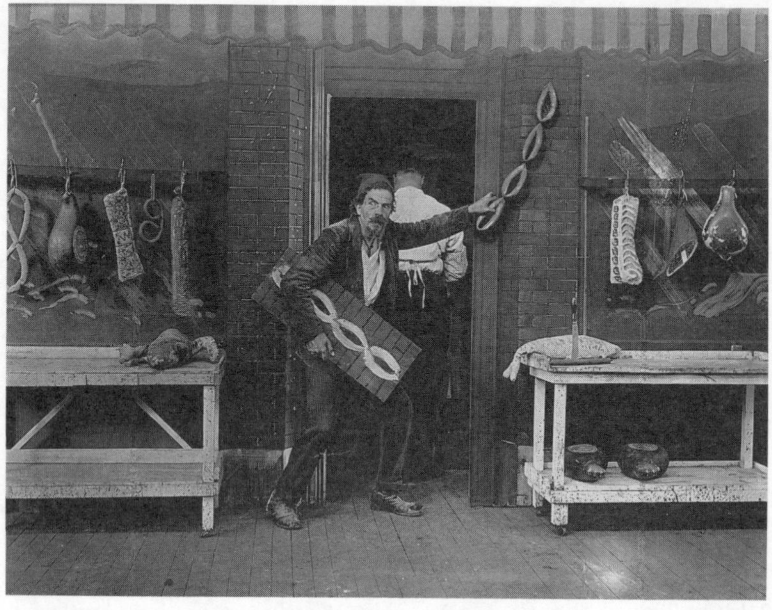

14 *The Starving Artist*, 1907

wild-looking character – in the act of stealing sausages from outside a butcher's shop; under his arm he carries a painting of sausages which he obviously intends to leave in place of the real ones. Evidently, the stereotype of the artist as a wild, struggling or starving man was being relayed by the cinema from the outset.

A few decades later fictional films had become long features recounting complicated narratives written by professional scriptwriters, who often took successful novels and plays as their starting points. The technical aspects of film-making, editing and projection had become much more sophisticated and the 'talkies' had replaced silent films. Furthermore, the star system had been instituted and the separation of films into different genres had taken place. The cinema had also become a substantial industry and business in Europe and the United States. Hollywood had established itself as the world centre of film production. Political leaders in many countries, but especially the dictators of the Soviet Union and Germany, had realised the tremendous value of film as a propaganda weapon and nationalised their film industries. The cinema had established itself as a vital leisure activity and source of entertainment: visiting the cinema twice a week had become a habit indulged in by many millions of British working-class people.

Four films dating from the 1940s to the 1980s are considered in detail and a broader survey is then undertaken of the spate of recent American movies featuring the artworld. Two of the movies – *The Fountainhead* and *The Belly of an Architect* – have American architects as their heroes, both of whom are modernists struggling to fulfil a personal vision. One architect triumphs over adversity, while the other fails and commits suicide. Since buildings and exhibitions are public phenomena and cost so much to erect, both films have to pay heed to the issues of patronage and the architect's social responsibilities. The films make an interesting contrast because the former was a Hollywood studio production, while the latter was a British-Italian art-house production.

In the case of cinematic portrayals of fictional artists and architects, there will not be the same need to evaluate their historical accuracy – although even fictional films are grounded in reality to some extent and can be read as cultural responses to historical events, to changes in politics, society, economics, technology and so forth. The Robert Redford vehicle *Legal Eagles*, for instance, is a fictional thriller but those familiar with the events surrounding the death and estate of the New York colour-field painter Mark Rothko will recognize the factual origins of the plot.

One aim of this book is to explicate ideologies underpinning apparently apolitical, entertainment movies about artists. In the case of *The Fountainhead*, for example, we shall encounter what is termed 'the ideology of absolute artistic individualism'. This film is exceptional in that its content is blatant propaganda in support of individualism, but the same ideology is also present – to a greater or lesser extent – in other films which valorise the lone artist and detach him or her from family, peer group and society as a whole.

Peter Greenaway, the director of two of the movies to be described, had an art school training and so we shall find that his work demonstrates a more sophisticated and complex understanding of art and artists than that typical of Hollywood in the 1940s. *The Draughtsman's Contract* is refreshing in its rejection of the artist-as-outsider stereotype. Mr Neville, his draughtsman-hero, is depicted as a skilled craftsman who performs useful work for his aristocratic employers.

Representing works of art in films about fictional artists is less of a problem than in films about real artists, but it can still present difficulties. If the movie is about a fictional male architect, for example, should his designs and plans be drawn by a real architect or by the film's art director? In *The Fountainhead* the latter solution was adopted but, as we shall see, the models and drawings of modern buildings supposedly designed by Howard Roark failed to convince or to please. *The Belly of an Architect* was much more successful because Kracklite, the fictional architect-hero, was engaged in organising an exhibition about a real French architect whose designs could be shown, and also because the film used the ancient monuments of Rome for its settings. Greenaway's earlier film *The Draughtsman's Contract* also took advantage of an authentic setting, in this instance an English country house. The draughtsman's drawings executed for the camera were obviously not historically genuine but they were sufficiently plausible to satisfy all but the scholar. In *The Rebel* the paintings by the character Paul Ashby, a supposedly talented painter, were executed by a real British artist and so carried conviction. We shall also discover that American fiction films set in the art worlds of New York and California routinely make use of real artworks, real artists and real art galleries.

Most films about art and artists are serious – indeed solemn – in their tone, because art is normally thought of as something spiritual and profound. Comedies about art are, therefore, rare. However, the high valuation of art – particularly modern art – is not shared by everyone: indeed, there are millions who are indifferent to the visual arts or who consider modern art to be a confidence trick perpetrated by a clique of self-serving artists, dealers and critics. Philistine attitudes towards modern art are often found in the news stories and cartoons of mass-circulation newspapers. Comedies too are one of the common means through which negative opinions find expression. The comedy film *The Rebel*, starring Tony Hancock, is worthy of consideration because of the ambiguity and scepticism it reveals towards contemporary art trends in Britain during the late 1950s.

What surveys of American films of the recent past reveal is that changes in reality have prompted a significant change in the nature of cinematic representation of artists, in the sense that the image of the artist as an alienated outsider starving in a garret is no longer tenable, at least not in the United States. Feature films made in the 1980s which refer to artists and the art world now recognise the fact that in New York contemporary art attracts enormous sums of money, that artists like Julian Schnabel and Jeff Koons have become millionaires and media celebrities as famous as rock music and movie stars. In short, the artist has become an insider and the artwork has become the ultimate commodity. This development means that it is has become virtually impossible for film-makers to suggest that American art has any critical or oppositional social functions left.

10 *The Fountainhead* (1948)

Ayn Rand's long, turgid novel *The Fountainhead*, the story of a modern architect, was published in the United States in May 1943.[1] Including paperback editions, the book sold several million copies worldwide. A film based on the book, directed by King Vidor and scripted by Rand, was made by Warner Brothers in 1948 and released in July 1949. This Hollywood movie now appears on television from time to time. It is clear that over the years Rand's ideas have reached a wide audience and, as the biography of Rand by Barbara Brandon reveals, exerted a considerable intellectual influence.[2] Since Rand was the author of both the novel and the screenplay, in the following discussion reference will be made to both.

The Fountainhead is set in America during the 1920s and 1930s – though it should be noted that the Wall Street crash of 1929 and the depression and unemployment which followed are hardly mentioned – and concerns the contrasting careers of two architects, Howard Roark – played by a miscast Gary Cooper – and Peter Keating – played by Kent Smith. Roark, the hero, is a loner, an honest, uncompromising, brilliant and ultra-modern architect who struggles throughout the film against the forces of prejudice, corruption and philistinism. Eventually he wins through to success without compromising his ideals. Keating, his rival, is handsome, weak and scheming. He is a mediocre architect prepared to borrow ideas from Roark and willing to compromise all aesthetic values and standards in order to further his career. To sum up the contrast between the two men: Roark represents the creative principle in mankind, while Keating

15 **Gary Cooper as Howard Roark.** ***The Fountainhead*****, 1948**

represents second-handers, those who are parasitic on original thinkers.

Another contrast occurs between Roark and Gail Wynand – played by Raymond Massey – a ruthless press baron. Wynand owns a populist newspaper called *The Banner* whose commercial values are the opposite of Roark's: it is a vulgar scandal sheet catering to the lowest denominator of taste. Wynand's total cynicism regarding human nature is explained by his struggle to escape from the misery and poverty of the New York waterfront. Apart from his pleasure in being a tycoon, one of the few consolations in life is his private art collection. When he meets the incorruptible Roark his faith in humanity is restored to some extent. The two men become friends: both are tough-minded individualists and so there is mutual respect. The contrast between them can be characterised as authentic egoism (Roark) and inauthentic egoism (Wynand).

The main villain of the film is an architectural critic, the self-appointed humanitarian and socialist Ellsworth Toohey, acted by Robert Douglas. He writes for *The Banner* and gives lectures on 'Art as a social symptom'. Toohey prefers Keating's mediocre buildings because the latter makes concessions to public taste. He hates Roark and tries to destroy him, because the existence of such independent thinkers threatens his hold over the masses. In the scheme of *The Fountainhead*, Roark represents individualism and Toohey collectivism. Rand based the character of Toohey upon several real people including Harold Laski, the British socialist, and Lewis Mumford, the American architectural writer.

Unable to obtain commissions because his designs are too radical, Roark is compelled to work for a time in a granite quarry. While a labourer he meets Dominique Francon – played by Patricia Neal – a beautiful but sexually repressed woman who writes on home decoration for *The Banner*. Dominique admires modern architecture and she falls in love with Roark after a rape-like encounter. Their relationship remains a perverse one, and as an act of self-punishment she marries Wynand whom she does not love. One reason why the scenes of passion in the film are so intense is that Cooper, aged forty-seven, and Neal, aged twenty-two, fell in love during the course of making the movie. Their relationship continued for some years afterwards but eventually ended because Cooper was unwilling to leave his wife and daughter.[3]

There are some blatant instances of phallic symbolism in the movie. For example, when Dominique first looks down on Roark from the brim of the quarry he is using a large rock drill. They exchange meaningful glances while the camera dwells on the drill penetrating rock. Skyscrapers – the ultimate phallic symbols – excite Dominique greatly. In the final shots of the film she travels in a hoist up and up towards the apex of the tallest tower in the world, and as she gazes upwards she sees Roark standing on the very top of the unfinished building with his legs splayed apart waiting to greet her. In the final scene, of course, the positions of domination and subordination communicated by their respective locations and directions of gaze in the quarry scene have been reversed.

Creativity, Rand seems to imply, is an exclusively masculine capability. Women in her novel show no desire or aptitude for creation, only an ability to serve powerful men. The source of creativity, the fountainhead of the title, is quite clearly located between Roark's legs. There is a paradox here in the sense that the blockbuster novel and the film script were both written by a woman. So, Rand seems to deny her own creativity and that of her sex when she celebrates that of her ideal male.

The climax of the film occurs when Roark is put on trial for destroying a public housing project which he secretly designed for Keating on condition that his specifications were carried out exactly. Keating does his best but he is unable to prevent Roark's plans from being altered by the committee in charge of the project. Rather than let his design be traduced, Roark dynamites the half-completed estate. Wynand decides, for once, to risk unpopularity and uses *The Banner* to defend Roark, but as a result he is ruined. At the trial Roark defends himself cleverly and, somewhat improbably, is acquitted. Wynand, now a broken man, decides to commit suicide but before he does so he commissions Roark to design the Wynand building, the tallest skyscraper in New York.

A summary of the plot and characters of *The Fountainhead* does not adequately convey its Sturm-und-Drang flavour. Rand's characters are wracked by extravagant emotions. They exist on a superior plane, luckily exempt from domestic chores and child rearing. Their behaviour often seems illogical and self-destructive, yet it is hard to understand what disturbs them. The explanation seems to be Rand's conception of the mass of humanity as sordid, unworthy and corrupt.

Humanity is redeemed only by the existence of certain rare beings, men of vision and indomitable will – supermen – who represent the unrealised potential of the species. (Friedrich Nietzsche's concept of the Superman was familiar to Rand because she studied Nietzsche's writings during the early part of her life.) Most of Rand's intellectuals punish themselves because they know they have 'sold out'. They feel guilt or resentment in the presence of Roark because he never compromises his ideals.

Rand's hero Roark is obviously a personification of absolute artistic individualism. Many descriptions of his character and behaviour establish his self-sufficiency, powerful ego and single-mindedness in pursuit of his architectural ambitions. Here are some characteristic statements from the Roark's speeches:

'You'll have to let me do this all alone, I don't work with councils. . . . I don't work with collectives, I don't consult, I don't co-operate, I don't collaborate. . . . My work done my way. A private, personal, selfish, egotistical motive. That's the only way I function. That's all I am. . . . the only quality I respect in men . . . a self-sufficient ego. . . . I don't like the shape of things on this earth. I want to change them. . . . For myself. . . . The first right on earth is the right of the ego. Man's first duty is to himself. His moral law is never to place his prime goal within the persons of others. His moral obligation is to do what he pleases.'

Normally it would be naive to assume that the views expressed by a fictional character are those of the author but, for reasons to be given later, there is no doubt that Roark's views are those of Rand. Individuals in Rand's universe are not social beings – beings who are human only because they are constituted by social phenomena such as language, who are embedded within social relations – but isolated 'atoms' existing independently of society. To them society seems an alien force, a restriction of their personal freedom. (Another right-wing thinker, Margaret Thatcher, once bluntly declared 'there's no such thing as society'.) From this perspective it is a misfortune that people have to have parents because this immediately places them within the social relations of the family. In the film we learn nothing of Roark's origins and we never meet any of his relatives. In some respects Roark resembles the typical hero of the Western, the lone gunman who rides over the horizon at the beginnings and ends of such films. Such a man has no family, friends or home; he is an outsider; he will not join any organisation; he has no sense of community.

Roark's antithesis – absolute collectivism, a condition in which individuals are completely dissolved in the mass – is advocated by various characters in Rand's novel and film but they are the villains of the story, consequently their ideas are only introduced in order to be denigrated and defeated.

For Roark, architecture is a calling, a passion, rather than simply a profession and specialism resulting from the division of labour within society. In fact, the particular characteristics of the practice of architecture – the long period of training, the need to belong to professional organisations and to work in teams, the dependence upon patrons – means that being an architect involves far more co-operation with others than, say, being a painter. (If Roark had been a painter or sculptor he would have been more plausible as an exemplification of individualism.) Most modern architects work successfully in teams (group practices). Rand does acknowledge this fact of architectural life but it is associated with the mediocrity of Keating and the firm of architects for whom he works. It is inconceivable to her that anything artistically worthwhile could be the result of a team effort.

Throughout *The Fountainhead* Roark is presented as a genius who is either misunderstood, neglected or persecuted. In his defence speech during the trial Roark also identifies himself with those creators and inventors of history who, he claims, were invariably misunderstood and persecuted by their contemporaries. It is true, of course, that one can find in history examples of artists and scientists who endured such experiences in their lifetimes, but equally one can find many examples of artists and scientists who were appreciated, acclaimed and rewarded by their societies. The idea of the embattled genius whose works are radically different from those of the academic artists and far in advance of public taste is a deeply entrenched myth of the modern age. Again, there is some material basis for the myth in that modernism was resented and resisted by various groups within society. Nevertheless, it had its supporters, patrons and collectors from the very beginning. Even Roark, it transpires, encounters some rich and powerful men who appreciate his radical designs and are willing to commission him. Art historians tend to reinforce the image of the artist as unappreciated genius by foregrounding early periods of poverty and struggle as against late periods of affluence and official recognition.

Even van Gogh, if he had not shot himself in 1890 at the age of thirty-seven, might have lived until the 1920s and ended his days a rich man.

Architects are far more dependent on patrons and clients than other visual artists because of the high capital expenditure involved in constructing buildings. Given this situation, how does Rand preserve Roark's absolute individualism while admitting that he enters into social relations with various clients? She solves this problem by allowing the 'atom' Roark to negotiate on equal terms with another 'atom' who is the client. Roark will not work for a board but only for another powerful ego such as Wynand. Like Roark, his clients 'come from nowhere', they are 'self-made' millionaires. As independent thinkers, they rely on their own judgement of the quality of Roark's buildings and therefore have no need to conform to existing public taste. They tell Roark what they want and he executes their demands entirely as he sees fit. In other words, there is no genuine collaboration. Although Roark designs buildings for others to live in and use, his concern is not primarily with their needs but with his own artistic satisfaction. At one point he says: 'I'm never concerned with my clients, only with their architectural requirements. . . . Bricks and steel are not my motive. Neither are my clients. Both are only the means to my work.'

The Fountainhead is an unusually didactic work in that its leading characters frequently deliver long speeches resembling lectures or political harangues. Roark's address to the jury in defence of his destruction of the housing project is the prime example. It provides the clearest account of the film's central ideology. From this speech we learn that the ethos of individualism is the very basis of American society and the reason for its success:

'Now observe the results of a society built on the principle of individualism. This, our country. The noblest country in the history of men. The country of greatest achievement, greatest prosperity, greatest freedom. This country was not based on selfless service, sacrifice, renunciation or any precept of altruism. It was based on a man's right to the pursuit of happiness. His own happiness. Not anyone else's. A private, personal, selfish motive. Look at the results. Look into your own conscience.'

We discover also that the ultimate goal of the human species is to achieve total individual autonomy and isolation: 'Civilisation is the progress towards a society of privacy. . . . Civilisation is the process of setting men free from men.'

Rand's novel was planned and written between 1935 and 1943, so we may presume that its glorification of individualism and the American way of life was prompted by concern about the collectivist regimes of Nazism and Stalinism. *The Fountainhead* is not, however, a critique of fascism or of Stalinism, indeed her hero Roark manifests several of the characteristics of dictators such as Hitler and Stalin. Instead it is an attack on any form of collectivism from the mildest social democracy to the most ultra-left communism. Rand even opposed the mild reformist policies of Roosevelt's New Deal administration. Modern architecture is the vehicle through which this attack is articulated, even though in reality many leading modern architects were socialists who envisaged their work as a means of achieving a more equal and just society.

A major contradiction of the *The Fountainhead* is that the values of modernism which it celebrates are denied by its own character. Formally speaking neither the book nor the film is a radical or experimental work. Rand's novel is a conventional narrative written in a popular literary style – which she herself called 'romantic realism' – while the film is a fairly typical Hollywood melodrama, though somewhat stylised. One can only accuse the novelist and film-makers of hypocrisy or double standards.

Furthermore, the ideal vaunted by the *The Fountainhead* – that the creative individual has the right to exercise complete artistic control – was at odds with the actual conditions of production in the film industry, as King Vidor well understood. (Any large-scale feature film depends upon teamwork, the co-operation of a considerable body of people, consequently compromises are inevitable.) Vidor, a leading Hollywood director whose previous films included *The Citadel* (1938), *Northwest Passage* (1940) and *Duel in the Sun* (1946), wanted to change Rand's story because he thought it wrong that a man who commits an illegal act should escape punishment, but his wishes were thwarted by Jack Warner.

Vidor confronted his boss with the moral dilemma of the film by asking if he would be forgiven for burning the film if unable to shape it the way he wanted. Warner replied; 'The studio won't forgive you, but a judge might.'[4] So, if Vidor had lived up to the example of Roark then he would have destroyed the film. If, on the other hand, he had succeeded in altering Rand's plot then her artistic integrity would have been compromised and she would have been compelled to dynamite the film set! The studio, in fact, was warned by Rand in advance that she would blow up the Warner Brothers lot if they altered or cut one word of her script. The studio believed her. All through the shooting Rand was present arguing with the director. At the premiere she discovered an important line had been cut from Roark's courtroom speech. She was furious and swore never to work for film companies again.[5]

Arguably, *The Fountainhead* is the mirror image of pop art (though of course they are not contemporaneous). Pop artists appropriated the imagery of mass culture. 'Low' culture became the content of 'high' culture, even so the distinction between high and low was maintained. *The Fountainhead* does the reverse: it appropriates and exploits modernism while not being in the least modernist. It could, therefore, be thought of as the revenge of low culture on high culture in the guise of its opposite.

Rand had reason to identify with Roark's long battle to achieve recognition because her novel was initially rejected by twelve publishers who deemed it 'too controversial, too intellectual' and 'non-commercial'. Even her eventual publishers – Bobbs-Merrill – had no inkling that the book would turn out to be a bestseller. As part of her research for the novel Rand read several texts about modern architecture including a biography of Frank Lloyd Wright. She also spent some time working incognito as a typist in the New York architectural office of Ely Kahn in order to gather first-hand information. Rand was later to meet Wright and when the film was being produced she informed Warners that the style of Wright's buildings was the only possible model for Roark's architecture. Warners asked Wright to design Roark's buildings but he demanded too high a fee. The drawings and models of structures supposedly by Roark were in the end produced by Edward Carrere, an art director who had received an architectural training.

Carrere's designs were poorly received: Rand disliked them thinking they were copies of unpleasant modernistic buildings, while Wright described them as gross caricatures of his work. The film was reviewed by at least two design periodicals – *Interiors* and *The Journal of the American Institute of Architects* – both of which printed negative reviews.[6] The architect and designer George Nelson, writing in

Interiors, described the sets as 'the silliest travesty of modern architecture that has yet hit the films' and 'a total perversion of formal and structural elements'. Donald Albrecht has argued that these judgements were too harsh: the sets met the requirement of a filmscript not a real architectural brief. He adds: 'As the film was *about* architects, its sets were *about* design'. This opinion is expressed in *Designing dreams: Modern Architecture in the Movies* (1987), a book which defends Hollywood's use of modern design on the grounds that such film decor in the 1920s and 1930s made modernism accessible and familiar to mass audiences.[7] By 1949, Albrecht thinks, the glamour associated with futuristic modernism had dissipated.

When Rand saw the rough cut of the movie she was disappointed. In spite of the fact that Gary Cooper was the ideal actor for the part of Roark as far as she was concerned, and the fact that she had kept control over the script, she still judged it 'no good'. Previews were favourable and on release the film had mixed reviews. *The Fountainhead* was not a tremendous success in 1949 but, like the book, it gradually gained admirers.[8]

Why a fictional creature such as Roark should have been devised in order to embody an extreme philosophy of individualism cannot be understood except in relation to Rand's life and political convictions. In her case, biography directly illuminates her work. Ayn Rand was born in St Petersburg in 1905 and died in the United States in 1982. Her Russian family was middle-class and Jewish (her original name was Alice Rosenbaum). As a result of the Bolshevik revolution of 1917, Rand's father lost his business and the family suffered great hardships during the civil war period. The consequence was that Rand became a fervent anti-communist. She emigrated to the United States in 1926 because she admired the free-enterprise capitalist system (apparently her loathing of Russia pre-dated the Revolution.) All her writings – fact and fiction – were a form of propaganda celebrating capitalism and damning communism. Gary Cooper was also an anti-communist and he, Rand and Ronald Reagan were members of the Motion Picture Alliance for the Preservation of American Ideals, an organisation dedicated to rooting out communists in the movie business. Both Cooper and Rand testified as 'friendly witnesses' at the hearings of the House of UnAmerican Activities Committee during the 1950s. Since the will of the individual was paramount as far as Rand was concerned, she even opposed organised religion. A particular target of her criticism was the Judaeo-Christian ethic of altruism: one should not live for others, only for oneself. This philosophy of selfishness she called 'Objectivism' and its logo was, appropriately enough, the dollar sign. Through her publications and lectures Rand steadily gained supporters. She inspired many young people and they established a network of groups to promote her ideas throughout the United States by means of newsletters and meetings. Eventually, Rand became famous enough to meet and influence leading industrialists and politicians. There was, however, a melodramatic climax to the cult of Rand worthy of a Hollywood script. She committed adultery with one of her leading followers, a married man; their affair became public, ended in bitterness and resulted in the disintegration of the Objectivist movement.

11 *The Rebel* (1960)

In 1959, the year before Anthony Hancock starred in *The Rebel*, he was hailed as comedian of the year. It was *Hancock's Half Hour*, a hilarious popular radio series of the mid 1950s (and later television series), with scripts by the talented duo Ray Galton and Alan Simpson, which established him as Britain's leading comic. Hancock (1924–68) came from a lower-middle-class background, a milieu he satirised mercilessly as 'East Cheam'. To a certain extent his humour was exportable. For instance, he was popular in ex-British colonies such as Australia but his dependence upon the British context may have been the reason why he never succeeded in the United States.

Like Charles Laughton, the star of *Rembrandt*, Tony Hancock was a tubby, neurotic perfectionist, a moody, melancholic clown. Offstage he often felt insecure and depressed. In his leisure time Hancock devoured encyclopedias in an effort to extend his education, and also serious works of philosophy in a vain attempt to discover the meaning and purpose of human existence; being a rationalist, religion did not appeal to him. Increasingly he turned to drink and eventually became an alcoholic. This resulted in violent brawls with his wives (he was married twice). At last, in 1968, alone in Australia, his marriage and career in ruins because of his drinking problem, he killed himself with an overdose of drugs at the age of forty-four.

The tragic, self-destructive end to Hancock's life, therefore, echoed that of visual artists such as Toulouse-Lautrec and van Gogh. There are in fact several references to van Gogh in *The Rebel*. Possibly, Hancock nursed a secret ambition to be a visual artist. Sean Kenny certainly thought so. He once said of him: 'Hancock wanted to become a serious artist. He was very talented. He could sketch very well, draw fantastic cartoons of people.'[1] It is not surprising, therefore, that Hancock's first starring role in a film should have been that of a frustrated artist. Many artists seek to resolve an inner, existentialist crisis through their art, but if this fails then the art in question becomes another source of anxiety. Self-destruction may well follow as it did in the case of Hancock. There is a certain irony in the fact that at one point in *The Rebel* the Parisian vogue for existentialism is parodied.

Humour is often ambivalent: there is affection as well as venom for its targets. *The Rebel* satirises the pretensions of artists and modern art, but it also affirms artistic aspirations. Since Hancock is the hero of the film, we identify with him in spite of his absurdities and sympathise with his desire to escape humdrum life in England to become an artist in Paris. There is also a serious character in the film – Paul Ashby (played by Paul Massie) – who is presented as a genuinely good painter.

The Rebel, a Technicolor movie shot at Elstree, was directed by Robert Day and featured a number of major British actors. Day (born 1922) is not one of the world's best-known directors. He began his film career as a cameraman and before *The Rebel* he made comedy, horror and space movies. Afterwards he directed Tarzan films and then worked more and more for television. The photographic style of *The Rebel* is consistently naturalistic: there is nothing experimental about Day's approach to film-making. The movie's script was written by Galton and Simpson from an original story by themselves and Hancock, while the musical score was supplied by Frank Cordell, a man known to art and design historians as one of the members of the Independent Group.

As the film's title indicates, it is about someone at odds with society. Hancock's own name is used throughout, thus entrenching the identification between him and the film's artist-character. He plays the part of an office worker in the City of London who, like thousands of others, wears a kind of uniform – dark suit, bowler hat, briefcase and

16 **Tony Hancock invents 'infantilism'. *The Rebel*, 1960**

umbrella – and commutes daily by train to work from his home in the suburbs, but secretly harbours an ambition to be an artist.

After a row with his boss, Hancock throws up his job and travels to Paris to study art. There he is befriended by Ashby, a worthy but poor English painter. The two artists share a garret and Ashby introduces Hancock to the bohemian subculture of Paris. It turns out Hancock has no artistic abilities whatsoever, but he soon achieves notoriety due to the false values of the avant-garde milieu he encounters. Later he becomes even more successful as a result of passing off Ashby's works as his own. For a while Hancock is taken up by the influential critic Sir Charles Brouard – played by the suave actor George Sanders – and by a wealthy patron with a ship in the Mediterranean. Eventually Hancock reveals the deception and enables Ashby to obtain the credit he deserves. Hancock, although disillusioned by his experience of the art world, does not give up. In the final scene he returns to the London apartment he rents from Mrs Cravatte – a philistine landlady played by Irene Handl – to continue his artistic struggle.

The opening scenes – which show Hancock's train journey to the office and the kind of tasks he performs when he gets there – rapidly establish what it is that the artistic ideal opposes: routine, regimented behaviour; uniformity, being one of a crowd rather than being an individual; faceless bureaucracy; working for others; working according to a clock; performing 'soulless' paperwork at a pace determined by time and motion experts simply for the wage packet; the prospect of a life of endless sameness lacking any kind of spontaneity, excitement, adventure or passion.

Although caricatured, the film's account of the daily existence of the urban office worker could almost be derived from a sociologist's textbook on alienation and anomie in a modern bureaucracy. There is no recognition here that the daily existence of many artists is, in fact, a regular schedule and long hours of hard work, that the smock and beret Hancock dons at home is as much a uniform as the City gent's suit. The truth of the contrast lies in the greater degree of freedom fine artists have over their labour; it is also work they respect and enjoy; it is done for its own sake, not simply for money. In short, the contrast is between alienated and unalienated labour.

Hancock's superior in the office – played by the lugubrious actor John Le Mesurier – discovers he has been drawing caricatures in the firm's time. The different values of art and business are sharply contrasted when Hancock is ticked off for spending hours 'illuminating' the letter 'S'. Hancock's comment that the decorated letter has 'charm' cuts no ice with his boss. A historical juxtaposition occurs here too: the totally different attitudes towards the meaning and value of human labour in medieval monasteries is implicitly contrasted with those pertaining in modern businesses.

Under pressure from his boss Hancock becomes overwrought and assaults him. The artistic personality, it would seem, has stronger feelings than ordinary mortals. An artist will become violent, 'a wild man', 'a madman', if the repression required by civilisation can no longer be maintained. Since the ethos of the office requires complete self-control at all times, the boss suggests that Hancock sublimate his emotions and fulfil his artistic leanings via the firm's amateur dramatic society but this proposal, representing as it does a half-hearted compromise, a conception of art as a hobby, is coldly rejected. Hancock wants to be a full-time professional, not a part-time amateur, hence his decision – taken in a 1950s Espresso coffee bar – to leave for Paris.

As far as the film's scriptwriters were concerned, Paris was the obvious choice because it was world's art centre. For more than a century this had been true, and once the Second World War ended many British artists did travel to Paris to study and to work. But, arguably, the film was anachronistic in this respect because New York had by then replaced Paris as the world's art capital. Nor did the scriptwriters notice that by the late 1950s it was much easier to become an artist in Britain: London was about to become famous for its pop artists and throughout the country thousands of teenagers – many from working-class backgrounds – were attending art and design colleges. It was they who would shortly produce the art, fashion, music, photography, graphics and design that would make the popular culture of the 1960s so distinctive. Of course, the fact that there was a respectable, higher educational, institutional route to becoming an artist fully supported by the state would have contradicted the artist-as-rebel/outsider premise of the film.

Two types of artwork appear in the film in order to establish a contrast between good and bad, authentic and inauthentic, traditional and experimental: Ashby's competent nudes and landscapes and Hancock's dreadful daubs and carvings. Ashby's paintings were executed by Alistair Grant, a Royal College of Art tutor and an artist exhibiting in London in the 1950s. Hancock's pictures are primitive and childish; in Paris he is said to belong to the 'Infantile School'. His ugly, badly carved 'sculptures' are if anything even worse, particularly the massive, half-finished stone statue of the Greek Goddess Aphrodite which makes several appearances. The film-makers were in no doubt about what signified bad art in the late 1950s. They little realised that a few decades later there would be a vogue for 'bad' painting and that artists such as Georg Baselitz and Bruce McLean would be exhibiting sculptures of an equivalent awfulness in major galleries.

Among the targets for *The Rebel's* satire was the post-war Parisian fashion for existentialism: at a party Hancock is admired by a group of existentialists, all similarly attired in black clothes and white make-up, who – unaware of the irony – condemn other social groups for their conformism. Another target was the obscure and pretentious jargon of the artworld: a café scene in Paris depicts a group of artists arguing among themselves in an effort to differentiate their art in the market place and to climb to the top of the heap. A third target was surrealism: Hancock visits the home of a rich, English eccentric and aesthete with the paradoxically plain name of Jim Smith: he wears a striped T-shirt, jodhpurs and half an upwardly curling moustache; he smokes cigarettes with a long holder, keeps a cow in his bedroom and is fond of resting underwater in a huge fish tank. This absurd character – played by Denis Price – was clearly intended as a parody of Salvador Dali, a hard target to hit because he was the past master of self-parody.

Writers of comedies take a cavalier attitude towards history: in their use of the past and the present, they are not concerned about consistency of period. For instance, in *The Rebel* there is a scene which includes a mish-mash of references to both nineteenth- and twentieth-century art. It is, in fact, one of the funniest scenes in the film: it shows Hancock attempting to produce an action painting. He is observed by a cow which supplies fresh milk for his breakfast and which also serves as a model. The presence of such animals in artists' studios was a feature of nineteenth-century realist art schools such as the one run by Gustave Courbet. Hancock unrolls a bolt of canvas on the floor, dons rubber hat and boots, picks up large cans of liquid paint, and proceeds to splash their contents onto the canvas, all the while talking to himself in an American, beat-style voice. Next he walks all over the slippery surface, squirts tubes of pigment over it, rides a bicycle across it and adds handfuls of sand.

Two topical targets were satirised here: first, the action-painting procedures of the recently deceased American artist Jackson Pollock (Pollock was also a heavy drinker and killed himself in a car crash in 1956. A large-scale exhibition of his work was held at the Whitechapel Art Gallery, London, in 1958. Hans Namuth's famous film of Pollock dripping paint was made in 1951); and second, the studio antics of the English artist William Green, who became notorious in the late 1950s for riding bicycles across canvases.

Arguably, in its depiction of Sir Charles, the film over-exaggerated the power of the art critic to make or break a reputation. Only a very few critics have this degree of influence – it more normally belongs to dealers and collectors. Nevertheless, the film was accurate in showing how, through exhibitions and press conferences, an artist can become a media celebrity virtually overnight. Wealthy collectors like to buy new art while it is still cheap and the artist is on the verge of fame. Once it becomes known that they value the art, its market value leaps up. If the original investors decide to sell, they can make huge profits. Hancock is taken up by a wealthy collector and his wife; the latter is a nymphomaniac who decides she wants Hancock. Only his incompetence as a lover and as an artist prevents him from becoming a plaything of the rich.

Hancock's contact with the patron provides the occasion for one of the best gags in the movie. Having botched a sculpted portrait of the man's wife, the artist flees to an airport to escape the patron's wrath. Since it is carnival time, Hancock is wearing a ludicrous budgerigar costume. (This outfit had served as the basis for one of his earlier stage sketches given at the 1958 Royal Variety performance.) Hancock tells the booking clerk he wants to fly to London; the clerk advises him to wait for an aircraft as it is rather a long way for a budgie!

The Rebel contained some acute criticisms of the world of modern art. As a deflation of that world's pretensions, it was salutary. In the contrast it set up between authentic and inauthentic strands of modern art and the difficulty of telling the difference between the two, the film articulated the anxieties of many lay people. Although the movie was extremely funny in places, it was too long. It was premiered at the Beirut film festival and first shown to the trade in London in January 1961. When released in Britain it was generally welcomed and it made money, but it failed completely in New York where it was shown in October 1961 under the title *Call Me Genius*. Bosley Crowther, film critic of the *New York Times*, was dismissive: Hancock, he said, 'stumbles vainly, giving a clumsy pretence of being funny'; he also claimed the repeated joke involving a statue that is so heavy it crashes through the floors of houses and ships had been stolen from *The Horse's Mouth*.[2] Hancock was in New York for the film's opening. He was so upset by the negative criticism, he left to seek solace, like the art-crazed hero of *The Rebel*, in the cafés of Paris.

Hancock's movie evoked no response from the British art press, but it did have a significant impact on a public schoolboy who was to become a well-known art critic. Peter Fuller (1947–90), in his book *Art and Psychoanalysis*, recalls seeing the film at the age of fourteen.[3]

Apparently, it prompted him to take up painting and to study modern art. He remarks: 'the film was silly enough . . . but the message I took away from it is that facility in "objective" representation was not decisive.' The influence of the film persisted into adult life: the term 'infantilism' became part of Fuller's critical vocabulary.

12 *The Draughtsman's Contract* (1982)

Peter Greenaway's *The Draughtsman's Contract* is a tour de force of art cinema. As a film and as a representation of an artist it is markedly different from the British and Hollywood examples already considered: it is far more sophisticated, self-conscious and intricate. The differences cannot be understood except in relation to the different social, historical and institutional contexts in which the films were made. Greenaway's movie, for example, was financed not by a major studio but by the British Film Institute in association with Channel 4 television (the BFI provided £180,000 and Channel 4 £150,000).

The film is also inconceivable except in relation to the growth during the 1960s and 1970s of film schools and film theory. Studies and analyses of the nature of cinema, film styles and genres produced a much more knowing generation of film-makers. The sophistication of audiences also increased during the same period so that films which are about the nature of film, which allude to other films, or which are allegorical or ambiguous as to genre, can now find an appreciative public. *The Draughtsman's Contract* quickly became a cult movie among the intelligentsia (especially on the continent of Europe) though there were some artist-intellectuals – Derek Jarman, for instance – who disliked its artificiality and cleverness. Alan Parker, a director of the kind of mainstream narrative movies Greenaway opposes, was one of those who angrily dismissed the film as 'pretentious' and 'pseudo-intellectual'. (He even threatened to emigrate with his children if this was to be the future of British cinema!) The fact is that Greenaway is a genuine intellectual who is interested in a cinema of ideas rather than a novel-based cinema of cheap emotions and sensations. His film is an exceedingly complex, ornate 'text' which, as one reviewer put it, was 'made to be analysed'.

The character of the film is partly explained by Greenaway's background and training: he was born in Newport, Gwent in 1942 into a middle-class family that later moved to north east London; he developed an interest in art and studied painting at Walthamstow College of Art during the early 1960s. (Ian Dury, the rock singer, was a fellow student.) The history of art is vitally important to Greenaway: virtually all his films and television work exploit the image bank provided by two thousand years of Western European art and architecture. As a student he had a penchant for 'speculative literature' and his paintings were criticized for being 'too literary'. He made one film – *Death of Sentiment* – while he was an art student. Film, he discovered, was a medium in which he could combine his interest in words and pictures (he both wrote and directed *The Draughtsman's Contract.*)

A seminal early influence was Ingmar Bergman's *The Seventh Seal* (1957). This film demonstrated that a metaphorical and allegorical approach to the cinema was possible. Greenaway subsequently studied the work of other European art cinema film-makers such as Alain Resnais, Pier Paolo Pasolini, Jean-Luc Godard and Michelangelo Antonioni. Resnais' demanding movie *Last Year in Marienbad* (1962) particularly impressed him. The brilliant camerawork was by Sacha Vierny. (Greenaway and Vierny have since made several films together.) Another seminal early influence – this time from the art of painting – was R. B. Kitaj's first one-man show held in London in 1963. Kitaj's paintings taught Greenaway that a scholarly, intertextual approach to art could succeed. He especially admired the way Kitaj combined images and words and used a compartmented structure to organize disparate items of information.

After art college Greenaway found employment in the film distribution department of the BFI where he was able to view a wide range of experimental films. Then, for a number of years, he worked for the film section of the Central Office of Information as an editor. There he learnt about the British documentary tradition and how propaganda films are constructed. Later still, he made a living as a freelance film editor. Simultaneously, he was making low-budget, avant-garde, independent films such as *Intervals* (1969), *H is for House* (1974), *Windows* (1975), *Dear Phone* (1976), *A Walk through H – or, the Reincarnation of an Ornithologist* (1978), *Vertical Features Remake* (1979) and *The Falls* (1980). Several of these films reflected an obsession with lush English landscapes which was to be developed even further in *The Draughtsman's Contract.*

17 **Anthony Higgins as Mr. Neville. *The Draughtsman's Contract*, 1982**

18 **Peter Greenaway, 'Mr Neville's drawing number 9'. *The Draughtsman's Contract*, 1982**

Greenaway takes a delight in arcane knowledge and in the activities of listing, classifying and cataloguing. Such systems – even bogus ones – are to be imposed on the world in order to contain its chaos. He took note of the vogue among avant-garde film-makers for 'structural-materialist film' and he shared with minimal and systems artists the habit of employing arbitrary compositional or structuring devices such as grids, numbers or the alphabet.

In sum, *The Draughtsman's Contract* can be seen as the result of a conjunction of fine art, avant-garde film, European art cinema and film theory. This might suggest that the film is dour and inaccessible but Greenaway is always conscious of the pleasures of imagery, language and scholarship; he also delights in playing games with the conventions of film and genre, consequently the movie is surprising, witty and visually stunning.

The film is set in Wiltshire in 1694 and is about a landscape artist and Scottish Roman Catholic called Mr Neville (played by Anthony Higgins) who makes a living drawing prospects of country houses for the landed gentry. On one level, then, the film is a period costume drama. However, mysterious incidents take place at Compton Anstey, the country-house setting, including two murders, so the film could also be regarded as an Agatha Christie-type 'who dun it?'. Yet neither of these descriptions exhaust the film: its form and content repeatedly raise the issue of the nature and purpose of art and so one could argue that the film is ultimately a reflection on art in general and, therefore, itself as a work of art. Creators are often the protagonists of Greenaway's films because they enable him to explore his own uncertainties about the role of the artist.

Groombridge Place – the real house chosen by Greenaway as the setting for his movie – is situated not in Wiltshire but on the border between Kent and Sussex. A brick structure surrounded by a moat, it was built by John Packer between 1652 and 1674. Legend has it that the pleasant formal gardens surrounding the house were designed by John Evelyn, the famous diarist and amateur landscape gardener. These gardens in turn are surrounded by fields with grazing animals.

It takes several minutes to reach the main title of the film because the credits are interspersed with short scenes which introduce us to the cast of characters. We meet the artist Neville, the landowners Mr and Mrs Herbert (played by Dave Hill and Janet Suzman), their daughter and son-in-law Mr and Mrs Talmann (played by Hugh

Fraser and Anne Louise Lambert), Mr Noyes the Herberts' estate manager (played by Neil Cunningham), and various others who make up a country-house party. Neville dresses plainly in black but most of the other males are foppishly attired in brocaded coats and enormous powdered wigs (the costume designer was Sue Blane).

At first the dialogue is hard to follow because the characters converse in a brittle, highly stylised form of English traditionally associated with Restoration novels and plays about the upper classes. Despite the problems this poses the audience, it is refreshing to hear in the cinema an articulate, complex form of speech. The music is foregrounded much more than is usual in films and tends to come in bursts; it was composed by Michael Nyman, who reworked the sounds and instruments of the seventeenth century. Nyman has explained that the instrumentation becomes richer as the film progresses in imitation of the way the drawings start with a single line and then gradually fill the whole sheet of paper. An eight-bar sequence is repeated with variations, again in imitation of the repeated visual elements.

It is high summer in an idyllic rural setting. Many scenes take place out of doors in the exquisitely beautiful gardens or fields, while others take place at night with illumination supplied by candles and lamps (several of the indoor night scenes' compositions are based directly upon paintings by Georges de la Tour and Caravaggio). So, throughout the movie, there is an alternation of light and dark, exterior and interior. The camera – operated by Curtis Clark – often holds a landscape view as if to provide a cinematic equivalent of a seventeenth-century veduta or, in the case of outdoor scenes with figures, to evoke a conversation piece.

A favourite repeated shot is of a landscape seen through Neville's drawing aid (a rectangular wooden frame with wires forming a grille which corresponds to a squared-up sheet of paper). The frame-within-the-frame device calls attention, of course, to the framing inherent in all painting, photography and filming; it also serves as a distancing mechanism. There is a pun here too because as the plot unfolds we discover that Neville is being set up or 'framed'. Greenaway recalls that at art-school he was told: 'paint what you see, not what you know.' Neville follows this rule but, paradoxically, by doing so he becomes blind to what is happening; he is thus easy prey for the female characters.

When the camera does move it tends to do so rapidly in a manner which calls attention to itself: tracking to the left or right in a long straight line recalling similar shots in Godard's *Tout va Bien* (1972). When such commonplace techniques as point of view and reverse shots are employed, they tend to be exaggerated as if to say to the viewer: 'You are familiar with this filmic convention, are you not?'

The film lasts nearly two hours (the first edit was three and a half hours) and principally consists of short scenes in which characters haughtily address or berate one another. One critic described the film's development as 'slower than a sedated sloth', but this is surely a mistaken impression, because the succession of scenes and rapid-fire conversations make for quite a brisk pace. What may contribute to a sense of slowness is the element of repetition: as the artist circles around the house day after day to produce drawings from different angles, there is necessarily a sequence of similar scenes. But the overall effect is musical or rhythmical, like the steps in a formal dance. Greenaway always likes to have a logical structure underpinning his films and in this case it was the twelve drawings which he set himself to execute at predetermined time intervals so that the light and cast shadows would be similar. As Robert Brown has remarked, all Greenaway's films create 'an idiosyncratic dialectic between narrative and structure'.[1]

Neville is a handsome, arrogant yet innocent young man who is determined to exploit his patrons to the maximum. As the film progresses, however, it becomes clear he is the one being used, that he is the victim. Reluctant to undertake a commission, he is eventually persuaded by Mrs Herbert and her daughter to make a dozen drawings of views of the family's country seat. A legal contract is drawn up by Noyes which includes the unusual provision that as payment the lady of the house will grant the artist any sexual favour he desires. Later on he comes to a similar arrangement with Sarah Talmann. The latter's German Protestant husband, it seems, is impotent and so a male heir for the estate is lacking. Neville does not realise it but it is he who is to serve as a breeding stallion; it is he who is being sexually exploited.

Imperiously, Neville sets about his task. Chairs and his drawing frame are placed day after day in different locations. Orders are given to keep prospects clear of people while he is drawing. Between times he disputes with the other guests as to whether or not there is any

English painting worthy of the name and submits Mrs Herbert to a series of humiliating sexual assaults. Franker than usual erotic scenes are, of course, the common currency of art-house movies.

Mr Herbert's dead body is discovered near an equestrian monument set in the moat. Has he been murdered? If so by whom? Who has a motive – his widow, daughter, son-in-law? Noyes is afraid he will be accused of the murder and he blackmails Mrs Herbert. She gives him her protection and money from the sale of the drawings in exchange for the incriminating contract. Mr Talmann acquires the drawings because he thinks they contain clues to Herbert's murder and his wife's infidelity.

It is now autumn. After a period away, Neville returns bringing Mrs Herbert a gift of pomegranates. These fruit are clearly of allegorical significance (they are ancient symbols of fertility). Indeed, Mrs Herbert informs Neville of the Greek myth associated with them. As a reciprocal gesture she orders her gardener to supply Neville with a pineapple (there is a reference here to a painting by Danckerts showing a gardener presenting King Charles with the first pineapple grown in England). The sexual liaison between Neville and Mrs Herbert is renewed one more time and the artist agrees to execute a final, thirteenth drawing of the house. Mrs Herbert, in the presence of her daughter, squeezes out the juice of the pomegranates into a cloth and remarks that the stains resemble blood. This heralds the demise of Neville who has now served his purpose.

As darkness falls, Neville completes the last drawing by the moat where Herbert's body was recovered. He is then surrounded by masked men carrying lamps. He recognises Talmann by his voice. The latter objects to his return and to the sexual affair with his wife. Neville protests that the women agreed to the contracts. His argument carries no weight; the men attack him, burn out his eyes, strip his body in order to scatter his clothes to make 'an obscure allegory', and finally they beat him to death and throw his corpse into the moat. In the final shots the stone rider of the equestrian monument dismounts and we see Neville's last drawing burning: it features the riderless horse (a sexual pun? Without Neville Mrs Herbert is riderless?). We are left not knowing who killed Herbert or why he was killed.

The above is a crude summary of an exceedingly complicated storyline which leaves out many asides and digressions. Greenaway's intention, one presumes, was to intrigue viewers by entrapping them in a mesh of references and to confound them with the labyrinthine niceties of the plot.

Composition is obviously crucial to the topographical views Neville specialises in and a comparable attention to composition is paid by the director and cameraman. The geometrical system of perspective underpins both the acts of drawing and of filming. Geometry is also present in the layout of the formal gardens of the house. Frequently, shots are so composed that the elements within them are symmetrical. This kind of ordering reflects the love of pattern typical of the period, but also the logical systems associated with so much modern art.

This order is not, however, all-powerful. It is in constant danger of breaking down. Neville has to give strict instructions each day to exclude random elements from his prospects. Even so, each view is disrupted by unaccountable objects such as a ladder against the house, a pair of riding boots in a field, a shirt on a bush. The mannered rituals of daily life are also disrupted by the rather brutal use Neville makes of the body of Mrs Herbert, and the social order is disrupted by the two murders. Beneath this controlled, ordered world, Greenaway implies, lie violent desires and actions. Indeed, the film suggests that the very maintenance of the social order depends on ruthlessness and killing. Greenaway's bleak and pessimistic view of the human condition is even more evident in some of his later films.

In the late seventeenth and early eighteenth centuries a contrast developed between ideal landscapes (idealised, invented scenes with classical buildings or ruins) and topographical studies (accurate representations of real places). Neville belongs to the latter school. He regards himself as an objective artist: from a particular point of view he records as precisely as possible what he sees though the drawing frame. There is no room in this naturalistic form of art for idealisations, inventions, subjectivity or expression, for the imagination or fantasy, or for any doubt that reality can be truthfully represented through its external appearances (hence the drawings seem dry and academic).

The historical models for Neville appear to have been artists like Wenceslaus Hollar (1607–77) and Leonard Knyff (1650–1722), two foreigners who found employment in England. Hollar (from Bohemia) was a graphic artist who made detailed prospects of aristocratic estates. Knyff (from Holland) was a painter and draughtsman of royal palaces and country houses. However, as Simon Watney has pointed out in a study of the film, real seventeenth-century draughtsmen tended to supply bird's-eye views of estates rather than the ground-level perspectives Neville provides.[2]

Photographs and film images have replaced such drawings as the epitome of objective statements about the world. In this film Greenaway uses the camera in a naturalistic way – in the sense that he avoids special effects – but this does not mean that the film is bereft of fantasy. Periodically he undercuts the viewer's certainty about what is real and what is not. For example, there are statues in the grounds of the house which are filmed as if they were made of stone, but half way through a scene one will come alive and we then realise the 'statue' was a man made up to look like stone posing as a statue. In one scene a 'statue' removes an obelisk from a plinth, then climbs on top of it, assumes a static pose and proceeds to urinate as if now a part of a fountain. Visual jokes of this kind – which are such a feature of the philosophical brand of surrealism practised by René Magritte – depend on the naturalistic and illusionistic qualities of the medium of film but simultaneously they undermine them. Such jokes call attention to the artificiality of films: viewers should not assume that films provide direct access to truth because appearances can be manipulated to deceive them. Seeing is not, therefore, the same as knowing.

At this point Greenaway's film poses fundamental questions as to the nature of art: is it a truthful reflection of reality or an artificial construction? His film seems to support the latter view because it is so contrived and mask-like. Yet, it includes the former. The movie can, perhaps, be thought of as existing in the tension between the two polarities.

Each of Neville's drawings is a document, a record of a particular place and time. And since they feature the anomalous objects referred to earlier, they can be interpreted as containing vital clues to the murder of Mr Herbert. Greenaway here insists upon the possibility that additional layers of meaning beyond surface appearances can be ascribed to visual images, that is, pictures can be symbolic, metaphorical, allegorical. The appearances of things, in other words, can be used to transcend mere appearance. Though, of course, this depends upon the viewers' possession of a certain body of cultural knowledge and the ability to read or interpret the contents of an image.

Like so much of English literature, *The Draughtsman's Contract* takes as its theme the obsession of the ruling classes with their ownership of property and their rights of inheritance. The focus of the film is entirely the indolent existence of the gentry. Sometimes we see gardeners and servants but we witness very little of their labour. The original, long version of the film contained a sub-plot about those below stairs. (Nor do we discover whence the Herberts' wealth derives – tenant farmers or sugar plantations in the West Indies?) In fact, the only 'worker' in the movie is Neville. At one point the industry of the artist is praised and is said to be of benefit to all. Neville, in contrast to conventional representations of artists, is shown to be a professional with a skill for which people are prepared to pay. We see him undertake and complete a specific task, a job of work. Proficiently, he fulfils his contractual obligations. The image of the artist Greenaway presents is therefore refreshingly different. However, Neville's fate implies that it is always the patron who has ultimate power over the artist.

While Neville is the central figure of the film and we learn about his sexual habits, nevertheless his inner being and private life are irrelevant to the concerns of the film. This is because Greenaway is not interested in the psychology of artists or their domestic lives (this will change with *The Belly of an Architect*), but in the mechanisms of art itself: how does a painting or a film work? How does it engage our eyes and minds? Within the film, characters refer to ingenuity, games, stratagems. This is how they behave and how Greenaway conceives of art. For him, art is a game played with the audience according to a shared set of rules and conventions, but requiring variations, innovations, tricks, diversions and so on if it is to delight and puzzle the public.

The Draughtsman's Contract is a film which approximates to a work of art. Approximates because it is, in part, a commentary on the nature of art and because it does not present itself as the product of a fine artist. Although an art-cinema movie, the retention of a conventional narrative, script and actors, and the use of the period costume and murder-mystery genres, set it apart from the kind of experimental films favoured by avant-garde artists. In fact, it could be argued that *The Draughtsman's Contract* is a re-working of an earlier genre of popular British cinema, the Gainsborough costume dramas such as *The Wicked Lady* (1945) starring Margaret Lockwood and James Mason. The latter film too was set in a country house, concerned the behaviour of the English gentry and included scenes of betrayal and murder.

On its release Greenaway's film was a hit with cinema buffs. It opened the London Film Festival in November 1982 and was also shown at festivals in Venice and Edinburgh, where it received standing ovations. The movie was even praised in New York. It was reviewed by the usual film magazines, but also by a leading British art critic in the fine-art journal *Studio International*.[3] Several critics described Greenaway as 'quintessentially English' and one judged the movie 'the most exciting English feature film for years'.

The most ambitious and scholarly critical response to the film was written by Simon Watney. He argued that the film was 'essentially an allegory. And . . . a film about allegory.'[4] Greenaway's intention, Watney maintained, was not to provide a historically accurate picture of Restoration England but to use the past as a pretext for commenting on contemporary England. Given Greenaway's cavalier attitude towards historical truth, there does not seem much point in discussing at length – as Watney does – the history of English society and landscape gardening in the seventeenth century. And even after Watney's interpretations, the film's comments on today's society also remain somewhat obscure. It seems more sensible, therefore, to accept Greenaway's own statement about the film's purpose: an invitation to consider the problems of pictorial representation by watching someone drawing a real landscape, by comparing image and reality, and by reflecting on the representation of both via the medium of film. More generally his aim was to make a movie with 'visual excitement and cerebral entertainment'.[5] *The Draughtsman's Contract* is certainly a delight to both eye and mind.

13 *The Belly of an Architect* (1986)

The Belly of an Architect, a British-Italian co-production written and directed by Peter Greenaway, is a remarkably assured piece of film-making. Like *The Draughtsman's Contract*, it contains exquisitely beautiful scenes in colour and a complex plot involving characters who belong to an upper-class milieu. However, in contrast to the earlier movie, the film is about an architect not a draughtsman, a city not a country house, and it is set in the late twentieth century not the seventeenth century. Stylistically the two films are similar: both contain symmetrically composed shots, allusions to art and to other films, and visual metaphors.

Greenaway's film has several themes: it is about the architecture and history of Rome; the organisation of an exhibition celebrating the French eighteenth-century visionary architect Etienne-Louis Boullée; the last months of the life of a fictional American architect called Stourley Kracklite; marital discord and betrayal; illness and mortality; the vexed relations between Americans and Europeans. All these disparate elements are interwoven to produce an exceedingly rich tapestry.

Kracklite, the film's main character, is a bearded, powerfully-built but overweight man. He is a modern, experimental architect who hails from Chicago and who is obsessed with Boullée. When the film opens he is about to fulfil a ten-year ambition to design and organise a Boullée exhibition in Rome. The part of Kracklite called for a strong physical presence: this was provided by the American character actor Brian Dennehy who normally plays the roles of heavies in crime movies. He gives such an outstanding performance that Greenaway's cerebral approach to film-making acquires an extra, emotional dimension.

Accompanying Kracklite is his wife Louisa – played by Chloe Webb – whose parents were Italian immigrants to the United States. She is much smaller than her husband and half his age. They have been married seven years but have no children. During the course of the film we learn that Kracklite has built very little because he fails to complete the projects he starts. This characteristic is echoed by his wife's inability to provide children: she has had several miscarriages. They journey to Italy in high spirits but in Rome their marriage will disintegrate.

The movie opens in scintillating fashion with a rapid succession of shots: it is May 1985, a train threads its way through a sun-soaked Mediterranean landscape near the France-Italy border; inside the train in a sleeping compartment are the Kracklites making love; they achieve orgasm as the border is crossed; 'What a way to enter Italy!' puns Louisa; another view of the train from a country cemetery hints at the many architectural monuments to death to be featured in the film. The scene shifts to an outdoor restaurant in front of the

19 **Brian Dennehy as Stourley Kracklite.** ***Belly of an Architect*****, 1987**

Pantheon in Rome during the late evening. In the background, illuminated by red flood-lights, is the magnificent classical building, while in the foreground the Kracklites are being wined and dined by their Italian patrons and co-organisers.

Chief amongst the Italians are Io Speckler – played by Sergio Fantoni – an urbane, sixty-year-old architect who has invited Kracklite to Rome; his slim, handsome and elegantly attired son Caspasian – played by Lambert Wilson – who is also an architect; Caspasian's sensual sister Flavia – played by Stefania Cassina – who works as an art and architectural photographer, and a mischievous young friend of Caspasian's called Frederico Boccini – played by Vanni Corbellini – who is the model-maker for the exhibition.

To celebrate Kracklite's arrival and his fifty-fourth birthday, two waiters bring a huge iced cake surrounded by candles which takes the form of Boullée's 1784 spherical design for a proposed cenotaph to Sir Isaac Newton. Kracklite appreciates this gesture and produces an

English pound note – a good luck token he carries – bearing a portrait of Newton which, he points out, includes apple blossom as a laconic reference to Newton's falling apple and the formulation of the law of gravity. A model of Boullée's Newton memorial and a pound note reappear in the final scenes of the film, as does a tragic demonstration of gravitational force.

It soon becomes clear that the suave, worldly-wise Italians will play havoc with the lives of the more naive Americans. In fact, Caspasian schemes successfully to replace Kracklite as the exhibition designer and he also has an affair with Louisa. Simultaneously, Flavia seduces Kracklite. Frederico, Caspasian's ally, proves an awkward assistant. He makes snide remarks at Kracklite's expense and is punished with a punch on the nose.

During the early part of the film, meals and press receptions take place in the grand architectural setting of the Victor Emmanuel building where the exhibition is to take place. Kracklite's pleasure is short-lived however because he suffers repeated attacks of stomach pains and vomiting. As a result he becomes obsessed with his belly and tours Rome stealing postcards of male statues with prominent stomach muscles which he enlarges on a photo-copying machine. He marks the images to indicate the site of his pain. Eventually, the whole floor of his lavish Roman apartment is covered with photo-copies of bellies. The result resembles Warhol's multiple-image, silk-screen pop-art paintings of the 1960s or the photo-copy art so fashionable in the 1980s.[1]

Reproduction – human and mechanical – is a recurrent theme of the film. Louisa becomes pregnant as a consequence of the love-making on the train and, since it takes nine months for the exhibition to come to fruition, she gives birth to a son at the opening of the show during the film's climax. Reproduction also occurs in the form of picture postcards of the major buildings of Rome. These images fill the whole screen as Greenaway delights in shifting back and forth between the postcard representation of a site and actual film of it from the same vantage point.

Another facet of reproduction is revealed when Kracklite visits Flavia's spacious, white-painted apartment/studio. He discovers a wall covered with a montage of black-and-white photographs recording, in chronological order, his stay in Rome and the affair of his wife and Caspasian. The montage of still images serves as a documentation of the film – up to that point – within the film. Flavia has linked her photos together with red tape which she also uses to entrap Kracklite as he accepts the inevitable and positions himself in the space Flavia has left at the end of the chronological sequence.

We identify with Kracklite and side with him against the devious Italians who are sabotaging his marriage and his exhibition, but he strains our sympathy because his obsession with Boullée causes him to neglect his wife and his behaviour becomes increasingly neurotic as he jumps to the wrong conclusion that Louisa is poisoning him. Why, we wonder, doesn't he seek medical advice? Eventually, a doctor diagnoses dyspepsia. Kracklite's health continues to deteriorate however and a hospital probe of his intestines reveals terminal cancer (both Greenaway's parents died of cancer). Rather than submit to a lingering death, Kracklite resolves to commit suicide at the opening ceremony of the Boullée exhibition. So although Greenaway's architect-hero is much more complex than the Hollywood norm, he conforms to the cinema's stereotype of the artist in so far as he is made to suffer and to die a martyr's death.

Boullée (1728–99) was a minor French architect, teacher and theorist who built several houses in Paris in a neo-classical style. He also undertook work for the King of Prussia. However, he is chiefly remembered for his fantastic, impractical schemes for huge, symbolic, geometric monuments, towers and ideal cities (like Kracklite, Boullée constructed very little). His present fame, in fact, is due to modern architects regarding him as a precursor. In the film, which is concerned with the relation between past and present, Boullée serves as a link between the classical period exemplified by Rome's historical buildings and the modern school exemplified by Kracklite who, significantly, is from Chicago, the city of the steel-frame buildings of Louis Sullivan, one of the founding fathers of modern architecture. The mix of classicism and modernism within the film places it clearly within the era of post-modernism. Furthermore, the film is so eclectic in its references and so obsessed with representations that it too can be regarded as a post-modern work of art.

It seems that Boullée was inspired by various Roman buildings even though he never visited the city. The Italians are somewhat contemptuous of the French visionary. Flavia points out that Hitler's architect Albert Speer was influenced by Boullée. The suggestion of a connection between Boullée and fascism is unsettling. It places a question mark over Kracklite's enthusiasm for the man, particularly since one of the Roman buildings we are shown is the 1942 EUR building (by Guerrini, Lapadula and Romano), a neo-classical 'Palace of Italian Civilisation' erected by the fascist regime, and since Caspasian is discovered to be milking the exhibition budget in order to fund the restoration of Mussolini's Foro Italico.

Greenaway seems to imply there are sinister overtones to the apparently innocent celebration of Boullée. In an understated way, the film explores the relation between architecture and politics. By showing the grandeur and power of the buildings of ancient and Renaissance Rome, the film necessarily implies: these structures were impossible without immense wealth and political power; such monuments are both magnificent and intimidating. When Kracklite learns of his impending death in the cloisters of a hospital, the doctor introduces him to the emperors of Rome as represented by a series of busts. Most were tyrants who met violent deaths. These were the ruthless people who commissioned the now-ruined structures of ancient Rome. The doctor comments philosophically that there is comfort to be derived from contemplating the folly of the dead and the continuity between then and now.

Our appreciation of Roman buildings is ambivalent because we cannot separate their aesthetic impact from their social function of domination. Greenaway also suggests that cultural manifestations such as architectural exhibitions are not innocent, disinterested events. As well as having political implications in the wider sense, they are also the site of micro-power struggles among the various parties organising such blockbuster shows.

During the course of the film we are introduced to eight of the famous monuments of Rome: the Mausoleum of Augustus, the Pantheon, the Colosseum, the baths of the Villa Adriana, the piazza and dome of St. Peters, the Forum, the piazza Navona, and the EUR building. Seven of these inspired Boullée and so they connect him to Kracklite. In total they also represent 2,500 years of architectural heritage and so their purpose, according to Greenaway, is to put Kracklite's nine-month predicament into perspective. Somewhat foolishly, Kracklite imagines he can make an impact on the city which has seen so many powerful men and architects come and go.

Rome is superbly recorded by Sacha Vierny, the cameraman.

Greenaway wanted the film to look as if it had been shot by an architect, hence the stress on symmetry and frontal views recalling architectural elevations and plans. The warm hues of Rome's buildings reminded Greenaway of those of a healthy human body and so he instructed Vierny to exclude, as far as possible, the natural colours of green and blue; this was achieved by means of filters and by shooting at noon. When the colour green did appear it had a negative connotation – green is the colour of decaying flesh. When Kracklite uses the photocopier, his face is repeatedly illuminated by livid green light. Cinema audiences will probably notice the somewhat strange colours, but one doubts they will understand the intended colour symbolism.

At times Greenaway could be accused of making an advertising film for Rome's tourist office but, in fact, by concentrating on the famous sites and insisting on picture postcards, he acknowledges that the architecture of the past and indeed the exhibitions of the present are inescapably part of the tourist industry. However, very little of the negative aspects of tourism appears in the film. Nor, apart from one beggar and a street trader who sells the marble noses he has chipped from antique statues, are the poor who inhabit all major cities shown.

At last in February 1986 the exhibition is finished. By this time Kracklite has been replaced by Caspasian but he is still due to perform the opening ceremony. Since he is missing, the duty falls to his heavily pregnant wife. As Louisa cuts the tape in front of a huge model of Boullée's spherical memorial to Newton, she collapses and gives birth to a son. The child's first cry is heard as Kracklite, who entered by a side door, gives a demonstration of Newton's law of gravity by falling backwards through a window to die sprawled on top of Caspasian's parked car far below. The conjunction of death and birth signifies, of course, the cyclical nature of human existence.

The Belly of an Architect was premiered in London in October 1987. It received favourable reviews and was warmly appreciated by the audiences of the art house cinemas where it was shown. A book containing a screenplay for the film was published by Faber & Faber in 1988, although it is a somewhat misleading text because it differs in several respects from what actually happens in the film.[2]

Kracklite is a plausible representation of a contemporary architect. We never see any of his buildings or designs but he has the strong public presence of a Norman Foster or a Richard Rogers. The fact that he is nonetheless flawed – physically and psychologically – makes him more believable and human; far more so than Rand's one-dimensional hero Howard Roark. Arguably, Greenaway is much more successful than other film-makers in blending art and life. Kracklite's work intrudes upon his marriage, his health, and vice versa. At one point Louisa says to him bitterly: 'Everything's permissible for Art. I mean, look at our marriage. Art first, Kracklite second, the rest a long way down the line.' So, while Greenaway is devoted to art, he recognises the price in human terms which is so often paid for it. The fact that Kracklite dies and Louisa and her child live also implies that the creation women are capable of is more enduring and worthwhile than the masculine striving for immortality through art, though feminist artists will no doubt object to this proposition.

In interviews Greenaway has explained that the subject matter of architecture appealed to him as an analogy for film-making. In both professions, for every project which comes to fruition, there are a dozen which fail. Furthermore, both arts require large sums of money. Clients and backers have to be satisfied, and so does the public who use buildings or visit the cinema. At the same time, architects and film-makers seek to maintain their artistic integrity. Evidently, the abilities demanded by architecture and film-making are much the same.

14 The American cinema's depiction of art in the 1970s and 1980s

Most of the feature films about artists considered so far share a veneration for their subject. They view art as the highest value that humankind can attain and they view the artist as a noble, idealistic individual who struggles and suffers in its cause. Is this how the American cinema of the 1970s and 1980s sees art and artists? Not according to the film critic Carrie Rickey. In a 1988 article she argued that while the American cinema had increasingly made reference to art and artists, it had done so in highly unflattering ways.[1] While agreeing that there have been significant changes in the cinematic representation of art and artists, I will argue that recent American fiction films nevertheless reproduce many of the long-standing clichés and stereotypes associated with the visual arts.

A spate of disaster movies in the 1970s suggested that Americans felt threatened by contemporary technology and by those professionals who had power over their lives. Irwin Allen's and John Guillermin's *The Towering Inferno* (Warner Bros, 1974), for instance, was about a new skyscraper in San Francisco which catches fire on its inaugural night, trapping and killing many people, because the builders cut costs by installing unsafe wiring. The style of the glass and steel skyscraper was international modern at its blandest, but during the course of the film cinemagoers were introduced to the structure's inner workings and mechanical services. The movie had a star-studded cast: Paul Newman played the architect of 'the tallest building in the world' while Steve McQueen played the heroic firechief. (Images of heroic firemen have a long history: they date back to the nineteenth-century paintings of Courbet and Millais.) By blaming the builders, the movie virtually excused the architect of responsibility for the disaster – he also redeemed himself by rescuing children – though it did insist architects should consult fire experts before designing high buildings. *The Towering Inferno* was a popular and competent example of the disaster-movie genre and it transmitted vivid warnings to the public about the dangers of tall buildings, and of putting profits before safety.

During the late 1970s American film-makers began to use the New York art world, in particular the district of SoHo (South Houston) as a setting. In such movies as Paul Mazursky's *An Unmarried Woman* (1978) and Woody Allen's *Manhattan* (1979) the art world is presented as a place of leisure and diversion, where people shop around for sex, homosexual as well as heterosexual. In the former film a link is established between sex and corruption: an art critic is willing to help budding artists if they will gratify his sexual desires. This film features the British star Alan Bates. He plays Saul, a worthy abstract painter, whose canvases were in fact the work of the American painter Paul Jenkins.

What the use of SoHo as a location signifies is the vastly increased size and visibility of the New York artworld since the 1960s. The art business is now an important micro-economy. However, as a sub-culture it still possesses a relative autonomy vis-à-vis the encompassing culture which endows it with an exotic appeal as far as film-makers are concerned. There is surely nothing new in the equation of art with eroticism and pleasure since these are characteristics of art itself and the conventional perceived characteristics of the bohemian subculture of the art world at least since the era of romanticism in nineteenth-century Paris. The presence of homosexuality is not new either because the arts have long been ssen as a haven for gays. What is new is the greater emphasis on unconventional forms of sex. This, of course, reflects the greater explicitness of our age and the constant need in popular culture to up the stakes in terms of shock-value. It is also a true reflection of the situation in the New York art world in the sense that the homoerotic images of a photographer like Robert Mapplethorpe have become extremely fashionable in recent years.

Manhattan, Allen's comedy of manners, satirises pretentious New Yorkers. Diane Keaton plays a wacky photographer (she must be strange: she actually likes minimal sculpture). The conception of the art world as the habitat of pretentious people and false values is a long-standing one (witness *The Rebel*). Given the prevalence of shady deals and forgery and the hyping of bad artists which take place in the art markets of the world, the public is right to be sceptical and suspicious.

Film-makers evidently believe it is but a short step from false values to crime itself. In *Beverly Hills Cop* (1984), a detective story directed by Martin Brest, a top American art dealer – played with icy menace by the British actor Steven Berkoff – uses his gallery as a cover for drug smuggling and murder. Axel Foley (played by Eddie Murphy) the street-wise cop from Detroit, is not fazed by the Ed Kienholz-like tableau (priced at $130,000) displayed in the dealer's Beverly Hills gallery. Associations between art and the lifestyles of the super-rich, and between art and crime, are asserted in the film which also implies that art is a con trick in its own right. There is little new here: the idea that modern art is a con trick is as old as modernism itself and Humphrey Bogart playing detectives like Philip Marlowe in crime movies of the 1940s also had to penetrate the fronts of art dealer or bookseller crooks.

A more complex view of the artworld is to be found in *After Hours* (1985), a black comedy-thriller directed by Martin Scorsese and starring Griffin Dunne, Rosanna Arquette and Linda Fiorentino. Griffin plays Paul Hackett, a straight office-worker who while looking for romance becomes involved with two women, one of whom is a sculptress with a loft in SoHo. Kiki, the artist, makes life-size, papier-maché, angst-ridden figures (the sculptures are actually by Nora Chavooshian). In fact three women characters in *After Hours* are artists. To have women routinely represented as self-confident artists is a new development, one which reflects the actual numbers of women who do now become professional artists and the impact of the feminist art movement since the late 1960s. Again the theme of perverse sex is present: Kiki indulges in sado-masochistic bondage games with her discipline-obsessed boyfriend. A sense of spiritual sickness pervades the milieu: Marcy, the woman Paul pursues, behaves in a disturbed manner and seems to be fascinated by the horrific things fire does to human flesh (so-called 'body art' involved much self-mutilation by artists.)

Paul encounters another woman, a barmaid, who later turns out to be an amateur artist. She is a relic of the 1960s and specialises in drawings of that era's rock and media stars. She draws a portrait of Paul which subsequently proves troublesome to him because it is duplicated and used as a 'wanted man' poster. Here at least the film recognises that art can fulfil directly practical functions.

Paul's contact with the art world results in a nightmare series of incidents. While fleeing from vigilantes, he meets another sculptress – June – who hides him by covering him with plaster so that he is transformed into a statue. Hence the culmination of his journey into the art world is imprisonment inside a work of art. The statue is then stolen by burglars, one of whom complains 'Art sure is ugly.' His partner responds: 'That's how much you know, the uglier the art, the more it's worth.' On the one hand, the view that modern art is 'ugly' is an old cliché, but on the other hand it may also reflect an awareness that exhibitions have been mounted in recent years with titles like '"Bad" painting'. When Paul finally escapes from the plaster cast, he is only too glad to return to the normality of his routine office job.

In this film the New York art world is represented as an enclosed realm with its own private codes, a place which promises sex and cultural nourishment, but which supplies nothing but trouble and danger. The whole film takes place at night – 'after hours' – when the daytime norms no longer apply. The view of the art world is conventional in this respect: a zone of weirdness, difference and suffering, a zone where the perverse desires of the unconscious find expression. The reviewer Pam Cook sums up the film as follows:

'*After Hours* is Scorsese's clearest and most pessimistic statement yet about the value of art. It can do nothing to change the world; it reflects the status quo, mirroring human misery and anxiety; it is both anti-social and outside society, its subject matter is the alienated individual; it is essentially ephemeral, subject to the same laws of disintegration and decay as human life; it is endlessly duplicatable, caught in a cycle of commodity production. . . . From this perspective, Scorsese himself could be seen as the other side of Paul: an artist trapped by the system, yet straining against it.'[2]

Perverse sex appears yet again as a theme in *9½ Weeks* (1985), a soft-core porn movie masquerading as art-cinema eroticism. It was directed, rock-video style, by Adrian Lyne and stars Kim Basinger as Elizabeth, a SoHo art gallery assistant, who has a sado-masochistic relationship with John, a wealthy Wall St commodities broker, played by Mickey Rourke. The film includes a masturbation scene in which the female lead climaxes while viewing slides of artists' works in an art-gallery basement. Among the fashionable New York artists whose work appears are Robert Longo, Jack Goldstein, Walter Robinson, George Segal and Sarah Charlesworth. A fictional, elderly male artist – Mathew Farnsworth – represents the visionary and spiritual values traditionally associated with art. However, this artist turns out to be so inarticulate that a critic is prompted to describe him as a 'pre-verbal' being.

Schematically, the film equates art with the feminine (Elizabeth) and money/business with the masculine (John). Since art depends on money and money needs some higher motivation, the two are strangely attracted. As the film progresses, Elizabeth increasingly submits to John's control and power games. Finally, near to a breakdown because of the corrupting effect of John's sadism, Elizabeth leaves him. One could conclude that the film's message is that when money seduces art, the values of art are in danger of corruption. As we shall see shortly, the art/money relationship becomes even more insistent in other films.

The art world as a site of strange behaviour (performance art), crime and corruption reappears in *Legal Eagles* (1986), a comedy-thriller and court-room drama directed by Ivan Reitman. Daryl Hannah plays Chelsea Deardon, a blonde beauty specialising in performance art. As a child she witnessed the death of her artist-father in a fire after an argument with two men. Her father's paintings (which we never see), presumed burnt, are in fact being kept in store while they increase in value by a crooked art dealer called Taft. A district attorney Tom Logan (Robert Redford) and a lawyer (Debra Winger) investigate the crime and help Chelsea recover a painting given to her by her father when she was a child. The plot is a thinly disguised variation on the real-life scandal and court case which followed the suicide of the noted American abstract expressionist Mark Rothko in 1970.

Like *Beverly Hills Cop*, the film dwells on the art/wealth nexus. We see Taft in luxurious New York galleries with Picassos on the walls and we visit Sotheby's in New York to witness the auction of an impressionist painting for over $2 million. Again, the untrustworthiness of the art dealer is signified by the British identity of the actor – Terence Stamp – who plays the role. Taft, like many real-life dealers, disdains performance art because he cannot buy and sell it as a commodity.

Fire is a motif which recurs throughout the movie. It is especially effective in a scene in which Chelsea gives a demonstration of her performance art to the artistically illiterate Logan. The piece – a mixed-media work involving words, sounds, photographs and the artist burning paper models and images of herself – is a reasonably plausible example of the genre. Laurie Anderson's multi-media performance art of the early 1980s was surely the source. Late in the film, the painting Chelsea seeks is discovered hidden inside a sculpture owned by Taft. Sculptures which conceal secrets or enclose live or dead bodies are commonplace in Hollywood movies about art. The popularity of the device may be due to a primitivistic effigy magic which, some art theorists argue, underpins the appeal of all figurative sculpture.

One theme of *Legal Eagles* is the struggle between those who value art for its own sake and those who value it for the profits it brings. In *Wall Street* (1987), a film about high finance directed by Oliver Stone, art is openly celebrated as the ultimate capitalist commodity. The movie is about the dishonest practice of insider trading in the New York financial markets of the 1980s. Michael Douglas plays Gekko, a rich and ruthless corporate raider and speculator whose luxury office and architect-designed home are decorated with modern works of art including a Picasso and a Miró. In one scene Gekko is shown bidding for works of art at an auction; the pop painter James Rosenquist is also there. Charlie Sheen plays the novice who wants to emulate Gekko and when he acquires some money he buys an expensive flat and hires an interior designer (played by Daryl Hannah) to provide him with 'instant culture' in the form of outlandish decor and a selection of works by contemporary American artists including Julian Schnabel (thus the contrast between the older Gekko and the younger man is exemplified by the fact that they own paintings from two different generations).

Art is thus presented as the visible sign of wealth and social prestige, a function it has of course served in many films. At one point it is also cited by Gekko as an ideal example of how money can be profitably invested and how value is created and increased via the consensus of a group of powerful people. In short, as the perfect commodity and the final reward for having made it. Although in *Wall Street* art is sullied by being associated with the greed and dishonesty of Gekko, this did not prevent the art world's willing co-operation: the film's credits include the names of several prestigious New York art galleries.

Art's relation to money and patronage is a significant issue in *The Moderns* (1988), a witty and intelligent movie written and directed by Alan Rudolph, which looks back to the origins of modernism in the Paris of the 1920s. It is in part a love story, in part a satire on the myth of Americans in Paris. The film mixes representations of real historical figures such as Gertrude Stein and Ernest Hemingway with fictional characters. One of the leading characters – Stone (played by John Lone) – is a rich gangster-type who is attempting to buy his way into Parisian society by acquiring a collection of modern art. At one point he arrogantly rejects the judgement of two art critics and tells them the cash he pays for art is what determines its value.

Keith Carradine plays Hart, the film's hero (whose name combines 'heart' and 'art'). Hart, an American cartoonist and artist who is unable to sell his paintings, is persuaded by a scheming art dealer (played by Genevieve Bujold) to compromise his ideals by forging a Cézanne, a Modigliani and a Matisse. Ironically, the 'originals' Carradine copies are themselves fakes – imitations made for the film and credited to a forger called David Stein. The convincing evocations of Paris are also false because the film was shot in Montreal.

Since the three forgeries appear at the end of the movie as part of the opening show of the Museum of Modern Art in New York, the implication is that the modernism transplanted from Europe to the United States is founded on a deception. Several of the film's characters comment on the fakery or artifice of art and since one repeatedly asserts that the future lies with Hollywood and the cinema, the

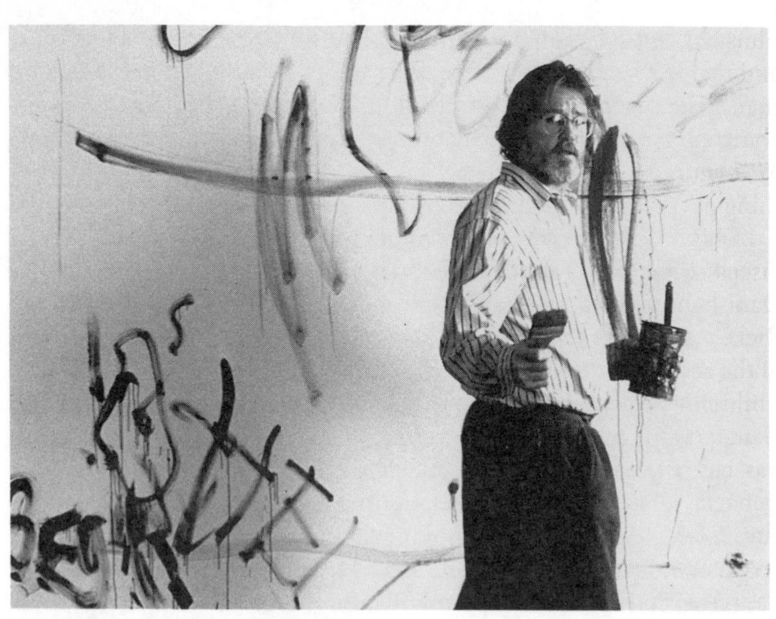

20 **Nick Nolte as Lionel Dobie in *New York Stories: Life Lessons*, 1989**

21 **Rosanna Arquette as Paulette in *New York Stories: Life Lessons*, 1989**

film-makers suggest that the cinema is the natural successor to fine art and that 'trickery' will be even more effective in the movie business than in the art business. Rudolph has explained that the film is a comment on the 'counterfeit times' we live in but, arguably, *The Moderns* is one of the few films about modern art which finds something positive in the proposition 'modern art is a fraud'.

In her article Rickey also mentions a film that has already been discussed, namely *The Wolf at the Door* (1986). Since this film was a Danish-French co-production it hardly counts as an American movie. Rickey claimed it depicted Gauguin as a paedophile, hence the image of the artist was tarnished yet again. If by 'paedophile' Rickey means 'child abuser', then the accusation is probably too strong, for although Gauguin had sexual relations with thirteen-year-old girls, in Tahiti it was customary for girls of that age to marry. Judith Molard, the teenager to whom he was attracted in Paris, was equally attracted to him.

After Rickey's article appeared another American movie about art was released, namely *New York Stories: Life Lessons* (1989). *Life Lessons* is a short film directed by Martin Scorsese with a script by Richard Price (it appears as one of a trio under the overall title of *New York Stories*). It is set in contemporary New York City and concerns the disintegrating relationship between a middle-aged male painter Lionel Dobie (played by Nick Nolte) and a young female painter Paulette (played by Rosanna Arquette). Paulette has been Dobie's mistress and technical assistant but she doesn't love him and wants to break away. Apparently, the story was derived from the diaries of Dostoevsky's mistress.

Most of the film is set in Dobie's huge studio loft where Paulette has her own room. However, there are several other scenes which take place in the New York art world. Dobie has been married several times and affects a worldly-wise attitude towards Paulette, offering her lessons in life as he pleads and exhorts her to stay with him. In fact, he is neurotically obsessed with her and repeatedly declares 'I love you, I would do anything for you, even stretch your canvases.'(!)

Dobie is a physically tough individual, bearded, a smoker and a drinker. He likes to work on his billboard-size canvases to the rock music of the 1960s – Bob Dylan, Cream, Procul Harum – played at top volume. He mixes his pigments on a dustbin lid and daubs them rapidly, instinctively, using brushes or his fingers. His heavily layered paintings are half-abstract, half-figurative; they are romantic in style, a cross between Monticelli and action painting. The model for Dobie was clearly an artist like Jackson Pollock, one of the hard-drinking, bar-room-brawling generation of the abstract expressionists. At one point Dobie even provokes a bar-room brawl with a fellow artist. Nick Nolte, who normally portrays he-man types, plays the part of Dobie with conviction and gusto.

Dobie is a famous, successful painter who shows in a major New York gallery. When the film opens he is anxious not only because Paulette has left his bed, but also because he has a show due to open in three weeks and his dealer is pressing him for new work. Paulette has a crush on Gregory Stark, an arrogant young performance artist. In one scene we see him giving a show to a crowd of trendy people dressed mainly in black leather: he performs on the tracks of an underground railway accompanied by flashing lights. His act involves telling humorous anecdotes about his daily life. Dobie is jealous of Stark because of Paulette's interest but he also resents him, one suspects, because the painter in Dobie despises the younger man's new-fangled form of art; as far as Dobie is concerned, performance art is fashionable trash.

The movie identifies far more with Dobie's point of view than with Paulette's. At times Dobie's tunnel vision in respect of his mistress is literally represented on the screen by an iris-like effect. She is secondary in terms of the film's emphasis and also in terms of her paintings: they are smaller, more figurative, but still loosely painted and romantic in style. While Dobie's are presented as being unproblematically those of a master, the quality of Paulette's remains in doubt. In fact, Paulette herself lacks faith in her talent and repeatedly asks Dobie for an honest evaluation. His refusal to give unqualified approval, she assumes, means that she has no future as an artist. Dobie reminds her she is a beginner and he urges her to stay in New York because the art market is there. Desperate to keep her, he offers to help her even more with her career. He repeats a standard cliché of art talk when he tells her that if she gives up art, then it means she wasn't really an artist in the first place. Real artists make art not out of choice but 'because they have to'.

In the end Paulette does leave Dobie to begin a different mode of life. The final scene is set in spacious white gallery where the opening of Dobie's one-man show is taking place. An attractive young woman serves Dobie some wine; she turns out to be an aspiring artist eking out an existence with part-time work; she wants to touch the charismatic Dobie for luck. Dobie's lustful gaze explores her flesh and he tells her he needs an assistant. One then perceives that Dobie's 'love' for Paulette was not as deep as he had maintained and that what we witnessed was a behavioural pattern in which older men use their fame, money and power to attract younger women, while such women use their good looks and bodies to obtain preferment.

Scorsese's representation of the art world context is more convincing than his depiction of the creative process itself. Dobie seems to paint in order to sublimate his emotional suffering and sexual frustration. Painting for him is a motor activity – it does not involve any intellectual work or any significant content. Nor does his art appear to serve any social or spiritual function apart from being sold to wealthy collectors. The paintings themselves were executed by Manhattan artist Chuck Connelly. Paulette's were executed by Susan Hambleton, so the male/female contrast in the movie was repeated in reality. Connelly's pictures have some degree of formal structure, but when Nolte is seen in close-up painting the already clotted surfaces he simply adds meaningless blobs and squiggles of streaky, multi-coloured pigment.

Life Lessons is by no means a major movie but it is a sharply observed portrait of a doomed romantic relationship and of certain aspects of the New York art world. In respect of the latter, becoming an assistant to a major, established artist is a well-known way of gaining valuable experience and becoming part of the art scene. For a woman, becoming the mistress of an older artist (or a dealer or a critic) is also a way of gaining access to the art world (witness *Camille Claudel*). Whether this method can be recommended by tutors teaching business-studies courses to art students is another matter.

It is evident that American film-makers have taken note of the significant changes which have occurred in the art world in the past two decades. The market in the art of the past and in contemporary art has grown enormously. Huge sums of money have been invested in art by a growing army of collectors and speculators. Opportunities for sharp practice, hype, market manipulation and corruption have increased, as the exposure of several art world scandals has demonstrated. Some artists have become extremely wealthy and have received the same kind of publicity as film and rock stars. Media coverage has often been more concerned with their financial success than with the quality of their art. Also, certain art dealers have become as celebrated and rich as the leading artists in their stables.

This shift explains the frequency with which dealers are now depicted in movies. Many people consider making money in such a way parasitic, so dealers tend to be despised. This is why they are often depicted as dishonest or criminal individuals. The link between art and money is now glaringly obvious, hence it is no longer possible to maintain art's 'non-commercial' image. Its claim to profundity and spirituality also seems more and more spurious as artworks rocket in value and scandals are uncovered. The fact that an artist such as Joseph Beuys could become world famous and affluent via installations involving slabs of fat, and by holding conversations with dead hares, encourages the view that contemporary art is a bizarre commodity whose values are determined by an exclusive cabal. Film-makers respond by asserting that art is a fraud. They clearly believe – and are probably right to do so – that this is a popular position, that when they pillory art they are expressing the views of everyone who does not belong to or benefit from the art world. Mass culture – in the form of the cinema – appears to be exacting a revenge on art for always being rated an inferior form of culture. Even so, American film companies have obviously found the subject of art attractive and useful. Earlier films focused almost exclusively on the figure of the artist. Today, the field of view is wider in that it encompasses dealers and collectors as well as artists. The art world – particularly that of New York – appeals to film-makers as an exotic, decadent domain, one with designer lifestyles, an aura of perverse eroticism, and the greedy accumulation of expensive commodities. Arguably, there is a good deal of truth in such cinematic representations, but what film-makers have ignored so far is the presence in the American art world of feminist and socialist artists who maintain an integrity of vision and who adopt a critical stance towards their local situation and the global context. And Rickey, by confining her analysis to American productions, neglects the much more subtle and satisfying representations of art and artists found in such British films as *Caravaggio*, *The Draughtsman's Contract* and *The Belly of an Architect*.

Most cinema has been simultaneously a form of entertainment and popular culture and an industry/business. Fine art, in contrast, has had a coy attitude towards buying and selling. Somehow art managed to appear to be above commerce. Perhaps one can explain the American cinema's recent interest in contemporary art and especially the marketing apparatus which now promotes it, in terms of an anxiety about the impact of commercialism on the aesthetic values of art, a concern which film-makers, as creative people, share with many fine artists.

III

ARTWORKS, DEALERS AND CRITICS IN FILMS

THE ARTIST IN HOLLYWOOD

15 Artworks, dealers and critics in films

Most of the films discussed so far emphasise the artist rather than the works of art he or she makes. This raises the question: are there any feature films in which the leading character is a work of art? The principal example which comes to mind is MGM's *The Picture of Dorian Gray*, a film released in 1945. It was directed by Albert Lewin and starred George Sanders, Peter Lawford and Angela Lansbury; Hurd Hatfield played Dorian. This movie was based, of course, on Oscar Wilde's famous novel of 1890 which tells the story of a handsome Victorian gentleman who sells his soul in exchange for eternal youth. Dorian's real age and inner corruption are registered in a 'living' full-length portrait he keeps hidden in an attic. In the final scenes Dorian attacks the portrait with a knife in the hope of ending its evil power. Instead, the figure in the painting becomes young again and Dorian is transformed into a hideous corpse.

Wilde's conceit was to reverse the ancient motto 'life is transient, art is eternal' by making the portrait age not the man. The picture of Dorian is an instance of what Kris and Kurz call 'effigy magic',[1] that is the primitive belief that a person's soul resides in their image or effigy (hence the belief that one can hurt a person by sticking pins into an effigy of them). Artists have often, in the past, been thought of as magicians because of their ability to make life-like images and statues. Film is an ideal medium in which to show Dorian's portrait because the painting's power to change over time can be realistically simulated

22 **Ivan Le Lorraine Albright**
'The picture of Dorian Gray', 1943–44

by means of dissolves.

Dorian's portrait in the film also carried conviction because it was painted by a remarkable 'magic realist', the American artist Ivan Albright (1897–1983). He was noted for his mastery of traditional oil-painting techniques and his fanatically detailed renderings of decaying human flesh. This skill Albright had acquired during the First World War when he had served as a medical artist recording the wounds of injured soldiers. He was also a painter whose work was often concerned with the theme of time. At the invitation of Albert Lewin, the artist went to Hollywood in November 1943 and spent almost a year working on the portrait. His twin brother Malvin, also an artist, executed a second painting with the same dimensions showing Gray as a young man (in the credits for the film Henrique Medina is cited as the painter of the young Gray).

Both artists worked from full-scale dummies of Hatfield, and Ivan also worked from a living model whose hands were covered with congealed chicken blood. Ivan was fascinated by the theory of complementary colour contrasts and he used iridescent blues, violets, purples, yellows and greens in order to generate the after-images strong hues can evoke (he realised that on the set the portrait would be subject to powerful lights). The completed movie was black-and-white except for two short Technicolor sequences in which we see the portrait of Dorian as a young man and as an old man. Clearly, the monochrome/colour contrast was intended to make the portrait especially vivid. In the final version of the portrait, Dorian's appearance is horrific: his eyes bulge, his face is covered with pustules, his hands ooze with blood, and his flesh seems to be eerily illuminated from within. Unusually, the painting was not relegated to a storeroom but acquired by a museum: it is now part of the collection of the Art Institute of Chicago.[2]

Portraits – of a more conventional type than Albright's – have appeared in a considerable number of Hollywood dramas where they have performed a variety of functions. Often they were used to represent an absent person who nevertheless exerted a powerful influence on the characters in the film. A famous example is *Laura* (1944), a crime story directed by Otto Preminger. A young woman is discovered battered to death on the floor of an apartment. Everyone assumes the corpse is Laura, the beautiful occupant of the flat, whose portrait dominates the living room. Dana Andrews plays a detective investigating the murder. Seeing the portrait many times and learning about Laura from her friends, he falls in love with her. It seems as if this is a love which can never be consummated but, eventually, about a third of the way into the film, Laura turns up alive and well – much to the astonishment of the rest of the characters.

Diane Waldman, the author of an article on hostile attitudes to modern art in American popular films and journalism of the 1940s, has argued that realistic portraits juxtaposed against examples of modernist abstraction were also employed by Hollywood directors 'to valorise an illusionist over a modernist aesthetic' (as in Alfred Hitchcock's *Suspicion* (1940)).[3] Realistic representation and a celebration of individuals were two important characteristics of the historical genre of portraiture. Both were also characteristic of Hollywood movies, hence the sympathy film-makers felt for naturalistic portraits.

Paintings and sculptures are, of course, routinely employed as props in feature films. They are an effective means of signalling a high level of income and culture. A case in point is *Rollover* (1982), directed by Alan J. Pakula and starring Jane Fonda and Kris Kristofferson. This movie is set in New York and its subject matter concerns the world of big business. Fonda plays a wealthy widow who resides in a lavish mansion on whose walls hang abstract paintings by American painters like Mark Rothko and Frank Stella. None of the characters in the film refer to the paintings nor does the camera dwell on them in any obvious way, consequently their role is virtually subliminal. Only the art specialist is likely to notice them consciously and to play the game of identifying their creators.

Directors of films aimed at art-cinema audiences are generally more interested in the issue of pictorial representation than directors of mainstream movies, consequently they are prepared to play complex games with still pictures. The plot of Greenaway's *The Draughtsman's Contract*, for instance, revolved around a series of topographical drawings. Another example is Raul Ruiz's *L'Hypothèse du Tableau Volé* (France, 1978). This is an exceedingly arcane film about the meaning and interpretation of images using as a pretext six mid-nineteenth-century academic paintings. Lina Wertmuller is another European film-maker who has frequently made use of historical works of art and monuments in her films about modern life in order to add an extra dimension of meaning. In an article about Wertmuller, Mark Le

Sueur argued that the role of these art treasures in her films was comparable to the 'disguised symbolism' function of certain objects in northern Renaissance painting.[4]

Finally, some general points about the appearance of works of art in bio-pics about real artists of the past. Film-makers frequently encounter difficulties in obtaining the objects they want to film, in meeting high insurance costs, in gaining access to museums and private collections, or in gaining permissions from copyright holders (some collectors refuse to co-operate with film-makers or demand too much money). The physical condition and shape of paintings may also make them unsuitable for the cinema screen. As we have already seen, producers and directors have adopted various strategies in order to overcome these problems. They can be listed as follows: recreate the motifs of paintings by means of tableaux; don't show any paintings at all or show them only from the back; have copies made by professional artists; have colour photographs made, enlarge them to the appropriate size and varnish them.

In addition to actual works, film-makers normally require a number of semi-completed paintings or sculptures for use in scenes where the artist is shown at work. Such items are usually furnished by a professional artist or copyist who attempts to simulate the style of the artist in question. In those instances where the artist-hero is fictional, the works of art are sometimes genuine – in the sense of being the work of a real artist (for example, the paintings of the character Gulley Jimson in *The Horse's Mouth* were in reality executed by John Bratby, a painter whose work was fashionable in Britain during the 1950s).

In certain movies a real artist's works appear alongside crude copies and completely invented pictures. Given these circumstances, it is obvious that confusion can easily arise in the layperson's mind as to what is and what is not authentic. The danger is that viewers who mistake poor simulations for genuine works will leave the cinema with a false impression of the quality of the artist's oeuvre.

Dealers

Dealers crop up as minor characters in quite a number of movies. In the art world dealers are widely regarded with distaste and suspicion because of the power they wield over the careers of their 'stable' of artists. Because dealers have a vested financial interest in the success of the artists they promote, there is always uncertainty concerning their true opinions and their commitment to art. The art world's low opinion is reflected in recent American movies where dealers are routinely represented as criminals. Exceptions to this rule are to be found in movies about nineteenth-century artists. *Moulin Rouge*, for instance, depicts Toulouse-Lautrec's dealer Maurice Joyant as a loyal friend, and *Lust for Life* represents Vincent van Gogh's brother Theo, who worked for a Paris gallery, sympathetically. The financial aspect of art is stressed in Robert Altman's *Vincent & Theo* (1990) and Theo's private life and work problems receive as much attention as those of Vincent. But while Altman represents Theo as a 'hero' because he supports Vincent, Gauguin and the impressionists, his employers are portrayed as unpleasant individuals whose only interest in art is the profit they can extract from it.

Critics

Another despised figure is the critic (witness *Caravaggio* and *The Fountainhead*). In the view of many people, art critics are non-creative parasites living off the body of art. Their power to pass judgement is resented and feared because adverse reviews can ruin an artist's career. It has already been argued that this power is greatly exaggerated, that dealers and collectors have much more power. One movie in which punishment is meted out to a critic by an artist is the five-part horror story *Doctor Terror's House of Horror* (1965) directed by Freddie Francis. During the episode entitled 'The crawling hand', a critic Franklyn Marsh (played by Christopher Lee) savages the paintings of Eric Landor (played by Michael Gough). Landor manages to humiliate the critic in public by getting him to praise a work which turns out to have been executed by a chimpanzee. Marsh exacts revenge by running Landor down with his car. As a result, the artist loses his hand and, unable to face the future, he commits suicide. The dismembered hand then attacks Marsh repeatedly until, at last, he is blinded. Thus the critic who could not see good art is punished by being prevented from seeing art altogether.[5]

Given that critics normally appear as minor characters in movies, it was a something of a surprise to find that the main character of *Melancholia* (1989) worked as an art critic. This movie, the first directed by Andi Engel, made use of the thriller genre in order to explore certain ethical and political issues. The German art critic David Keller – played by the rugged Dutch actor Jeroen Krabbé – is in his forties, writes reviews for glossy art magazines and lives alone in a comfortable flat in central London with a phone, typewriter, paintings, piles of magazines, books on van Gogh, videotapes and a reproduction of Dürer's 'Melancholia'. In 1968 Keller had been a left-wing student activist, one who believed that violence in a good cause was justified, but now he is disillusioned and emotionally numb; his life is a routine lacking in purpose or passion.

We follow Keller as he visits upmarket galleries and submits his copy at the smart premises of his agent. Nostalgic remarks about the radicalism of Joseph Beuys and a conversation with a cynical gallery director about post-modernism signal to the viewer that there is little meaning to be derived from the commercial art world of the 1980s. Even this film subscribes to the view that art criticism is not truly creative: at one point a female friend urges Keller to stop writing about the work of others in order to complete his half-finished novel.

Keller's morose existence is interrupted by a phone call from Hamburg asking him to live up to his 1960s ideals by executing a Chilean torturer staying at a hotel near Tower Bridge. The critic is

23 **Jeroen Krabbé as David Keller.** ***Melancholia*, 1989**

taken aback but he undertakes the task. By the end of the film he has committed two murders and isolated himself in a Tuscan farmhouse. Engel's main character is a plausible figure: there are a number of left-wing critics, radicalised in the 1960s, whose hopes for a better world were dashed in the 1970s and 1980s. But Keller's direct actions seem to fulfil his personal needs, a Sartre-like existentialist agenda, rather than any contemporary political function. His actions are after the event – after the student movement, after Chile – hence they do not concern the immediate political issues of Britain in the 1980s. What the film also fails to consider is that contemporary art criticism might be a significant site of ideological struggle, that it might be a subject worth making a film about. One has only to think of the passion and anger that has been aroused in the art world by such critics as Clement Greenberg and Peter Fuller, or the heated debates that have occurred between the supporters of Prince Charles and modernist architects, to see that there is scope for drama in the realms of contemporary art and architectural criticism, much more indeed than Engel manages to infuse into his somewhat melancholy movie.

16 The artist in Hollywood: *Spellbound* (1945)

This chapter could also be entitled 'A surrealist in Hollywood: Salvador Dali's dream sequence for *Spellbound*', or 'Selling a surrealist dream to the dream factory'. An examination of *Spellbound* is relevant to this text, first because it is a rare example of a leading modern artist being employed by a Hollywood studio, and second, because by comparing it to *Un Chien Andalou* the differences between Hollywood cinema and surrealist cinema can be highlighted.

Spellbound (Selznick International), a black-and-white, murder-mystery and romance movie released in the USA in 1945, was notable in several respects: it was directed by the British master of suspense Alfred Hitchcock and produced and largely edited by the American, David O. Selznick (famous for *Gone with the Wind*). Its screenplay was written by the respected writer Ben Hecht and it starred the Swedish beauty Ingrid Bergman and the handsome, virtually unknown Gregory Peck. Also, the film tackled an offbeat subject: the relatively new science of psychiatry. Finally, it included a dream sequence by art director James Basevi based on designs by the notorious Spanish painter and surrealist Salvador Dali.

Work on the film took place in 1944 towards the end of the Second World War. Psychiatry, Selznick thought, was going to be of value after the war in the rehabilitation of disturbed ex-servicemen. He was keen, therefore, to use the popularising power of the cinema to promote its healing potential. It was also becoming established as a fashionable therapy for stressed civilians including those in the film industry. Both Hecht and Selznick visited psychiatrists and the latter employed his analyst, May E. Romm (a top Los Angeles psychiatrist), as psychiatric advisor to the film. During pre-production several visits were also made to mental asylums for the purposes of research. One worry the film-makers had was that psychiatry might prove too high-brow for many in the American cinema audience, especially those in rural areas. They persisted in their attempt to popularise the subject, but made many compromises to ensure the film's content was not over complicated.

Dali too was a mixed blessing. On the one hand, his international fame as an avant-garde artist would improve the cultural status of the film and help the publicity department, but on the other hand his input might prove too 'difficult' and 'inaccessible'. The weird eroticism of his art might also cause censorship problems (one of Selznick's assistants dubbed Dali's paintings 'phallic frescoes').

Apparently, Selznick thought Hitchcock chose Dali purely as a publicity gimmick but the director had other, stylistic motives:

'I felt that if I was going to have dream sequences, they should be vivid. I didn't think we should resort to the old-fashioned blurry effect they got by putting Vaseline around the lens. . . . I used Dali for his draftsmanship. I wanted to convey the dreams with great visual sharpness and clarity. . . . Chirico (Giorgio de Chirico, the Italian metaphysical painter) has the same quality, the long shadows, the infinity of distance, and the converging lines of perspective..[1]

On another occasion Hitchcock recalled:

'What I really wanted to do, and they wouldn't do it because of the expense, was to have the dream sequences shot on the back lot in the bright sunshine, so that they would have to stop down the camera to such a degree that the picture would have been needle-sharp, as a contrast to the rest of the picture which was slightly diffused.'[2]

From the first quote it almost sounds as if Hitchcock would have preferred to have engaged de Chirico. Dali had the advantage of being in the United States. Also, outside the art world, he was more famous than the Italian painter. Dali's painting technique fitted Hitchcock's prescription because it employed the highly detailed, smooth-surfaced, trompe l'oeil, perspectival manner of depiction that northern European oil painters had developed during and after the Renaissance. This mode of representation had in fact been mechanised by the inventions of photography and cinematography. The contents of Dali's pictures may have been peculiar – soft watches, burning giraffes, distorted limbs propped up by crutches, etc. – but the naturalistic way they and their landscape settings were rendered accorded perfectly with the clarity of standard film images.

There was another parallel between Dali's painting methods and cinematic techniques: in some of his paintings figurative images emerge from and blend with landscape backgrounds; the effect is reminiscent of dissolves in movies. A remark by Leonard Leff that Hitchcock liked to make everyday objects strange, to reveal the horror in 'things', suggests a further bond with Dali.[3]

During the 1930s Dali lived in Italy and France to further his career and to avoid the civil war raging in Spain. He also made several visits to the United States; in 1939, for example, he designed an installation for the World's Fair held in New York. In 1940 he and his wife Gala moved to the States to escape the Second World War in Europe. They were to remain there for the next eight years. During his American trips and residence, Dali produced many oil paintings – including portraits of society men and women – drawings and book illustrations. He also designed costumes and sets for ballets, advertisements and shop-window displays. In 1941 he was honoured with a retrospective exhibition at the Museum of Modern Art.

Dali was thus widely known to the Americans as a 'surrealist' even though he had been 'excommunicated' from the movement in 1938 for his reactionary politics, his return to the Catholic faith and his commercial exploitation of surrealism ('Avida Dollars' was André Breton's sardonic anagram of Dali's name). An invitation to work on a Hollywood film no doubt appealed to Dali: it would be well paid, it would attract lots of media attention and it would be a golden opportunity to widen still further the audience for his art. Dali, a self-obsessed exhibitionist, thrived in the glare of the spotlight.

Another reason why Dali would have been attracted by the offer was the fact that he already had some film-making experience: he and Luis Buñuel had collaborated to produce the two seminal surrealist films *Un Chien Andalou* (1929) and *L'Age D'Or* (1930). His designs for *Spellbound* were more or less bound to draw on the imagery he and Buñuel had devised to scandalise the European bourgeoisie. Of course, in practice the two experiences were very different: the surrealist films were privately financed, independent projects whereas *Spellbound* was a mainstream studio production, a commercial movie. Dali's role in the relation to the latter film was that of an external consultant. He had little power, therefore, to determine what finally appeared on the the screen. As Dawn Ades has observed, in Hollywood the contents of the dream sequence had to serve the needs of the scenario.[4] In short, the conditions of production characteristic of Hollywood studios meant that Dali did not enjoy the individualism and creative freedom typical of fine-art practice and independent film-making.

Besides collaborating with Buñuel, Dali had written articles on the history of the cinema and a scenario for a film of his own. As a young man he had been unimpressed by the cinematic experiments of European avant-garde artists, that is, abstract films. He had preferred American movies, in particular the 'surreal' comedies of Max Sennett, Harry Langdon and the Marx Brothers. In 1937 Dali had visited Hollywood to paint Harpo Marx's portrait and to work with him on a script for a film to be entitled *Giraffes on Horseback Salad*. Then, in 1939, he had paid homage to one of Hollywood's most famous child stars with the painting *Shirley Temple, the youngest sacred monster of the cinema*. He had also designed, during the 1930s, a sofa in the shape of Mae West's lips and an interior based upon her face (*The face of Mae West – usable as a surrealist apartment* [1934–5]). Clearly, Dali was keenly interested in popular cinema before popular cinema became interested in him.

After some haggling with Selznick, Dali agreed to work on *Spellbound* for a fee of $4,000. He is reported to have generated more than a hundred sketches and five black-and-white oil paintings.[5] These were delivered in June 1944 and Dali later spent about a month in Hollywood (most of September and early October 1944). Dali's extravagant ideas included a proposal to use fifteen grand pianos loaded with sculptures suspended over the heads of dancing couples 'immobilised in exalted poses' in a speeded-up perspective that 'disappeared into an infinite darkness'.

Dali's designs were passed to Basevi, the studio's set designer. A first costing yielded a figure of $150,000; Selznick considered this excessive and so the budget was drastically reduced to $20,000 (the total cost of *Spellbound* was $1.6 million and it earned $7 million at the box office, so it made a healthy profit). As already indicated, Hitchcock's original intention had been to shoot the dream sequence in sunshine in order to achieve the sharp-focus effect he wanted but, for reasons of convenience and economy, the sequence was in the end shot in studios. Rex Wimpy, a trick photographer, was Hitchcock's cameraman, and he shot fifteen minutes of film relating to the dream sequence. Selznick was unhappy with the results and employed William Cameron Menzies for a time to photograph additional footage using sets, miniatures and rear projection. Menzies shot the gambling-house section and the rooftop miniatures.

It was common practice in those days for studios to edit the picture once shooting was over. Hitchcock's involvement in the final cut of the film was, therefore, minimal. Selznick took charge and ordered more work on the dream sequence.[6] Although he was dissatisfied, he did not blame Dali. Work on the troublesome sequence continued into January 1945; the retakes contributed to the long delay in the film's release.

A dream sequence lasting fifteen minutes in a mainstream movie would have been truly remarkable and so one is not surprised to learn that Selznick considered it much too long and complicated and that he decided to cut it during post-production to under two minutes. Bergman, in retrospect, regretted the loss: in her memoirs she recalls the hard work that went into the 'beautiful' dream scenes.[7] For one scene she was covered in plaster to become a flying statue of a Grecian Goddess with an arrow piercing her neck; a death mask was also made; the plaster cracked to reveal the real woman underneath (which according to Bergman meant that the film had to be run backwards so that she could be seen to be breaking out of it) while the mask splintered releasing streams of ants. The ants and much more were lost on the cutting room floor.

Before discussing the actual content of the dream in the completed movie, a reminder of the plot. *Spellbound* centres around a mental asylum called 'Green Manors'. Peck arrives there as Dr Edwards, the new head doctor, even though he is really John Ballantine. Bergman plays the part of Dr Constance Peterson, a straight-laced psychiatrist on the staff. She soon notices that Ballantine exhibits signs of mental disturbance and as she treats him she falls in love with him (thus breaking the psychiatrist's rule about avoiding counter-transference). It emerges that Ballantine is suffering from amnesia and that he fears he has committed a murder: he may have killed the real new head of the hospital and taken his identity. Dr Edwards has in fact been murdered but not by Ballantine. Constance becomes convinced that Ballantine's illness can be traced back to a guilt complex dating from childhood (we later discover he has suppressed the memory of a childhood accident in which he killed his brother). He suffers from nightmares and the plot requires their decipherment to resolve the mystery and to identify the real killer of Dr Edwards. In the scenes preceding the dream sequence, Ballantine and Constance take refuge from the police in the home of Brulov (Constance's friend and teacher; the part was played by Michael Chekhov). While Constance sleeps, Ballantine picks up an old-fashioned straight-edge razor to shave but then becomes hallucinated by the whiteness of the shaving cream and the bathroom fittings; he enters the darkened room where Constance lies in bed; as he stands by the bed holding the razor in his right hand, he poses a threat of violence and sexual violation. This scene resembles the prologue of *Un Chien Andalou* where a smoking man (Buñuel, in fact) is shown gleefully sharpening a razor and testing it on his thumb-nail; later on in the film a woman is pursued and menaced by a lustful man (Pierre Batcheff). Ballantine does not molest Constance; instead he goes downstairs where Brulov is waiting in his study. Shortly afterwards, Constance and Brulov listen while Ballantine recalls his nightmares. Strictly speaking, therefore, the dream episodes in *Spellbound* are flashbacks, recollections of dreams.

Selznick made Peck/Ballantine give a verbal description of everything that happens visually in the dream passages because he was afraid that otherwise the audience would not be able to follow them. In Leonard Leff's opinion 'the heavy narration demotes the images to illustrations' and undermines Hitchcock's subjective shooting (that is, showing what the character saw). In justification one could argue that the voice-over commentary is logical because Ballantine is telling the story of the dream to the two 'dream detectives'.

The film's dream sequence is presented in three short episodes lasting approx thirty-five seconds, twenty seconds and forty seconds.

24 **Salvador Dali, 'The Eye', study for *Spellbound*, 1944**

To begin, the camera closes in on Ballantine's face and then dissolves into the first part of the dream – a close up of a single large eye. Ballantine recalls a gambling house with no walls but with drapes hanging from the ceiling. The drapes have enormous eyes painted on them. Again the camera zooms forwards into the set to draw the viewer into the dream – a device repeated in all three episodes. While people play cards at tables, a man goes around cutting through the painted eyes with a gigantic pair of scissors. We then return to the study where the two psychiatrists compare notes and proffer off-the-cuff interpretations.

Anyone who has seen *Un Chien Andalou* will remember the horrific shots of a razor slicing open what appears to be a woman's eyeball while clouds cut across the face of the moon – here is surely the origin of the painted eyes cut with scissors in *Spellbound*. Typically, the disturbing content of the surrealist film was transformed in the Hollywood movie into something much milder and safer. The similarities between certain parts of *Spellbound* and *Un Chien Andalou* are so striking one is driven to conclude that Hitchcock was influenced by Buñuel's and Dali's film at the scriptwriting stage, even before Dali made his contribution. Biographies of the director confirm that he was influenced by surrealism. Indeed, Hitchcock specifically cited *Un Chien Andalou* in conjunction with certain dream and fantasy sequences in his own films.

Also in the first dream episode, a semi-naked female wanders around kissing the gamblers. Brulov claims the she is simply an expression of Ballantine's desire for Constance. By means of dissolves and superimposition the scene appears to take place within the iris of an eye. One of Dali's most striking painted studies was used as a backdrop at this point: a painting called *The Eye* showing a disembodied eyeball floating in the sky above a desert landscape. The image of an eye is an ancient motif as far as artists are concerned. It was also a significant object/symbol for many surrealist artists and poets, witness René Magritte's painting *The False Mirror* (1928) and Georges Bataille's *Histoire de l'Oeil* (1928). Bataille's pornographic 'masterpiece' was one of Dali's favourite books. (Later on in the dream sequence, Dali introduces a pyramid; freemasons employ the eye and pyramid as symbols and they appear on the Great Seal of the United States.) In *Spellbound* the analysts Constance and Brulov interpret the eyes as the guards of Green Manors. The strange behaviour of the scissor-man is, therefore, a sign he was one of the patients.

In the second part of the dream Ballantine plays cards with a bearded man sitting opposite across a vast table top. The camera occupies Ballantine's point of view and his hands and cards loom large in the foreground. (Situating the viewer in this way and using over-size props such as cards, glasses of milk and guns in the foreground space are techniques Hitchcock repeats throughout the movie. Besides placing the viewer in the point of view of the protagonist, the devices establish a powerful contrast between near and far.) Ballantine plays the seven of clubs. His opponent says he has twenty-one but his cards turn out to be blank (according to the psychiatrists, the numbers of the cards are a disguised reference to the name of a New York club). Again the camera moves forward as the man with the blank cards is threatened by a 'proprietor' wearing a hood over his head so that all his facial features are blurred. This hooded man closely resembles figures that appear in Magritte's 1928 paintings *Les Amants* and *L'Histoire Centrale*. It seems reasonable to assume that Dali knew these two works.

Episode three of the dream is set in a landscape. On the left are dark cliffs with crude facial characteristics. In the middle distance rocks form an explicit head with a tree growing out of it. A large pair of pincers appear on the horizon while on the right is the sloping roof of a house with a tall chimney. Again the camera moves forward as the card player leans over the edge of the roof and falls head over heels to his death. Behind the chimney stack – out of which tree roots grow – the masked 'proprietor' lurks. In his hand he holds a small distorted wheel which he then drops. The camera pans down to it until the wheel fills the screen (with Brulov's help, Constance later interprets the sloping roof as a mountainside and the wheel as a symbolic representation of a revolver). There is a dissolve to puffs of smoke. A long shot follows in which Ballantine is seen running down the side of a pyramid pursued by the shadow of some winged creature.

Episode three obviously owes much to Dali's desert landscape paintings of the 1930s with their disembodied heads, anthropomorphised rocks and stylised clouds. In terms of their harsh black and white contrasts and cast shadows, the scenes are also indebted to the work of de Chirico. Given the fact that none of the dream was shot out of doors and the fact that effects such as dissolves and superimpositions were used, the final result was a long way from Hitchcock's original conception of a harshly realistic dream.

Those sketches and studies for the dream sequence that exist in museums and private collections today show that the film-makers did use some if not all of Dali's ideas and designs. For instance, Dali's sketches of Ballantine running down the side of the pyramid being pursued by a winged shadow was faithfully recreated in the film. One of his painted studies for the rooftop sequence was also followed in most respects.

Arguably, Dali cynically exploited his own back catalogue of paintings rather than devising something new and original. In the world of cinema certain films have been called 'exploitation movies'. This concept can be extended to the fine arts: Salvador Dali was perhaps the first exploitation artist in the sense that during his years in the United States he mined his early achievements and that of surrealism in general for cash and publicity. Warhol, a later exploitation artist, owed much to Dali's example. One way in which exploitation artists disarm criticism of their behaviour is by being absolutely brazen about their base motives: Dali frankly admitted in interviews his desire for and love of money and gold, while Warhol cheerfully expounded a philosophy of 'business art'. After 1940, 'selling out' became a way of life for Salvador Dali.

A comparison of *Un Chien Andalou* and *Spellbound* reveals the crucial differences between authentic surrealism and the sanitised, watered-down version retailed by Hollywood. *Un Chien Andalou* lasts only seventeen minutes; its speed and economy are very striking. *Spellbound*, in comparison, seems slow and ponderous. Although Dali and Buñuel drew on residues from their own dreams, their film did not simply recount a particular dream, rather it was constructed in a way analogous to dreams.[8] *Un Chien Andalou* was fantastic, anarchic, cruel, disturbing and immoral. In terms of its content, everything was intended to be irrational, consequently the film was designed to resist logical explanations (of course, this has not prevented film theorists from producing extremely detailed and erudite interpretations of its meanings). According to Buñuel, the film was conceived as 'a desperate and passionate appeal to murder'; its intention was 'to provoke in the spectator instinctive reactions of attraction and repulsion'. In its rejection of rationality and conventional standards of morality such a film would have outraged the censors of Hollywood in the 1940s, and in its depiction of the relations between men and women as one of mad lust it would have alienated the mass public.

In contrast, the whole purpose of *Spellbound* was to restore order, to normalise, that is, to provide a rational interpretation of the nightmare, to heal Ballantine, to clear up a murder, and to resolve all the initial problems and tensions in the flowering of romantic love between the hero and heroine. By the end of the movie Constance has helped Ballantine undergo a cathartic cure (during a dash down a ski slope) and has decoded the whole dream and explained all its symbolism. The makers of *Un Chien Andalou* had completely different intentions for, according to them, nothing in their film symbolised anything. As far as Selznick was concerned, psychoanalysis was a talking cure, whereas for the surrealists it was a key to unlock the door of the unconscious. In his memoirs, Buñuel acknowledges a debt to Freud but, citing unhappy encounters with psychoanalysts in the United States, he dismisses psychoanalysis as 'a form of therapy reserved for the upper classes' (because of its high cost).[9] Buñuel had nothing but contempt for an American psychoanalyst who had viewed *Un Chien Andalou* and been horrified by it. Buñuel wondered how such a person could cope with the actual contents of the unconscious.

Spellbound is a significant instance of the interaction between modern art and the mass media (and also between European high culture and American popular culture) which has taken place throughout the twentieth century. As far as Dali, Hitchcock and Selznick were concerned, there was a mutual benefit to be gained from the transaction (on the whole the film was received favourably and it succeeded at the box office), but from the standpoint of the radical poetic and political ambitions of the original surrealist movement, the film was simply another example of the recuperation and de-politicisation of modern art by the culture industry. The film may have served to popularise psychoanalysis and a facet of surrealism, but its construction still maintained a sharp division between the world of dreams and the real world, whereas the aims of the original, left-wing surrealists had been to shatter the barrier between the conscious and the unconscious, between the inner, subjective realm of dreams and the outer, objective world, and to further the revolutionary cause of the proletariat by taking desires for reality.

Can anything be said in favour of *Spellbound* as against *Un Chien Andalou*? As a genre picture – a mystery and romance entertainment movie – it has many fine qualities and original touches. It is also a sufficiently complex film to have prompted at least one subtle psychoanalytic review by William Van Wert.[10] From a feminist perspective, the most positive aspect of *Spellbound* is the leading female character: despite the tension in the part between Constance's nature as a woman and her professional role as a doctor (the alternating roles are signified in the film, according to Van Wert, by the putting on and taking off of spectacles), she is shown to be caring, intelligent, resourceful and brave.[11] It is she who protects Ballantine, solves the mystery and, in the final scenes, confronts the real murderer.

In contrast, women in *Un Chien Andalou* are simply the passive or frightened objects of male brutality and lust: women are treated with sadistic cruelty (an attack with a razor and sexual harassment). In retrospect it seems clear that the male surrealists, in abandoning the repression Freud considered essential to civilisation, were willing to tolerate the release of all kinds of sinister, masculine erotic fantasies and behaviour.[12] No doubt they would argue that it was better to sublimate such desires in art than to suppress them, and that feeding back those fantasies to the public was a confrontational and subversive act, but today – in the light of critiques of pornography – we are not so certain of the social value of such images.

IV

ARTISTS' FILMS AND ARTS DOCUMENTARIES

17 Artists' films

Film's status as art has always been problematic. The cinema emerged in the 1890s, hence it was a latecomer as far as the fine arts were concerned. Furthermore, its reliance on mechanical reproduction, industrial methods of production, its blatantly commercial character and function as popular entertainment, militated against its acceptance as an art form. Subsequently, of course, a small fraction of films came to be regarded as works of art and the concept of 'art cinema' was established. Film as fine art is something different; it results from the fact that some visual artists have acquired cameras and made films.

Writers on artists' films have tended to discuss them as part of the categories avant-garde/independent cinema and abstract/creative/experimental/poetic/structural-materialist/underground/visionary film. For the purpose of this text, 'artists' will be defined as those recognised as such by the art world. These individuals have generally been trained at art school (film and video departments are to be found in a number of art colleges), have created paintings and sculptures as well as films, have exhibited in art galleries and museums, and have been reviewed in the art press.

During the twentieth century a considerable number of artists, designers and photographers have made films at some point in their careers. The list includes Marcel Duchamp, Hans Richter, Man Ray, Salvador Dali, Fernand Léger, László Moholy-Nagy, Joseph Cornell, Bruce Connor, Yoko Ono, Andy Warhol, Eduardo Paolozzi, Bruce Lacey, John Latham, Stuart Brisley, Derek Boshier, David Dye and Gilbert & George. A much smaller number have made film their principal medium of expression: Peter Gidal, William Raban, Mike Dunford and Malcolm Le Grice are four British examples who spring to mind. Some artists, like Walter Ruttmann, Viking Eggeling, Robert Breer, Paul Sharits, Ed Emshwiller, George Landow, Derek Jarman and Peter Greenaway, switched their allegiance from painting to film while others, like the surrealist Luis Buñuel, made cinematic contributions to a radical modern art movement before gravitating towards mainstream cinema.

Artists' films are identifiable by their makers' artistic status, by certain formal characteristics, and by their particular modes of production and distribution. Unlike mainstream movies which involve the labour of large teams of people, artists' films tend to be work of one person (or a small group) – they are thus highly personal or individualistic. Often they are filmic extensions of the artist's aesthetic concerns as articulated in drawing, painting or sculpture. This means they are unlikely to make sense to viewers unfamiliar with the artist's oeuvre as a whole or with the aesthetic programme of the art movement to which he or she subscribes. Some historians have classified artists' films in terms of art movements: abstraction, cubist, futurist, surrealist, pop, minimalist, etc. There are also instances of film and art directors being influenced by the style of a major art movement. A well-known example is expressionism: Karl Grune's *Die Strasse* (1923) even had sets designed by the German expressionist painter Ludwig Meidner.

Most artists' films are shot on 8mm, Super-8mm, 16mm and Super-16mm rather than 35mm. Budgets are extremely modest and the films are funded by the artists themselves, by their parents, by wealthy private patrons, or by grants from public organisations such as arts councils. The Arts Council of Great Britain was founded to promote the arts and the public's appreciation of them at the end of the Second World War, but it did not begin to fund artists' films until 1969. Three years later it established an artists' film committee to vet grant applications. For a time, the British Film Institute also set aside funds for experimental films. Support for artists' films began much earlier in the United States: the Museum of Modern Art in New York began collecting and distributing them in 1937. From time to time avant-garde film-makers have founded self-help groups and co-operatives in order to exhibit, sell and distribute their work.

Modern artists are more interested in experimenting with techniques and the form and content of films, with addressing issues of duration, perception and representation, than in telling dramatic stories performed by professional actors. Indeed, much artist film-making can be regarded as a meta-discourse on the nature of film as film. (However, it should be remembered that technical innovation and formal experimentation have also occurred throughout the history of mainstream cinema.) Artists' films frequently refer to the history of the fine-arts rather than to the history of motion pictures. The arts of painting and sculpture involve the direct physical manipulation of certain materials, hence film-makers emerging from a fine arts background are more willing than other movie makers to alter the film itself; for instance, by scratching or painting on the celluloid. (The European pioneers of abstract films such as Richter, Ruttmann and Eggeling are normally discussed in histories of experimental animation.) Innovators have even made films using no lenses and resprocketed a filmstrip with the aid of a sewing machine.

Artists whose work involves live performances – for instance, Stuart Brisley, the Viennese Aktionismus group, Gilbert & George – have often resorted to film as a way of obtaining a permanent record of their activities. Such films could be considered arts documentaries, but the close involvement of the artists in the film-making process normally ensures that they remain artists' films rather than arts documentaries.

Typically, artists' films are more self-referential and intellectually demanding than mainstream movies; entertaining the audience is not a prime objective. Indeed, the values of art and entertainment are seen by many artist film-makers as mutually exclusive; their aims are to challenge the expectations of viewers and to subvert the narrative codes and visual grammar of mainstream commercial cinema. The existence and character of experimental film-making cannot be understood except in relation to the background presence of dominant cinema.

Artists' films are not normally encountered in high-street and suburban cinemas; instead they are shown at festivals, during happenings, in private art galleries, art-house cinemas, museums, arts labs, film societies and co-ops, college circuits and art schools and, occasionally, on television. Their projection sometimes involves mixed-media installations that are site-specific; in these cases normal methods of distribution via cinema chains are out of the question. Nevertheless, many artists' films are of the conventional type and there are organisations that distribute them. In Britain the Arts Council published a catalogue of artists' films available for hire (subsequently the distribution agency became Concord Films). Art school lecturers were one group who made regular use of this service.

From a Hollywood studio's point of view, artists' films are non-commercial, minority products. Frequently they earn no money for their makers. In general, fine artists make films for personal reasons, that is in order to satisfy their own desires and interests; consequently, they make little or no effort to conform to the major established cinematic genres or to appeal to mass audiences; they are content with peer-group approval and small specialist audiences. Some critics, irritated by the refusal of artists to imitate Hollywood production values, have accused artists' films of being poorly made, pretentious, self-indulgent, elitist, obscure, difficult, boring and unpleasurable. In many instances these criticisms are justified, but some of these characteristics are inevitable given the aim of most artist film-makers to generate a critical alternative or 'antidote' to Hollywood-type films.

The specialist nature of artists' films does not mean that they never have a public impact. When Buñuel's and Dali's *Un Chien Andalou* (1929) was screened in Paris it proved a box-office success despite the fact that some viewers complained to the police that it was cruel and obscene. Audiences may have been shocked by the violence and eroticism of the imagery, but they were certainly not bored. Most commercial movies of the 1920s and 1930s have been forgotten and are no longer screened whereas *Un Chien Andalou* is still being shown. Hollywood studios hope their films will be instantly popular so that they can recover the millions of dollars they have invested, but in the fine arts popularity may take decades to achieve. There are many instances of works of art that began by being known to a handful of people but which much later became known to millions.

Alfred Hitchcock's acknowledgement of the influence of surrealist cinema on his own work is another instance of the wider effects of artists' films. As histories of the interaction between the fine arts and the mass media have demonstrated, sooner or later the ideas and innovations of fine artists percolate through to the mass media of film, advertising and television. Arguably, artists' films perform a 'research and development' function in respect of the mass media (in spite of their avowedly oppositional stance). As in pure scientific research, it is inevitable that there are many failures and dead ends.

Given the large number of artists' films that have been produced in Europe, the Soviet Union, Japan, Australia, north and south America since the 1920s, a comprehensive survey is impossible in one chapter. For this reason, I propose to discuss the films of two important artists – one a European working in the first half of the twentieth century and one an American working in the second half – in order to flesh out the points made above.

Moholy-Nagy

László Moholy-Nagy (1895–1946) was a Hungarian avant-garde artist who had an international career: he worked in Germany, France, Britain and the United States. An enthusiastic educationalist, he taught at the Bauhaus and later established his own Institute of Design in Chicago. By the end of his life he had become one of the major figures of modern art. What was remarkable about him was his versatility and adaptability, his willingness to experiment with a wide range of media: painting, photography, sculpture, kinetics, architecture and film. In addition, he designed industrial products, theatre sets and shop-window displays and wrote and designed books. As one might expect, Moholy-Nagy was against specialisation. He had an optimistic, utopian, totalising vision and was a fervent believer in the revolutionary potential of modern art, design and technology.

One of Moholy-Nagy's books is entitled *Painting, Photography, Film* (it was first published in German in the 1920s); the sequence of terms implies a technological and historical progression. He became convinced that easel painting was outmoded and that painters should become film-makers. In the ten-year period 1926–36 he made eleven films. *Light Display: Black–White–Grey* (1930), made with the aid of his wife Sybil, is only a few minutes long. It depicts a machine constructed from an electric motor, chain belts, coloured light bulbs, perforated sheets of metal, wood and transparent plastic. It evolved during the period 1922–30 and was called *The Light-Space Modulator* (Busch-Reisinger Museum, Harvard University). This five-foot-high kinetic device was made with the help of an engineer and a German electrical company (AEG) and shown at the Deutscher Werkbund exhibition held in Paris in 1930. It was intended as a receiver and transmitter of light; in a darkened room the machine rotated, reflected and deflected coloured lights projected on to it, and cast changing patterns of

25 **László Moholy-Nagy, 'Light space Modulator', 1923–30**

26 [*facing*] **Frames from *Light Display: Black – White – Grey*, 1930**

shadows. The artist envisaged such light displays as forms of public entertainment akin to fountains.

Moholy-Nagy's writings on film reveal an obsession with the play of light and colour (he had hoped to make the film in colour but had to be content with black-and-white). According to him, the purpose of the medium of film should not be limited to showing dramatic action and to reportage; it should permit the creative exploration of the essential characteristics of the medium which were, in his opinion, light, motion and sound. *Light Display* is a film recording the operation of a real apparatus – a machine for painting with light – but it probably seems abstract to new viewers and it is certainly an example of formal experimentation. A screening of *Light Display* took place in 1932 at the Film Society in London. John Grierson, the documentary film-maker, acquired rights to it and used clips from it in various films and trailers: it is to be glimpsed in a 1933 telephone film entitled *The Coming of the Dial*.[1]

Paradoxically, Moholy-Nagy's commitment to the artistic use of film did not prevent him from making other films that were naturalistic studies of cityscapes and social documentary-type subjects, for example, Berlin; gipsies; the old-port district of Marseilles; the life of lobsters; the new architecture at the London Zoo. Moholy-Nagy's abundant writings include a number of scenarios for films including one that is surrealist in character.

In 1932 he penned a highly critical open letter to the film industry (published in English in 1934 in *Sight and Sound*) in which he blamed commerce for a decline in the cinema. Business, the pursuit of profit, he claimed, had driven out art and excluded experimenters and independent film-makers. He demanded that experimenters be freed from censorship and taxation and be given allowances and access to production and distribution facilities and educational institutions. What he wanted did not really come to pass in Britain until the 1960s. Arguably, the light displays he envisaged in the 1930s also found their fulfilment in the 1960s, that is, in the multi-media discos (with their coloured lights projected on to revolving mirrored balls) and the rock concerts of the period.

Another intriguing aspect of Moholy-Nagy's film experience was the contact he had in London with the mainstream film producer and director Alexander Korda (a fellow Hungarian) who was planning the science fiction film *Things to Come* (1936). Korda had seen and been impressed by *Light Display*, and he wanted a special light effect for his movie. He therefore commissioned Moholy-Nagy to construct some models of sets for the film. Apparently some sequences of special effects were shot but in the end they were not used. (The actual set designer for *Things to Come* was Vincent Korda, the director's artist-brother.) Photographs of the models reveal that Moholy-Nagy constructed futuristic cityscapes from metal, plastic and glass. There was an emphasis on contour and perforation, space frames and lightweight geometric structures, some of which were suspended in space. Transparency and light were again very much in evidence.

Moholy-Nagy's excursions into film-making reflected both the diversity of his interests and the diversity of the situations and commissions he encountered as an itinerant avant-garde artist-designer. As we have seen, in the 1930s his films evoked a response in the British cinema world, but today they are little known and little seen.

Warhol

Although the aesthetic quality and ethical value of Andy Warhol's art is a matter of debate, there is no doubt that he was one of the most significant artists of the second half of the twentieth century. Warhol (1928–87) is best known as a pop painter but in fact he produced work in many media including film and video. In 1963 he began to concentrate his attention on film-making because, he said, it was easier than painting. At the time his policy was to 'expand sideways' in order to achieve fame in as many fields as possible. Using money earned from the sale of his pop pictures, Warhol funded his own films. At first they were made very cheaply and it was some years before he began to see a financial return on his investment. Operating from the silver-foil-covered space of the Factory, in New York, he parodied the practices of Hollywood studios by churning out films with 'superstars' selected from among his exhibitionist friends. For a time everyone who visited the studio was offered a 'screen test'. Warhol and his assistants were highly productive: filmographies list over sixty films made between 1963 and 1968. Hollywood studios take months or even years to shoot a film; Warhol thought nothing of making one in a day.

Warhol's interest in the cinema was long standing. Since childhood he had been attracted by the fame and glamour of movie stars like

Garbo and Harlow; as an adult he took a perverse pleasure in watching 'bad' movies, both mainstream and underground. His pop paintings had included homages to movie stars such as Marilyn Monroe, Elizabeth Taylor, Natalie Wood, Warren Beatty, Marlon Brando and James Cagney. There was also something filmic about the repeated strips of nearly identical images that criss-crossed many of his canvases. Warhol, the voyeur, the man who wanted to be like a machine, placed a machine – the film camera – between himself and reality. He was obsessed with recording and documenting daily life, in particular the bohemian milieu of the Factory. No artist's studio in the history of the world has received so much attention from its master or the public. The film camera made the process of documentation easier.

As an artist Warhol thrived in the space between popular culture and avant-garde art: his paintings combined images culled from the mass media with formal structures derived from minimal and abstract art (there was also an anti-art, dada-like element and a strong emphasis on the conceptual). Similarly, his films related both to Hollywood cinema and to underground films. During the 1960s New York became the centre of a thriving underground film movement. Warhol himself called his films 'experimental' and subsequently they have been included in histories of the movement. At the time Warhol was recognised by the leading figures of the New American Cinema (for example, the film-maker and critic Jonas Mekas), even though some underground movie makers (for example, Stan Brakhage) found his films hard to accept. 'Underground' in this context can be taken to refer both to experimental films by independent film-makers and to porn movies shown in the red-light districts of New York. Warhol, the man, was a homosexual with a camp sensibility. As Peter Wollen has pointed out, in his films Warhol combined minimalism with camp theatricality.

When he began in 1963 Warhol knew nothing about the technicalities or rules of film-making; nor did he wish to serve an apprenticeship. He re-invented the medium from zero, as it were, by making silent black-and-white movies and he then repeated the evolution of the cinema by gradually introducing camera movement, sound, colour, scripts, narrative, etc. His first camera was a motorised Bolex which took 100-foot rolls of 16mm film. A year later he purchased an Auricon newsreel camera which took 400-foot rolls; soon afterwards he purchased a yet more sophisticated camera that could take 1200-foot rolls and was capable of synchronous sound recording. A tripod with a swivel-head and a zoom lens were also acquired.

Warhol placed the Bolex in a fixed position (pans and hand-held camera movements came later), pointed it at a subject, pressed the start button and let it run. Static viewpoints, close-ups and long takes became characteristics of many of his early films. The camera simplified and automated the image-making process; it enabled Warhol to get on with other things such as phoning his press agent. When one can of film was used up he inserted another. Afterwards the reels of film were crudely spliced together. At first, therefore, the orthodox montage and editing techniques of dominant cinema were ignored. Warhol found editing tedious and lab work expensive and uncertain.

Warhol's films are curious in their mixture of similarities to and differences from Hollywood movies. Both, for instance, believed that people are the proper subject for cinema because we are all fascinated by other human beings and love to watch them unobserved. In the case of Hollywood, the people on screen are specially selected and trained ones called 'stars' who obey the orders of directors and who speak lines written by others. Warhol could not afford to hire existing stars so he invented his own. His 'superstars' were drawn from friends and hangers-on who visited the Factory regularly. Besides other artists, poets, actors, rock musicians, art critics, curators, dealers and collectors, Warhol's circle included socialites, poor little rich girls, fashion models, drug addicts and transvestites. In one sense Warhol's superstars were unknown, ordinary people, but in another sense they were special – Warhol attracted eccentrics, people who loved to talk, show off, dress up and role play. Initially, Warhol could not afford to pay his performers, so his entourage provided a pool of free labour, people willing to work for nothing for the cachet of being associated with Warhol and the promise of 'fifteen minutes of fame'.

In the beginning Warhol did not bother with scripts or rehearsals because he wanted people to be themselves. Chance and random factors were willingly accepted. This attitude was inherited from the dada movement and it was also manifested in the work of John Cage the happenings and fluxus movements of New York. The advantage of letting the camera run and run was that after a while people lost their inhibitions and behaved 'naturally'. Of course, the very presence of the camera alters reality and people act and pretend all the time, so 'being themselves' involved improvising and faking it for the camera. What was real and what was fake in this situation was one issue that intrigued Warhol and the journalists who interviewed him. Later on, scripts establishing 'situations' and 'incidents' were provided by Ronnie Tavel and Chuck Wein but Warhol still insisted 'no stories, no characters'. If what happened in front of the camera reminded him of Hollywood, he rejected it.

In spite of Warhol's interest in film as film, he did not make abstract films nor was he a formalist. His films nearly always had a human content. At the same time they differed markedly from Hollywood movies in terms of their lack of action (audiences complained that 'nothing happened'), camera movement, finish, professionalism and gripping plots, and in their inordinate – by Hollywood standards – length. In accordance with his aesthetic of acceptance, Warhol's direction of the actors was minimal. Editing was also kept to a minimum: standard-length rolls of film were just assembled like the basic units favoured by minimal artists. Camera shake, dim or harsh lighting, variable sound quality, out-of-focus footage, strobe cuts, crude zooms, dirt and scratches on the film were all welcomed by Warhol on the grounds of anti-illusionism, that is, they reminded viewers they were watching a film. The raw, primitive quality of Warhol's early films was paradoxical in the sense that it simultaneously signified artifice (this is film not reality) and realism (these are real people not professional actors, their behaviour is spontaneous).

Sleep (1963) is often cited as Warhol's first film. It is a silent, black-and-white film depicting a naked man – John Giorno – sleeping for six hours. The construction of the film turns out to be more complex than one might assume. It does not record a single night's slumber. It was made over several evenings and consists of three hours of ten-minute segments (each segment is shown twice); the camera angle was changed for each roll and therefore it focuses upon a different part of Giorno's body. Also, the film is intended to be projected at a speed of sixteen frames per second instead of the regular twenty-four frames per second. Warhol wanted to slow the film down in order to make up for the time he lost when he changed the magazine.

Clearly, this is a concept movie in the sense that the bizarre idea is crucial. Does one really need to see it? Many who saw it quickly became bored, but those who persisted reported that a different kind of attention came into play in which every detail took on a heightened significance. (Boredom is relative to the observer. To those who dislike cricket, the length and slowness of the game are intolerable.) Hollywood's treatment of time in films is false to reality because it is truncated; Warhol's was more truthful because in many instances reel time equalled real time. Clearly, this latter characteristic serves to heighten the viewer's consciousness of duration. A entertainment movie is designed to divert the mind, to provide a way of 'killing time', whereas the artist's film is designed to emphasise the passage of time. Some critics of Warhol's films equated 'dragtime' with 'drugtime'.

It could be argued that *Sleep* was also a descriptive, realist film. After all, it documented an actual event and took as long to project as a night's sleep. Where it differed from conventional social documentary films and television programmes was in its mundane subject matter and its lack of commentary and conventional editing. A banal subject, a common human experience, and yet one that is a basic necessity. The one-word titles of other films – *Eat* (1963), *Haircut* (1963), *Drunk* (1965) – indicate the extent to which Warhol took the banalities of everyday life as a starting point. Eventually, however, his films tackled more important subjects such as women's liberation.

Empire (16mm, black-and-white, silent, 1964), another of Warhol's early films, was co-directed by John Palmer and the cameraman was Jonas Mekas. The film showed the Empire State skyscraper in New York, as seen from the 44th floor of the Time-Life building, over a period of eight hours during which time there is transition from daylight to night-time. The idea is striking, eight hours in the life of . . . The subject could be regarded as a phallic symbol, as a popular icon. If one complains that such subjects are trivial, then one must also object that a Chardin still-life painting of pots and pans also features unimportant objects. Artists' films frequently relate to the history of art in a way mainstream films do not. For instance, *Empire* can be regarded as an extension of the traditional genre of western European painting – landscape (or, more precisely, townscape). Claude Monet's studies of the Cathedral at Rouen can be cited as an art-historical precedent for *Empire*. Portraiture was another traditional genre that Warhol addressed in his film-making. Henry Geldzahler, a curator friend, for example, was filmed in 1964 resting on a couch silently smoking cigars for 100 minutes.

27 **Andy Warhol, two frames from *Empire*, 1964.**
© 1992. The Andy Warhol Foundation for the Visual Arts, Inc.

We do not study a painting hanging on a living-room wall continuously for hours on end. Instead we look at it from time to time. Some of Warhol's films were like paintings in the sense that they were projected as background stimuli, as images which viewers could glance at now and then. The word 'environmental' has been used to characterise such films. The British artist-musician Brian Eno was later to extend this idea by making videotapes with images that, like a view through a window, changed very slowly.

Warhol's films were often radical and disturbing in their content as well as their form. Naked men with erections, blasphemy, foul language, heterosexual, homosexual, bisexual and sado-masochistic behaviour were all unflinchingly portrayed. Drug addicts were filmed injecting heroin into bottoms and rinsing their dirty needles in Coca Cola. 'Filthy', 'degraded' content typical of the pornography industry, the homoerotic and drug subcultures of New York were transposed by Warhol into a high-culture context. Dealers who ran galleries felt uneasy when asked to project a film like *Blow job* (1963), which depicts the face of a man for over half an hour while he is being fellated.

Certain superstars got carried away in front of the camera: in *The Chelsea Girls* (1966) Ondine, a manic, cruel drug addict, plays the part of the Pope of Greenwich Village. On camera he injects himself with drugs, confesses his homosexuality and verbally abuses a woman – Rona Page – who has come to make confession and then slaps her hard across the face. Warhol – a Catholic who attended church regularly – did not intervene, nor did he censor the scene afterwards. The artist's amorality, his refusal to condemn and judge was unnerving to people on the left as well as the right.

During the 1960s Warhol's films reached disparate audiences by being shown in various New York venues: the Factory, the Filmmakers' Cinematheque, the Bridge cinema, the New Cinema Playhouse, the Regency, Cinema Rendezvous, the Cafe au Go Go and the Washington Square Gallery. They were also seen on college campuses. *The Chelsea Girls* was Warhol's first commercially successful film and from then on his work played in art houses as well as art world and 'underground' venues.

Warhol experimented not only with the medium of film but also with the audience. He set out to see how much could they endure. Once he remarked that his films would enable members of the audience to get acquainted. When people are provoked by what they see on the screen they are likely to talk to one another. Warhol didn't mind if people booed, chatted, ate, drank, smoked or went out for a while during screenings of his movies. His films did not have to viewed continuously in the conventional manner. Their aim was not to blot out the audience's awareness of their surroundings and draw them into a world of escape and fantasy as Hollywood movies attempt to do.

Some consideration has to be paid to the way Warhol's films were presented because this was another dimension in which a difference between artists' films and most mainstream cinema emerged. The device of changing the speed of projection has already been mentioned. Warhol's films were sometimes projected two at a time side-by-side, thereby setting up contrasts of imagery, sound/silence, black-and-white/colour. Two or three reels from the same film were also projected onto a single screen so that the imagery was superimposed. (One cannot imagine a normal cinema audience tolerating superimposition for very long.) Projection was treated in a fairly casual way so that no two presentations were likely to be identical.

Since his early films were silent, Warhol engaged a rock band – the Velvet Underground plus a singer, Nico – to provide a sound accompaniment when they were first publicly screened at the Cinematheque in New York in February 1966. More elaborate mixed-media events soon followed. The 'Exploding Plastic Inevitable' (EPI) for instance, was a multi-media discotheque held in The Dom, an old Polish social club in New York, in 1967. Multiple projection of films, strobe lights and coloured filters occurred while the Velvets played and various Factory superstars performed whip dances on stage. The EPI visited several American cities but clearly a complex presentation such as this could not be reproduced very often; it could not be distributed to hundreds of cinemas in different countries the way conventional films are.

Warhol's most radical and innovative period as a film-maker was from 1963 to 1968. In 1968 he nearly died as a result of being shot by Valerie Solanas. After that he increasingly relinquished control of production to collaborators such as Paul Morrissey (who began to work with Warhol in 1965), and he permitted the films to become more conventional in their construction so that they would be more 'commercial', in fact, a half-way house between underground and overground. *Lonesome Cowboys* (1968), for instance, was shot on 16mm Eastman Colour stock but released on 35mm. Raw footage was edited down so that the film ran for 116 minutes. Filming took place at an outside location in Arizona and there was a crude storyline. The film satirised the macho values of Westerns by depicting the sexual antics of a group of gay cowboys. Since this film was a direct parody of a major Hollywood genre, it was accessible to a wide audience. Sherpix, Inc., a distributor specialising in art films with forty art-house theatres across the country, took charge of circulation.

Warhol was not content as an artist to struggle in poverty and isolation, or even to be satisfied with art world acclaim. His desire was to become as famous and powerful as the American movie and rock stars he so much admired, and to be as financially successful as many people who run their own businesses. These aims he achieved: he became a media celebrity known throughout the world and a wealthy businessman. Thus he undermined the stereotype of the artist as alienated outsider associated with figures like Gauguin and van Gogh. In 1963–4 Warhol's 'home' movies were known only to his intimates and to New Yorkers involved in the underground movie scene, but gradually, as Warhol's fame as a pop artist spread, his films or clips from them were seen globally. Young avant-garde film-makers in many countries were influenced by his work. So was mainstream cinema itself: the plot of the feature film *Midnight Cowboy* (1969) directed by John Schlesinger and starring Dustin Hoffman and Jon Voight was evidently influenced by the contents of Warhol's films; its cast even included extras drawn from Warhol's entourage. During the 1970s and 1980s several television documentaries about Warhol ensured that knowledge of his work reached many millions. Some of Warhol's films can now be bought in videotape form for home viewing, though these tend to be the later ones directed by Morrissey. (Even so, many of his films have been seen by only a few people and remain unavailable.) Although the example of Warhol is somewhat untypical, it does show that, over time, artists' films can have an impact far beyond the art world ghetto.

Warhol was fond of saying that if a film didn't make sense, then it was art. As we have seen, film as art involved other criteria: the artistic status of the film-maker, references to the history of the fine arts, radical experiments with form, content and presentation, foregrounding the material and medium of film itself. For a time Warhol was committed to films as art rather than films as entertainment and commerce but, as already explained, he eventually allowed commerce to displace art. Warhol was always a peculiar 'auteur': all his products had a distinctive brand image, yet he tried progressively to detach himself from the production process. Eventually, he made the transition from cameraman to studio head.

Much of the dynamic of experimental cinema stems from its love-hate relation with dominant cinema. But the political significance of this relationship has been the subject of much debate. For instance, in the mid 1970s Mike Dunford, a British film-maker and theorist, accused Warhol of appropriating the 'radical energy of the experimental film movement' and claimed that his emergence as a film-maker signified the movement's 'recuperation into the institutionalised radicalism of the cultural avant garde'.[2] From Dunford's left-wing revolutionary standpoint, 'the dispute between experimental film-makers and industrial film-makers' was 'a confrontation between philosophies of the same class – the bourgeoisie'. Warhol, of course, was not a leftwinger. Furthermore, overtly political subject matter rarely entered into his work (although it could be argued that his frankness about homosexuality contributed to the struggle for gay liberation). Nevertheless, for a time during the 1960s Warhol's films were subversive of both dominant cinema and dominant American values. The FBI certainly thought so: in 1968 they placed him under surveillance in order to gather evidence regarding the offence of 'interstate transportation of obscene matter'. When *Lonesome Cowboys* was screened in Atlanta in August 1969 the cinema was raided by the police. As a result of these official attentions, cuts had to made in the film and Warhol's earnings were curtailed.

18 Arts documentaries

Arts documentaries make up a small fraction of the total number of documentary films produced for the cinema during the twentieth century. Even so, there are thousands of them. In addition, many thousands of arts documentaries – shot on both film and videotape – have been made for television in recent decades. In Britain during the 1950s John Read regularly made black-and-white 35mm films about living artists for transmission on BBC television. Since another book would be required to do justice to Read's work and other arts documentaries made for television, this chapter concentrates on arts documentaries made with cinema exhibition in mind.

Films about art are usually shot on 16mm. They vary considerably in their length (they normally fall within the range ten minutes to one and a half hours). They are funded by a variety of sources: private individuals, independent production companies, cultural organisations, charitable foundations, national film agencies, museums, arts councils, television channels and businesses. As 'shorts' they have been shown as second features, but more often they have been screened in art-house cinemas, film societies, museums, arts centres and art schools. Their social purposes are to celebrate human cultural achievements, to instruct and to educate.

In the literature on film and photography, the deceptively simple term/concept 'documentary' has generated much discussion.[1] For our purposes it will be sufficient to remark that, compared to fictional features such as *The Moderns*, documentaries make a greater claim to realism and truth: in an arts documentary we expect the works of art illustrated to be genuine ones (here, of course, the film-maker is dependent on the work of attribution and authentication performed by curators, connoisseurs and art historians), we expect to see a real artist not an actor, we expect the factual content of the images and the commentary to be based on research and scholarship and to be as accurate as possible. We also anticipate that the creativity of the film-maker will be subordinated to the creativity of the artist portrayed. Nevertheless, the constructed nature of audio-visual representations – the assumptions underlying the choice of subject and the approach taken, the selectivity of the raw material, the reliance on human witnesses with fallible memories and the capacity to lie, the compression of time, the narrative organisation of sounds and images – means that not even documentaries can escape ideological determination.

Those who make arts documentaries are not normally fine artists: they tend to be photographers, film directors, critics and art historians. Their external vantage point is some guarantee of critical scrutiny and objectivity, even though most directors make films about artists they admire.

Obviously, works of art and artists are the principal subjects of arts documentaries. Let us consider first how works of art are represented. Neither the cinema nor television can duplicate exactly the experience of seeing a work of art in the flesh; nevertheless a film camera loaded with colour film is capable of recording the visual appearance of paintings, sculptures and buildings with a fair degree of verisimilitude. The cinema's reproduction of the detail and colour values of a painting is normally superior to television's. However, some documentary film-makers do not make it clear when they are filming from a slide or a photograph (via the use of a rostrum camera) rather than from the original. Some also mislead the viewer by showing details but not the whole picture. Tiny drawings can be blown up to mural scale on the cinema screen so, ideally, the film-maker should include some shots which enable the viewer to judge the actual size of the original. If the object in question has a surface texture (as in the case of van Gogh's heavily impasted Arles canvases) then angled shots are needed to reveal it.

Filming sculptures and buildings requires shots from various distances and angles to illustrate their three-dimensionality and their environmental settings. In both cases lighting is crucial because changes of illumination can radically alter the appearance of the objects in question. A raking light across a stone carving will reveal the marks left by the sculptor's chisels and the surface texture will stimulate the viewer's tactile sense. In the case of buildings, interiors as well as exteriors should be shown and evaluations of the structures' functions should be given via interviews with people who have actually lived or worked in them. Architecture needs to 'work' both aesthetically and practically; it is a poor documentary which discusses a building's style but not its performance and durability.

The film camera stands in for the viewer's eyes; in the cinema it also harnesses and directs the viewer's gaze. (When the camera's movements fail to accord with those desired by the viewer, irritation may follow.) As Philip Hayward has pointed out, during the 1940s and 1950s arts-documentary film-makers like Luciano Emmer and Enrico Gras 'concentrated on using the specific technical facilities of film technology to produce detailed readings of individual pictures which employed both close-ups to focus on individual pictorial elements and the use of pans and edited sequences to bring out dramatic tensions and/or *narrativise* elements of individual pictures'.[2] Essentially, what these film-makers did was to animate a still image by fragmenting it and then presenting the fragments in a temporal sequence. Clearly, the various fragments could be presented in different orders to tell different stories.

Lauro Venturi, a co-director of Emmer, in a theoretical article published in the 1950s which attempted to classify films on art, explained that a film-maker who begins with a close-up of a detail of a painting and who then pulls back to reveal more is able to surprise the viewer – to create a sense of suspense that is purely cinematic – compared to the opposite procedure of seeing/showing the whole picture first.[3] This example highlights the difference a cinematic representation can make compared to direct vision.

Film-makers command a battery of techniques – long shots, close-ups, tracking shots, pans, zooms, focus in/out, dissolves, freeze frame, etc. – which they can use while recording works of art. And if they so wish, they can foreground these devices during the editing process in order to make an emotional impact and to impose a particular 'reading' of an artist's work. For instance, in Alain Resnais's and Gaston Diehl's early black-and-white documentary *Van Gogh* (Paris, Pantheon Productions, 1948), camera movements across the surfaces of canvases were increased in speed until the paintings became unreadable, focus was also pulled to create blurs, and montage was accelerated as the film neared its end. Clearly, the film-makers' intention was to communicate the growing agitation and crisis in van Gogh's life through visual inscriptions (reinforced by music and commentary).

Many viewers regard such a treatment of van Gogh's work as perfectly valid and natural, but others believe it involves a melodramatic manipulation of his work dependent on a conception of art as diary, autobiography and personal expression. Film-makers who stress the subjectivity of the artist rather than the objectivity of his vision interpret the flame-like, agitated cypresses in van Gogh's St Rémy pictures as signs of the creator's mental disturbance, whereas anyone who has been to Provence and seen the effect of the Mistral wind on these trees will be impressed by van Gogh's realism. From this example, it is clear that cinematic techniques are never ideologically innocent.

Soundtracks normally accompany the images of a documentaries. There are several options: (a) silence; (b) actual sounds recorded at the time of shooting; (c) a voice-over commentary and/or music added later. In regard to the image/sound montage juxtaposition, there are two main possibilities: (a) 'anchorage': the sounds parallel the images in the sense they confirm what the viewer sees; (b) 'relay': the words or music extend meaning by supplying additional information. Clearly, sound can also be used in a contrapuntal manner to contradict the images. Most documentaries include a voice-over commentary read by an actor or the director from a prepared script. This may include the voice of the artist or quotes taken from his or her writings. Paul Cox's 1987 homage to van Gogh – *Vincent* (Illumination Films, Australia) – is a ninety-nine-minute colour film that blurs genres because it is a mix of documentary and dramatised biography. Actors appeared in this movie but van Gogh himself was not impersonated except in terms of a voice-over: the British actor John Hurt read extracts from van Gogh's letters. Hurt's voice is familiar to millions of cinemagoers and so it gave a particular flavour to the film. For some listeners the relentless monotony of Hurt's voice proved in the end somewhat tiresome. Relying on quotes from the artist naturally privileged his account of the work, thereby excluding critical or historical comment.

Besides the voice of Hurt, the soundtrack also featured music by Vivaldi, Rossini and others. Solemn classical music on the soundtrack of a film about painting is the sure sign of a 'serious', 'profound' arts film. In fact, music is a powerful, insidious and little-considered factor. Much of the time it is not registered by the conscious minds of those watching the screen. John Berger and Mike Dibb, in part one of the BBC2 television series *Ways of Seeing* (1972), set out to explain the role of silence and music in relation to shots of a painting. Extracts from different types of Italian music were cut rhythmically to details taken from a Caravaggio. What the film-makers succeeded in showing was that the kind of music chosen can easily inflect the meaning of a painting recorded on film.

Arts documentaries that concentrate on the artist rather than the work may be called 'profiles'. They can take as their subjects both dead and living artists. If footage of a famous artist of the past exists, then posthumous films can be compiled. Some of the earliest film of an artist at work was shot by Sacha Guitry in 1919: it shows Auguste Renoir, in the last year of his life, painting with a brush tied to a crippled hand. (If the artist lived before the birth of the cinema, then the preferred form is the dramatised biography or bio-pic.) Normally, however, profiles concern living artists. They usually include footage of the artist's studio and interviews with him or her and with critics.

curators, collectors, dealers, models, friends and relatives.

Several positive characteristics of the living artist's profile can be identified: first-hand information from the creator of the works about the circumstances of their making, about underlying intentions, aesthetic principles, and questions of materials, techniques, form and content. By filming the artist at work, the process of production can itself be shown. Contextual information – about the artist's appearance, dress, manner, voice, place of abode and general life style – can also be conveyed.

However, there are limitations too: when interviewed artists may prove uncommunicative or inarticulate; or they may lack insight into their own unconscious motivations. Location shooting frequently takes place in the studios of artists, but even on home ground many artists find it hard to talk sensibly in the presence of a camera-crew with their lights, microphones and cables. One recurring obstacle is the conviction many artists hold that the character of visual art cannot be adequately translated into words: 'my painting speaks for itself, if I could put it into words there would be no point in doing it'. Interviewers frequently encounter resistance to their questions for this reason. (It should be acknowledged that there is some justification for this view: each medium has a specificity which precludes a complete translation into another.) Sometimes artists interviewed on camera come across as simpletons because their intelligence finds expression through their drawing or painting not through their speech.

Artists, like non-artists, are flattered by the attention of film-makers but they can also feel uncomfortable about the interviewer's request for self-exposure and self-analysis. All interviews presuppose the subject's ability to make sense of their experiences and histories. And because time is at a premium, a whole career has to be represented by a few memories and anecdotes. Questions to artists sometimes require them to do more than talk about intentions and techniques: they also require them to engage in interpretation and evaluation – tasks normally reserved for the critic or historian. Individuals are, of course, experts on their own lives but their memories may be faulty, and they are generally much less expert on the question of the relationship between their personal experiences and the wider social and historical contexts.

In 1950 very few artists expected to be filmed. A decade later, filmed interviews with leading artists had become a matter of routine, especially in the United States. One American artist who was interviewed hundreds of times and who developed strategies for thriving in the glare of publicity – Andy Warhol – mastered the mass media and adapted them to his own purposes. When interviewed he would subvert the process by answering all questions with just 'yes','no', or with mumbles or prepared aphorisms and paradoxes. By throwing back the interviewer's queries and by denying there was any inner being to be revealed, he acted like a mirror. Once he even sent a look-a-like on a lecture tour of American campuses. These maddening tactics only served to stimulate curiosity about Warhol's persona and sex life. Capitalising on the public's fascination with celebrities, Warhol founded *Interview* magazine and began to conduct tape-recorded interviews himself.

Sometimes interviews with artists fail because the interviewer is ineffective. Clearly, the quality of the questions put to an artist is important: banal questions are likely to elicit banal replies. Interviewers need to be knowledgeable about the artist's work but at the same time to have a sense of what a less-informed audience might wish to learn. Abstract art is one of the most intractable subjects and it is rare to find an interviewer sufficiently in tune with this kind of work to be able to formulate intelligent questions. If an interviewer or director is over-friendly and over-reverential then a bland, uncritical account of the artist's work may result. There is a real risk of this because documentaries are generally made by people who are enthusiastic about the work of the artist in question and who are also dependent on the artist's co-operation and hospitality. Far too many documentaries are like extended adverts for the artist and their work. The gushing approach can also result in pretentious and portentous arts documentaries that produce derisive laughter from audiences.

The more fundamental objections to 'monographic' accounts of artists made by such left-wing scholars as Nicos Hadjinicolaou and Griselda Pollock have already been discussed. Profiles of artists are certainly open to exactly the same criticisms that have been directed towards feature films and books focussing upon individual artists: they are more or less bound to reinforce the 'auteur' conception of art.

Earlier, the value of seeing an artist at work was cited as one advantage of the artist's profile. This point will now be elaborated via a discussion of two famous examples. It would be hard to over-estimate the influence of Hans Namuth's and Paul Falkenberg's 1951 film o

Jackson Pollock (1912–56) or Henri-Georges Clouzot's 1956 film *Le Mystère Picasso*. In the 1950s certain film-makers seem to have been fascinated by the act of creation and imagined they could capture it on celluloid.

In fact, in spite of the valuable information such documentaries provide, the enigma of the creative process remains because the viewer rarely discovers the reasons for the actions recorded. For instance, we may see a painter applying a certain shade of colour to canvas but do we learn from this why that hue was chosen and not another? Films necessarily record outward behaviour, consequently they are poor at revealing inner motivation. A voice-over commentary by a critic or by the artist concerned can, of course, provide explanations of the actions recorded, but where the artist's decisions are largely habitual or intuitive, explanations may be lacking. In the case of art which is improvisational in character, the artistic decisions may be split-second ones determined primarily by what marks have already been made.

Another reason why viewers should be sceptical of such documentaries is that artists do not normally work while being filmed, consequently the very presence of the camera may cause a stilted performance. Viewers can never be certain what difference the intrusion of the film crew into the artist's studio made. As the detailed account of the shooting of Namuth's film given in Steven Naifeh's and Gregory White Smith's 1990 biography of Pollock reveals, the whole procedure was very contrived.[4] (Presumably, the most accurate record of an artist at work would result from a 'candid camera' approach, that is, filming a day's labour with a hidden camera.) Many 'creative act' films were really factions: visual records of acting performances – self-impersonations, one might say – given by artists at the behest of directors. Often the artworks generated during the course of filming were not preserved. In these instances, therefore, the creative act was simulated for the benefit of the camera.

Hans Namuth (1915–90), a German-American photographer, was noted for his photos and films of artists. He met Pollock in 1950 and persuaded him to be photographed at work in his Long Island barn-studio. Pollock must have sensed that such photos would be useful for publicity purposes. Many of Namuth's stills of Pollock in action convey his rapid movements by means of blurs. The idea for a film stemmed from Namuth's desire to capture, in a temporal medium, the painter's movement: 'the dance around the canvas, the continuous movement, the drama'. In August 1950 he made a false start by shooting seven minutes in black-and-white using a hand-held Bell & Howell 'Turret' camera of Pollock at work inside his studio.

He then persuaded a film editor, Paul Falkenberg, to act as a producer and to provide $2,000 working capital. In the Autumn Namuth shot 16mm colour footage over several weekends. To avoid the expense of lights, Pollock was shown out of doors pouring paint on canvas laid out on a concrete base near his studio. Pollock had to be directed and lots of reshooting proved necessary. A passage showing the shadow of the artist was a later simulation. The outdoor location was windy and this interfered with the fall of pigment. Minutes of painting took days to capture on film. Footage of Pollock hanging one of his drip paintings was also shot in the Betty Parsons gallery New York. Falkenberg viewed the rushes and made suggestions for further shots for use in the editing phase. For example, he advised Namuth to take close-ups of Pollock's working shoes and a discarded cigarette.

One memorable sequence was the result of Namuth lying on the floor shooting Pollock through a sheet of toughened glass serving as a canvas. (This painting – *Number 29, 1950* – is now in the National Gallery, Ottawa, Canada.) Namuth had wanted to show the artist at work but with his face in full view. In effect, Pollock is seen through his art. It was a visualisation of Pollock's stated desire to be literally in the painting.

Once location work was over, a six-minute script consisting of quotes from Pollock's previous statements about his methods was prepared by the artist, Namuth and Falkenberg. In a monotone voice, Pollock read it into a tape recorder. Finally, Morton Feldman composed some music 'as if in response to choreography'. The music was for one instrument only – a cello (played by Daniel Stern) – because of shortage of money.

Jackson Pollock was premiered at the Museum of Modern Art, New York in June 1951. In August it was also screened at the first American Art Film Festival held at Woodstock, New York State. Initially, the film seems to have met with a cool reception: a critic writing in the *New York Times* claimed that Pollock 'belittled and denigrated his own work by a precious and pretentious presentation'; George Grosz told Falkenberg in 1952 that he had promoted 'inhumanity in the arts' by filming an abstract expressionist. The documentary was subsequently made available for hire on the college circuit. There was a slow response but by 1956 – the year of Pollock's violent death in a car crash – it had been seen by thousands of students.

Although the film was only ten or eleven minutes long, it was to play a vital role in publicising Pollock's art, or at least one aspect of it: the film resulted in an lopsided appreciation of Pollock's oeuvre because it showed only some late pictures and the drip-painting technique. (Pollock scholars now insist he didn't drip the paint, he poured it.) The cinematic portrayal of the existential act of creation was a kind of visual confirmation of Harold Rosenberg's influential theory of action painting (published in *Art News* in 1952). The film's stress on the performance of the artist was also instrumental in helping to establish the genre subsequently called 'performance art'.

Namuth's pictures of Pollock as a tough but vulnerable man, a chain--smoker who dressed in worker's blue denim and paint-spattered shoes, have been seen by Ellen Landau, one of the artist's biographers, as purveying the same 'rebel hero' image as certain male film stars of the 1950s, namely James Dean, Marlon Brando and Montgomery Clift.[5] Especially telling are the moody photographs Landau juxtaposes of Pollock and Brando. Americans in the 1950s, it seems, needed a new kind of culture hero. Barbara Rose comments: 'the conversion of reality into myth, the essence of media culture, began with Namuth's documentation of Pollock painting'.[6]

In the case of Clouzot's *Le Mystère Picasso* (Filmsonor Production, 1955), there was a more or less equal partnership between film-maker and fine artist. Picasso's exceptional ability to work quickly directly from his imagination meant that works of art could be produced specifically for the camera. The film was unusual in two respects: its length (eighty-five minutes) and its technical ingenuity. The camera – operated by Claude Renoir – faced the back of the artist's easel. Picasso worked with inks that bled through sheets of white paper that were filmed from behind. The result was that Picasso's marks appeared on the cinema screen as if by magic. The audience was allowed to follow the evolution of a work of art through all its stages. Only later in the film did another camera placed at right angles to the easel make visible the studio set up. Clouzot – famous for his thriller *Wages of Fear* – disliked the way most films on art showed details of paintings. He believed this practice disrupted their integrity, and so he was determined to show only whole images. Hence, there was no

28 **Pablo Picasso (left) at work in *Le Mystère Picasso*, 1955–6**
© E. Quinn

camera movement and, at first, no editing of takes.

A change of tactics, however, was called for when Picasso, who had become highly involved in the filming, decided to work in oils on linen canvas. A stop-motion camera on the same side of the easel as Picasso was then used to record painstakingly each brush-stroke. Dissolves were then employed to link the separate shots. Shooting took place in studios in Nice during the heat of summer. Picasso's biographers report that the days of filming left him exhausted.

During the course of the film Picasso executes a series of drawings and paintings using such materials as charcoal, inks and oil paint. His first drawing – an artist and nude model – is made in silence apart from the scratching sound of charcoal on paper. After a slow, deliberate beginning Picasso picks up speed and starts working with washes of colour as well as line. As he does so, music composed by George Auric is introduced which matches the pace and theme of Picasso's mark making. Auric used the full gamut of sound from two pianos to full orchestra. Each piece of music was specially written to suit the visual performance in mood and length. Short periods of silence were incorporated at the end of each piece so that viewers could contemplate the completed artwork for a moment without distraction.

Watching Picasso at work one is impressed by the apparently limitless fecundity of his invention and yet time and time again he baffles by his habit of ruining or re-working perfectly satisfactory results. There seem to be no discernible criteria for deciding when a painting is finished. The effect is rather like observing someone endlessly doodle. One suspects Picasso spun out his designs to play up to the camera. There is no verbal explanation or critical commentary as such, though a few remarks are passed during the interval in which we see the studio. Picasso's ability to play infinite variations on themes derived directly from his imagination is somewhat vitiated by the clichéd, touristic nature of his iconography: Spanish bullfighting scenes for instance which are, all too predictably, accompanied on the soundtrack by Spanish guitar music.

Although the film received a prize at the Cannes Film Festival, excited critical attention in the art press, and was praised for its fusion of two media, it was a box-office failure in France and the United States. A feature-length movie about a modern artist at work was hardly likely to appeal to the mass of cinemagoers and so it was shown in art houses. Distribution agreements soon lapsed and for nearly three decades the film remained unavailable. It was shown again on television in Europe and the United States in late 1980s.

There are some arts documentaries that resemble printed biographies and bio-pics like *Lust for Life* in that they are more interested in the artist's private life and personality than in the artist's work. Of course, life and work are always interwoven but the extent to which art is autobiographical varies from artist to artist and from work to work. David Hockney is an artist whose art is more autobiographical than most. He has often depicted incidents from his own life and painted portraits of his family and close friends, and recorded the places where he has lived. He is an openly gay artist and so his imagery reflects his homosexual desires. Anyone looking at a major exhibition of his work is likely to gain a vivid impression of Hockney's sexual habits and luxurious life style. This was certainly the response of the film-maker Jack Hazan when he examined a catalogue of Hockney's work in 1970. He immediately decided he wanted to make a film about Hockney. Hazan, a heterosexual, had previously made films for television, including one about the British artist Keith Grant

29 **David Hockney being filmed in 1972 by Jack Hazan during the making of *A Bigger Splash*, 1974**

and another about the American writer James Baldwin. With fou others, he founded a production company called Solus Films.

At first, Hockney refused to co-operate but Hazan began anywa and over the next three years shot footage of the artist and his circl whenever the opportunity arose and finance permitted. (The movi was funded by Hazan who had to take out a second mortgage on hi house.) Hockney treated the episodic filming as a joke and so he wa shocked when he finally viewed *A Bigger Splash* (1974) and discovere it was a serious, ambitious movie that dealt honestly with his privat life. Afterwards, he claimed that Hazan acted 'surreptitiously disguising what he was really up to.

With the smallest possible cameracrew, Hazan shot the film c 35mm; its running time is feature length. At the time it was mac Hockney was breaking up with his long-term lover Peter Schlesinge Hazan's movie is a candid exploration of this painful event and i impact on Hockney's circle of friends. It also provides a vivid pictu of the sybaritic life style of its affluent participants. The pace of t film is slow and the narrative is fragmented but it has a cumulative strength. Some scenes were straight fly-on-the-wall documentary: a fashion show, a mock Miss World competition, Hockney being ticked off by his dealer Kasmin for not working hard enough. Several scenes reveal Hockney's photographic and painting procedures; repeatedly we see him struggling to resolve a large, poolside picture which includes the standing figure of his ex-lover in a pink jacket staring down at a submerged swimmer. Other scenes are dramatic reconstructions and dream sequences created especially for the camera. An especially lyrical scene depicts several naked young men frolicking in a swimming pool.

Peter Webb, a Hockney scholar, claims the content of the film is a mix of fact and fiction. Hockney himself thought it exaggerated the role of sex in his life: 'Sex doesn't dominate my life . . . painting does'.[7]

Hazan often brings Hockney's friends into contact with the paintings he did of them. He also recreates the tableaux vivants on which they were based. For instance, in one scene Hockney visits the New York apartment of Henry Geldzahler and discovers Henry and Christopher Scott sitting in the poses they adopted for his double portrait. Hockney speaks to them but the frozen figures do not respond. Philip French, in a review of the film, pointed out that Hockney's paintings often employ the device of the picture within the picture. He concluded: 'Hazan has seized upon this aspect of Hockney's work, putting it together with the artist's ability to make the technical problems of art do service for the emotional problems of his life. In doing so he has made a film which successfully merges its own form and style with those of its subject'.[8]

Initially, Hazan's film met with censorship because of its nude, erotic scenes and gay content, but eventually it was widely seen and appreciated.[9] From the point of view of art history, such documentaries are of questionable value, but given the inherent limitations of the genre, *A Bigger Splash* was probably the most successful and frankest exposé of an artist's private life in the history of the cinema.

An upsurge of interest in films on art occurred on both sides of the Atlantic during the 1980s. Annual and biennial festivals of films and videos on art, architecture and archaeology were established in Brussels, Barcelona, Madrid, Paris, Bordeaux and Rotterdam. Festivals were also mounted in such north American cities as Chicago and Montreal. Meanwhile, in New York, the J. Paul Getty Trust in association with the Metropolitan Museum of Art founded, in 1984, the 'Program for Art on Film'.[10] The aim of the Program is to improve the quality of film and videos about the visual arts and to enhance the public's awareness of art through the media of film and video. A 'critical inventory', that is a computer database listing 17,000 items, has been compiled; it is international in scope and serves as an information resource for those wishing to trace and hire films and videos.

In 1986 a 'production laboratory' was also founded to facilitate the making of new innovatory documentaries. Analysis of the database revealed that the majority of items were about twentieth-century art, so the laboratory decided to restrict its funding to films and videos dealing with pre-1900 subjects. As one might expect, the analysis of the database also revealed a massive bias towards Western art and English-language films dealing with the art of painting.

Conclusion

What this book has shown is that stories about fictional artists written for mass audiences began in the nineteenth century with the publication of artist-novels. In the twentieth century fictionalised biographies of real artists became bestsellers. They helped to make certain artists into popular cult figures. From the 1930s onwards it was the cinema which sporadically imitated and adapted these literary genres for the big screen and gave rise to the bio-pic celebrating the life of a famous white, male, European genius. While some of these movies were serious and sincere, they tended to reproduce, uncritically, the myths and stereotypes that had been associated with artists for centuries, and the theoretical shortcomings of the discipline of art history.

While the profit motive may not have been the primary reason for making artist-movies, the necessity to reach and entertain a popular audience meant that only a particular type of artist could serve as a subject for such films. Rational, unemotional abstract artists with uneventful private lives never stood a chance.

The film-makers' need to compress and dramatise the events of an artist's life meant that even films based on historical research involved many omissions and distortions. Historical truth is probably an impossible ideal but the irony is that those who most manipulate the past are the very ones who believe it can be faithfully reconstructed on screen if only the acting is good enough and if only enough money is spent on costumes, props and sets. As we saw, it was the British film-maker with the smallest budget – Derek Jarman – who set out in *Caravaggio* to question the validity of such illusionism.

Analysis showed that historical accuracy varied from film to film. The periods of training most artists undertake tended to be ignored by scriptwriters and the recurrent emphasis on the private lives and love affairs of artists meant that art itself had to be content with a supporting role. Comparisons between the film-maker's versions of an artist's life and historical data about that artist revealed in several cases instances of self-censorship and sanitisation. Film-makers, it would seem, are not prepared to be as frank about their subjects as biographers.

The need to show at least some works of art during the course of a movie caused considerable problems for producers and art directors. The practice of including real, copied and invented works in the same film was criticised because of the confusion it was likely to produce in the minds of those not expert enough to tell the difference.

The artist-movie genre does not include many examples. Clearly, it was never going to be as popular a genre as, say, the Western. Even so, finalising audience figures and reaching conclusions about influence in respect of movies is difficult because, after their initial run in the cinema, they can appear on television or they can be rented from video shops. Their potential to influence, in other words, still exists.

One of the most significant points confirmed by this study is the way mass-media representations of art and artists 'contaminate' the originals. For example, is it possible for anyone who has seen *The Agony and the Ecstasy* to think of Michelangelo without also evoking the image of Charlton Heston as Michelangelo? (If we had a film showing the real Michelangelo then it might be easier to separate the two.) Such superimpositions are compounded by those television art programmes which use extracts from artist-movies as if they were documentaries.

Some fine artists contributed to mainstream commercial cinema by being employed as art directors and set designers, others painted portraits and made sculptures for use as props but, as our study of the relation between Salvador Dali, Hitchcock and Selznick showed genuine collaborations between artists and Hollywood were rare and not necessarily fruitful. The lessons of *Spellbound* were that some modern artists have had no qualms about selling their artistic principles for money and that dominant cinema could use and popularise radical modern art, but only at the cost of emasculating it. However the comparison between *Spellbound* and *Un Chien Andalou* also showed that the Hollywood film was not without it virtues and the surrealist film not without its vices.

During the 1980s art-house films about artists and architects directed by the British art school graduates Jarman and Greenaway showed that the medium was capable of more complex and subtle representations. In the same decade American film-makers adopted much less reverential attitude towards the subjects of art and artists

They also recognised that many leading contemporary artists are now female. However, the focus of their attention shifted away from the figure of the artist towards the infrastructure of the art world – critics, dealers, salerooms, etc. – and to the commodity nature of art. American film-makers could not help noticing the blatant commercialism of the art worlds of New York and Los Angeles and this produced a disillusionment with the avant garde which became evident in the cynicism of their crime stories and comedies. Fine art finally lost its aura of cultural superiority in relation to the movies.

From the 1920s onwards many fine artists dabbled in film; a smaller number renounced their commitment to painting and sculpture and embraced film wholeheartedly, convinced it was the medium of the future. It was argued that artists' films were conceived in opposition to dominant cinema and that their refusal of the entertainment and production values of Hollywood-type movies meant that they were condemned to the margins. Aside perhaps from the work of Andy Warhol and Paul Morrissey, artists' films remain known only to the art world cognoscenti. During the 1960s Warhol's New York Factory parodied Hollywood film studios with their stars and assembly-line type of production, but later on his collaborator Morrissey realised that commercial viability depended upon making a compromise with industrial cinema. The films he made under the Warhol brand name, therefore, were uneasy hybrids – half Hollywood, half avant garde. Many artist film-makers were interested in formal experimentation and their discoveries in this realm did have an influence on the mass media.

Thousands of documentary films about art and artists have been produced in the twentieth century. A particularly important decade was the 1950s, both in terms of profiles of artists and also in terms of theoretical articles. What many documentary film-makers hoped to capture on film was the creative act itself. After Hans Namuth's documentary showing Jackson Pollock at work, more and more artists realised the promotional value of film to their careers. Documentaries may have been seen by small specialist audiences but over time they contributed to the steady expansion in the audience for art, particularly once television rather than the cinema had become the main means by which such films reached the public.

From 1950 onwards it was the mass medium of television which brought documentaries about art, drama-documentaries about artists and reviews of exhibitions into the homes of millions. In Britain in particular several generations of television producers took on the responsibility to inform and educate as well as to entertain: they devised factual programmes of various kinds in order to communicate knowledge about the visual arts to the public at large.

Notes

Introduction

(**1**) The term 'matte shot' has been defined by James Monaco as follows: 'A matte is a piece of film that is opaque in part of the frame area. When printed together with a normal shot it masks part of the image of that shot and allows another scene, reversely matted, to be printed in the masked-off area. If the matte changes from frame to frame, the process is called "travelling matte" or "blue screen".' The term 'chroma key' refers to an electronic, television method of melding separate images. See J. Monaco, *How to Read a Film: the Art, Technology, History and Theory of Film and Media*, New York, Oxford University Press, 1977, pp. 400, 416. In the case of *Dreams*, special visual effects were provided by Industrial Light & Magic and Den-Film Effects. The effects required the use of both film and television technologies: besides a matte camera, HDTV (High Definition Television) was also employed.

1 Introduction to Part I

(**1**) For an in-depth discussion of faction and drama-documentary see Derek Paget's *True Stories? Documentary Drama on Radio, Screen and Stage*, Manchester, Manchester University Press, 1990.
(**2**) Marcuse quoted in: B. Katz, *Herbert Marcuse and the Art of Liberation*, London, Verso, 1982, p. 41.
(**3**) J. A. Gaertner, in his useful article 'Myth and pattern in the lives of artists', *Art Journal* XXX (1), Fall, 1970, pp. 27–30, identifies a number of recurrent myths or patterns associated with the lives of artists: 1) the infant prodigy; 2) the genius who dies young; 3) the artist as bohemian; 4) the artist as madman or sick genius; 5) the decadent artist; 6) the artist as suicide; 7) the tragic artist who achieves posthumous glory; 8) the forgotten artist; 9) the great or princely artist; 10) the healthy artist; 11) the primitive artist; 12) the divinely inspired artist; 13) the artist as businessman; 14) the alienated artist; 15) the socially integrated artist. These patterns, Gaertner argues, are often 'dialectically opposed'; for example, the existence of healthy artists implies the existence of sick artists.
(**4**) There are some movies that depict female artists, most of them fictional beings: Vincente Minnelli's romantic drama *The Sandpiper* (MGM [Metro-Goldwyn-Mayer], 1965) tells the story of an independent female painter called Laura Reynolds; she was played by Elizabeth Taylor (this film also featured a male sculptor played by Charles Bronson!). During the 1980s the situation began to alter as more and more films appeared which depicted women as artists, either as main or subsidiary characters. For instance: *Frida: Naturaleza Viva* (1984), a Mexican film about Frida Kahlo directed by Paul Rosenzweig; the Canadian movie *I've Heard the Mermaids Sing* (1987) (this was directed by Patricia Rozema and concerned the relationships between three female characters – a photographer, an art dealer and a painter); the characters of Marcy and Kiki in *After Hours* (1985); the character of Chelsea Deardon in *Legal Eagles* (1986); the character of Sabina in *The Unbearable Lightness of Being* (d. Philip Kaufman, 1987); the character of Paulette in *New York Stories: Life Lessons* (1989).

2 Rembrandt

(**1**) G. Greene, *The Pleasure Dome: the Collected Film Criticism 1935–40*, London, Secker & Warburg, 1972.
(**2**) S. Callow, *Charles Laughton: a Difficult Actor*, London, Methuen, 1987, pp. 107–9.
(**3**) G. Schwartz, *Rembrandt: His Life, His Paintings*, New York, Viking, 1985, p. 363.
(**4**) G. Schwartz, *Rembrandt*, p. 364.

3 Moulin Rouge

(**1**) La Mure went to live in the United States. *Moulin Rouge* was the first novel he wrote in English. He is also the author of a novel about Mona Lisa, the subject of Leonardo's famous portrait.
(**2**) J. Huston, *An Open Book*, London, Macmillan, 1981, pp. 210–11.
(**3**) Lautrec's life and works are well documented both in terms of written material and photographs. There is also a good deal of information about his music hall subjects. For a detailed, generously illustrated, account see R. Huisman and M. Dortu, *Lautrec by Lautrec*, London, Macmillan, 1964. Two more recent publications are *The Letters of Henri de Toulouse Lautrec*, ed. Herbert Schimmel, Oxford, Oxford University Press, 1991 and the scholarly catalogue of the 1991 Hayward Gallery exhibition: *Toulouse-Lautrec*, London, South Bank Centre/Paris, Réunion des Musées Nationaux, 1991 with essays by Richard Thomson and others. The Hayward exhibition gave rise to much speculation concerning the Lautrec's character and his attitude towards the prostitutes he depicted.
(**4**) T. Pulleine, 'Obituary: John Huston', *Films and Filming*, Oct. 1987, p. 12.

4 Lust for Life

(**1**) Information on Douglas's life is drawn from Michael Munn's *Kirk Douglas*, London, Robson Books, 1985, and Kirk Douglas's *The Ragman's Son: an Autobiography*, London, Simon & Schuster, 1988.
(**2**) Douglas, *The Ragman's Son*, pp. 268, 475.
(**3**) R. Parker, 'Flashback: The Hand-in', *American Film*, XI (2), November 1985, pp. 58–60, 80.
(**4**) P. Tyler, 'Lust for lifelikeness', *Sex, Psyche, Etcetera in the Film*, Harmondsworth, Penguin Books, 1971, pp. 153–8.
(**5**) J. Berger, 'The myth of the artist', in *Artist, Critic and Teacher*, ed. A. Jacobs & P. Whannel, London, Joint Council for Education through Art, 1959, pp. 17–22.
(**6**) Berger, 'The myth of the artist'.
(**7**) A. Artaud, 'Van Gogh le suicide de la société', *Oeuvres Completes*, Paris, Gallimard, 1974.
(**8**) G. Pollock, 'Artists mythologies and media genius, madness and art history', *Screen*, XXI (3), 1980, pp. 57–96; reprinted in *Picture This*, ed. P. Hayward London, John Libbey, 1988, pp. 75–113.

5 The Agony and the Ecstasy

(**1**) J. Rovin, *The Films of Charlton Heston*, Secaucus, NJ, Citadel Press, 1977, p. 149.
(**2**) Rovin, *The Films of Charlton Heston*, p. 146.
(**3**) Rovin, *The Films of Charlton Heston*, p. 146.
(**4**) E. Kris, *Psychoanalytic Explorations in Art*, London, Allen & Unwin, 1953, p. 47.
(**5**) N. Wapshott, *The Man Between: a Biography of Carol Reed*, London, Chatto &

18 **Arts Documentaries**

(**1**) John Grierson's definition of documentary as 'the creative interpretation of actuality' has become famous. Three publications concerned with different facets of documentary are: William Stott's *Documentary Expression and Thirties America*, New York, Oxford University Press, 1973; Dai Vaughan's *Television Documentary Usage*, London, British Film Institute, 1976; and Paul Swann's *The British Documentary Film Movement 1926–46*, Cambridge, Cambridge University Press, 1990.
(**2**) P. Hayward, 'Beyond reproduction' *Block*, (14), 1988, pp. 55–9.
(**3**) L. Venturi, 'Films on art: an attempt at classification' *Quarterly of Film, Radio and Television*, Summer 1953, pp. 385–91.
(**4**) S. Naifeh & G. White Smith, *Jackson Pollock: an American Saga*, London, Barrie & Jenkins, 1990. See also H. Namuth's *Pollock Painting*, ed B. Rose, New York, Agrinde Publications, 1980.
(**5**) E. Landau, *Jackson Pollock*, New York, Abrams, 1989.
(**6**) H. Namuth, *Pollock Painting*, introduction.
(**7**) 'I didn't want to be a movie star' *Time Out*, April 11–17, 1975, p. 9 (interview with David Hockney).
(**8**) P. French, 'A Bigger Splash' *Sight and Sound*, 44 (2), Spring 1975, pp. 120–1.
(**9**) A more detailed account of *A Bigger Splash* can be found in Peter Webb's biography *Portrait of David Hockney*, London, Chatto & Windus, 1988.
(**10**) Information about the Program has been kindly supplied by special consultant Nadine Covert. The address of the Program is 980 Madison Avenue, New York, NY 10021, USA.

Bibliography

General

Appleyard, B. *The Culture Club: Crisis in the Arts*, London, Faber & Faber, 1984.
Armes, R. *On Video*, London, Routledge, 1988.
Aumont, J. *L'Oeil Interminable: Cinéma et Peinture*, Paris, Séguier, 1989.
Balzac, H. de, *The Unknown Masterpiece*, London, Caxton, 1899, first published in French in 1837.
Berger, J. 'The myth of the artist', in *Artist, Critic and Teacher*, ed. A. Jacobs & P. Whannel, London, Joint Council for Education through Art, 1959, pp. 17–22.
Booker, C. *The Neophiliacs*, London, Collins, 1969.
Bonitzer, P. *Peinture et Cinéma: Décadrages*, Paris, Seuil, 1985.
Buck, L. & Dodd, P. *Relative Values: or What's Art Worth*, London, BBC Books, 1991.
Carver, R. ed. *Ariel at Bay: Reflections on Broadcasting and the Arts, a Festschrift for Philip French*, Manchester, Carcanet, 1990.
Caughie, J. ed. *Theories of Authorship*, London, Routledge, 1981.
Donoghue, D. *The Arts without Mystery*, London, BBC, 1983, revised versions of the Reith Lectures of 1982.
Edgerton, G. ed. *Film and the Arts in Symbiosis*, Westport, CT, Greenwood Press, 1988.
Egan, C. ed. 'The "mediazation" of the Arts', *Perspectives on Film*, (4), 1983.
Fraser, G. M. *The Hollywood History of the World*, London, M. Joseph, 1988.
Gaertner, J. A. 'Myth and pattern in the lives of artists', *Art Journal*, XXX (1), Fall 1970, pp. 27–30.
Giddings, R. & others. *Screening the Novel: the Theory and Practice of Literary Dramatisation*, London, Macmillan, 1990.
Gimpel, J. *The Cult of Art: Against Art and Artists*, London, Weidenfeld & Nicolson, 1969.
Gough-Yates, K. 'Film: Robert Altman's Vincent & Theo', *Art Monthly*, (137), June 1990, pp. 28–30.
Haas, P. de. *Cinéma Intégral: de la Peinture au Cinéma dans les Années Vingt*, Paris, Ulysse, 1985.
Hayward, P. 'Beyond reproduction: art, audio-visual culture and the implications of technological media', *Block*, (14), 1988, pp. 55–9.
— —. ed. *Picture This: Media Representations of Visual Art & Artists*, London, John Libbey, 1988.
Heisner, B. 'Movie scenery and popular architecture: Morris Lapidus' Miami Beach hotels', *Postscript*, I (1), Fall 1981.
Homberger, E. & Charmley, J. eds. *The Troubled Face of Biography*, London Macmillan, 1988.
Katz, B. *Herbert Marcuse and the Art of Liberation: an Intellectual Biography*, London Verso, 1982.
Kostof, S. *The Architect: Chapters in the History of the Profession*, New York, Oxford University Press, 1977.
Kris, E. *Psychoanalytic Explorations in Art*, London: Allen & Unwin, 1953.

Kris, E.. & Kurz, O. *Legend, Myth and Magic in the Image of the Artist*, New Haven & London, Yale University Press, 1979, first published in Vienna in 1934.

Le Sueur, M. 'The use of works of art in the films by Lina Wertmuller', *Artibus et Historiae*, VI (3), 1982, pp. 151–61.

McArthur, C. *Television and History*, London, British Film Institute, 1978.

Paget, D. *True stories? Documentary Drama on Radio, Screen and Stage*, Manchester, Manchester University Press, 1990.

Pinxteren, K. & others. *Vincent van Gogh on Film and Video: a Review 1948–90*, Amsterdam, Stichting van Gogh, 1990, lists seventy-five examples!

Saint, A. *The Image of the Architect*, New Haven & London, Yale University Press, 1983.

Short, K. *Feature Films as History*, London, Croom Helm, 1981.

Smith, P. *The Historian and Film*, Cambridge, Cambridge University Press, 1976.

Sorlin, P. *The Film in History: Restaging the Past*, Oxford, Blackwell, 1980.

Thompson, J. B. *Ideology and Modern Culture: Critical Social Theory in the era of Mass Communication*, Cambridge, Polity Press, 1990.

Tyler, P. 'The artist portrayed and betrayed', in *The Three Faces of Film*, New York, Thomas Yoseloff, 1960, pp. 49–55.

— —. 'Lust for lifelikeness' & 'Megalomaniascope and "The Horse's Mouth" ', in *Sex, Psyche, Etcetera in the Film*, Harmondsworth, Penguin Books, 1971, pp. 153–8, 159–63.

Viatte, G. ed. *Peinture–Cinéma–Peinture*, Paris, Hazan, 1989.

Walters, M. *The Male Nude: a New Perspective*, London, Paddington Press, 1978.

Wittkower, R. & M. *Born under Saturn: the Character and Conduct of Artists*, New York, Random House, 1963.

Wyver, J. *The Moving Image: an International History of Film, Television and Video*, Oxford, Blackwell, 1989.

Zola, E. *The Masterpiece*, London, Paul Elek, 1959, first published in French in 1886.

2. Rembrandt

Callow, S. *Charles Laughton: a Difficult Actor*, London, Methuen, 1987.

Greene, G. *The Pleasure Dome: the Collected Film Criticism 1935–40*, London, Secker & Warburg, 1972.

Higham, C. *Charles Laughton: an Intimate Biography*, London, W. H. Allen, 1976.

Korda, M. *Charmed Lives: a Family Romance*, London, Allen Lane, 1980.

Kulik, K. *Alexander Korda: the Man who could Work Miracles*, London, W. H. Allen, 1975.

Lanchester, E. *Elsa Lanchester Herself*, New York, St Martin's Press, 1983.

Schwartz, G. *Rembrandt: His Life, His Paintings*, New York, Viking, 1985.

Singer, K. *The Laughton Story*, Philadelphia, John C. Winston, 1954.

Street, S. 'Alexander Korda, Prudential Assurance and British film finance in the 1930s', *Historical Journal of Film, Radio and Television*, VI (2), 1986, pp. 161–79.

Tabori, P. *Alexander Korda*, London, Oldbourne, 1959.

3. Moulin Rouge

Eyles, A. 'Behind the camera: Oswald Morris', *Focus on Film*, (8), 1971, pp. 28–37.

Hammen, S. *John Huston*, Boston, Mass, Twayne Publishers, 1985.

Huisman, R. & Dortu, M. *Lautrec by Lautrec*, London, Macmillan, 1964.

Huston, J. *An Open Book*, London, Macmillan, 1987.

Kaminsky, S. *John Huston: Maker of Magic*, London, Angus & Robertson, 1978.

La Mure, P. *Moulin Rouge: a Novel based on the Life of Toulouse-Lautrec*, London, Collins, 1951.
McCarty, J. *The Films of John Huston*, Secaucus, NJ, Citadel Press, 1987.
Mage, D. A. 'The way John Huston works', *Films in Review*, III (8), October 1952, pp. 393–8.
Pratley, G. *The Cinema of John Huston*, Cranbury, NJ, A. S. Barnes, 1976.
Schimmel, H. ed. *The letters of Henri de Toulouse Lautrec*, Oxford, Oxford University Press, 1991.
Thomson, R. & others. *Toulouse-Lautrec*, London, South Bank Centre/Paris, Réunion des Musées Nationaux, 1991, catalogue of an exhibition held at the Hayward Gallery, London.

4. **Lust for Life**

Berger, J. 'The myth of the artist', in *Artist, Critic, Teacher*, eds. A. Jacobs & P. Whannel, London, Joint Council for Education Through Art, 1959, pp. 17–22.
Douglas, K. *The Ragman's Son: an Autobiography*, London, Simon & Schuster, 1988.
Harvey, S. *Directed by Minnelli*, New York, Harper & Row, 1990.
Munn, M. *Kirk Douglas*, London, Robson Books, 1985.
Parker, R. 'Flashback: the hand-in', *American Film*, XI (2), November 1985, pp. 58–60, 80.
Pollock, G. 'Artists mythologies and media genius, madness and art history', *Screen*, XXI (3), 1980, pp. 57–96, reprinted in P. Hayward, ed., *Picture This*, London, John Libbey, 1988, pp. 75–113.
Preziosi, D. *Rethinking Art History: Reflections on a Coy Science*, New Haven & London, Yale University Press, 1989, pp. 21–7.
Stone, I. *Lust for Life*, New York, Longman, 1934.
Tyler, P. 'Lust for lifelikeness', in *Sex, Psyche, Etcetera in the Film*, Harmondsworth, Penguin, 1971, pp. 153–8.

5. **The Agony and the Ecstacy**

Crowther, B. *Charlton Heston: the Epic Presence*, New York, Columbus Books, 1986.
Heston, C. *The Actor's Life: Journals 1956–76*, New York, Dutton, 1979.
Moss, R. *The Films of Carol Reed*, London, Macmillan, 1987.
Rovin, J. *The Films of Charlton Heston*, Secaucus, NJ, Citadel Press, 1977.
Stone, I. *The Agony and the Ecstasy*, London, Collins, 1961.
Wapshott, N. *The Man Between: a Biography of Carol Reed*, London, Chatto & Windus, 1990.

6. **Caravaggio**

Carrier, D. 'The transfiguration of the commonplace: Caravaggio and his interpreters', *Word & Image*, III (1), January-March 1987, pp. 41–73.
Finch, M. 'Caravaggio', *Monthly Film Bulletin*, LIII (627), April 1986, pp. 99–100.
Friedlaender, W. *Caravaggio Studies*, Princeton University Press, 1955.
Januszczak, W. 'The assassination of Caravaggio', *The Guardian*, 24 April, 1986, p. 13.
Jarman, D. *Dancing Ledge*, London, Quartet Books, 1984.
——. *Derek Jarman's Caravaggio: the Complete Film Script*, London, Thames & Hudson, 1986.
O'Pray, M. 'Fierce visions: Derek Jarman', *Art Monthly*, (117), June 1988, pp. 34–6.
Posner, D. 'Caravaggio's homo-erotic early work', *Art Quarterly*, XXXIV (3), 1971,

pp. 301–24.
Prendergast, M. 'Caravaggio: the making of a dream', *Films and Filming*, (376), January 1986, pp. 27–30.
Rayns, T. 'Unnatural lighting: Derek Jarman's Caravaggio', *American Film*, XI, September 1986, pp. 44–7.
Thorton, L. 'Recreating Caravaggio', *Observer Magazine*, 20 April, 1986, pp. 42–7.
Walters, M. *The Male Nude: a New Perspective*, London, Paddington Press, 1978.

7. **The Wolf at the Door**

Andersen, W. *Gauguin's Paradise Lost*, London, Secker & Warburg, 1972.
Brettell R. & others, *The Art of Paul Gauguin*, Washington, DC, National Gallery of Art, 1988.
Danielsson, B. *Gauguin in the South Seas*, London, Allen & Unwin, 1965.
Hoog, M. *Paul Gauguin: Life and Work*, London, Thames & Hudson, 1987.
Mongan, E. & others. *Paul Gauguin: Catalogue Raisonné*, Berne, 1988.
Reiner, J. 'Film review: "Wolf at the Door"', *The Hollywood Reporter*, July 29, 1987, pp. 3 & 6.
The Wolf at the Door, Copenhagen: Dagmar Film Production, 1986, publicity booklet.
Thomson, B. *Gauguin*, London, Thames & Hudson, 1987.

8. **Camille Claudel**

Cherry, D. 'On the screen of representation: viewing Camille Claudel', *FAN*, III (2), 1989, p. 39.
Gaudichon, B. & others. *Camille Claudel*, Paris, Imprimerie Blanchard, 1984.
Gray, M. *Depardieu*, London, Sinclair-Stevenson, 1991.
Milne, T. 'Camille Claudel', *Monthly Film Bulletin*, LVI (663), April 1989, pp. 108–9.
Mitchell, C. 'Intellectuality and sexuality: Camille Claudel.' *Art History*, XII (4), December 1989, pp. 419–47.
Paris, R-M. *Camille: the Life of Camille Claudel, Rodin's Muse and Mistress*, London, Aurum Press, 1988)
Paris, R-M. & De La Chapelle, A. *L'Oeuvre de Camille Claudel*, Paris, Adam Biro, 1990.
Smyth, R. 'Love that turned to stone', *The Observer*, 5 February 1989, pp. 33–4.
Witherell, L. 'Camille Claudel rediscovered', *Women's Art Journal*, VI (1), Spring-Summer 1985, pp. 1–7.

10. **The Fountainhead**

Albrecht, D. *Designing Dreams: Modern Architecture in the Movies*, London, Thames & Hudson, 1987.
Baxter, J. *King Vidor*, New York, Monarch Press, 1976.
Brandon, B. *The Passion of Ayn Rand*, London, W. H. Allen, 1987.
Durgnat, R. 'The Fountainhead', *Film Comment* IX (5), September-October 1973, pp. 92–4.
Higham C. & Greenberg, J. 'Interview with King Vidor', in *The Celluloid Muse: Hollywood Directors Speak*, London, Angus & Robertson, 1969.
McGann, K. 'Ayn Rand in the stockyard of the spirit', in *The Modern American Novel and the Movies*, eds. G. Peary & R. Shatzkin, New York, Frederick Ungar, 1978, pp. 325–35.
Neal, P. *As I Am: an Autobiography*, London, Century Hutchinson, 1988.
Nelson, G. 'Mr Roark goes to Hollywood', *Interiors*, April 1949, pp. 110–11.

Rand, A. *The Fountainhead*, New York, Bobbs Merrill, 1943.
Petley, J. 'The architect as Übermensch', in *Picture This*, ed. P. Hayward, London, John Libbey, 1988, pp. 115–25.
Saint, A. *The Image of the Architect*, New Haven & London, Yale University Press, 1983.
Swindell, L. *The Last Hero: a Biography of Gary Cooper*, New York, Doubleday, 1980.
'The Fountainhead', *Journal of the American Institute of Architects*, July 1949, p. 27.

11. The Rebel

Hancock, F. & Nathan, D. *Hancock*, London, W. Kimber, 1969.
Holmes, A. *The Rebel*, London, Mayfair, 1961.
'The Rebel', *Monthly Film Bulletin*, XXVIII (326), March 1961, pp. 33–4.
Walker, J. A. 'The Rebel: a comic portrayal of the avant garde artist', *AND: Journal of Art & Education*, (18/19), 1989, pp. 41–4.
Warner, T. 'Tony Hancock . Matinee Idol', *Railway Cuttings*, (35), 1988, pp. 13–8.

12. The Draughtsman's Contract

Andrews, N. 'A walk through Greenaway' *Sight and Sound*, XLVIII (2), Spring 1979, pp. 94–5.
Brown, R. 'Greenaway's Contract', *Sight and Sound*, LI (1) Winter 1981/2, pp. 35–8.
— —. 'The Draughtsman's Contract', *Monthly Film Bulletin*, XLIX (586), November 1982, pp. 254–6.
Januszczak, W. 'The Draughtsman's Contract', *Studio International*, CLXLVI (999), 1983, pp. 21–3.
Watney, S. 'Gardens of speculation: landscape in "The Draughtsman's Contract"', in *Picture This*, ed. P. Hayward, London, John Libbey, 1988, pp. 183–92, previously published in *Undercut*, (7/8), Spring 1983.

13. The Belly of an Architect

Clarke, J. 'Architecture and mortality' (Interview with Peter Greenaway), *Films and Filming*, (397), October 1987, pp. 6–8.
Forbes, J. 'The Belly of an Architect', *Monthly Film Bulletin*, LIV (645), October 1987, pp. 299–300.
Greenaway, P. *The Belly of an Architect*, London, Faber & Faber, 1988.
Ranvaud, D. 'The Belly of an Architect' (Interview with Peter Greenaway), *Sight and Sound*, LVI (3), Summer 1987, pp. 193–6.
Strick, P. 'The Belly of an Architect', *Films and Filming*, (397), October 1987, pp. 29–30.

14. The American Cinema's Depiction of Art in the 1970s and 1980s

Rickey, C. 'Cinema: going SoHollywood', *Art in America*, LXXVI (7), July 1988, pp. 45–9.
Walker, J. A. 'Aesthetics of the billfold', *The Times Higher Educational Supplement*, March 17, 1989 p. 16.

15. Artworks, Dealers and Critics in Films

'Albright twins paint gruesome masterpieces', *Life*, March 27, 1944, pp. 63–70.

Combs, R. 'The Picture of Dorian Gray', *Monthly Film Bulletin*, LII (622), November 1985, pp. 355–6.
Croydon, M. *Ivan Albright*, New York, Abbeville Press, 1978[?].
Elsaesser, T. 'The Hypothesis of the stolen painting', *Monthly Film Bulletin*, LI (611), December 1984, pp. 368–9.
Ivan Albright: a Retrospective Exhibition, Chicago, Art Institute, 1964.
Van der Marck, J. 'Ivan Albright: more than meets the eye', *Art in America*, LXV (6), November-December 1977, pp. 92–9.
Wilde, O. *The Picture of Dorian Gray*, London, J. M. Dent, 1976, first published in 1890.

16. The Artist in Hollywood: *Spellbound*

Ades, D. *Dali*, London, Thames & Hudson, 1982.
Bergman, I. & Burgess, A. *Ingrid Bergman: My Story*, London, M. Joseph, 1980.
Bigwood, J. 'Solving a *Spellbound*puzzle', *American Cinematographer*, LXXII (6), June 1991, pp. 34–40.
Buñuel, L. *My Last Breath*, London, Flamingo Edition/Fontana, 1985.
Doty, A. *Alfred Hitchcock's Films of the 1940s: the Emergence of Personal Style within the American Studio System*, PhD dissertation, University of Illinois, 1984.
Dali, S. 'The Surrealist conception of "sexual freedom"' (1930) (reprinted in M. Nadeau's *The History of Surrealism*, Harmondsworth, Penguin Books, 1973, p. 305).
Drummond, P. 'Textual space in "Un Chien Andalou" ', *Screen*, XVIII (3), Autumn 1977, pp. 55–119.
Gabbard, K. & G. *Psychiatry and the Cinema*, Chicago & London, University of Chicago Press, 1987; this book surveys over 250 American films featuring psychiatrists – the earliest film mention is dated 1906.
Gassner, J. & Nichols, D. eds. *Best Film Plays 1945*, New York, Crown, 1946; includes Ben Hecht's script for *Spellbound*, pp. 57–113.
Haver, R. *David O. Selznick's Hollywood*, London, Secker & Warburg, 1980.
Hecht, B. 'Spellbound', in *Best Film Plays 1945*, eds. J. Gassner & D. Nichols, New York, Crown, 1946.
Leamer, L. *As Time Goes By: the Life of Ingrid Bergman*, London, Hamish Hamilton, 1986.
Leff, L. J. *Hitchcock & Selznick*, London, Weidenfeld & Nicolson, 1987.
Spoto, D. *The Life of Alfred Hitchcock: the Dark Side of Genius*, London, Collins, 1983.
Van Wert, W. F. 'Compositional psychoanalysis: circles and straight lines in "Spellbound"', *Film Criticism*, III (3), 1979, pp. 41–7.

17. Artists' Films

Abrahams, A. *Warhol Films*, Amsterdam, Rongwrong, 1989.
'Avant garde film', ed. S. Field & P. Sainsbury. *Afterimage*, (2), 1970, (thematic issue).
'Avant garde film in England & Europe', ed. R. Cork. *Studio International*, CXC (978), November-December 1975, (thematic issue).
Battcock, G. ed. *The New American Cinema: a Critical Anthology*, New York, Dutton, 1967.
Brakhage, S. *Film at its Wit's End: Eight Avant Garde Film-makers*, New York, McPherson & Co, 1989.
Cornwall, R. *Films by American Artists*, London, Arts Council of Great Britain, 1981.
Curtis, D. *Experimental Cinema: a Fifty Year Evolution*, London, Studio Vista, 1971.
Curtis, D. ed., *The Elusive Sign*, London, British Council, 1987.

Bibliography

Dunford, M. 'Experimental/avant garde/revolutionary film practice', *Afterimage*, (6), Summer, 1976, pp. 96–112.

Dusinberre, D. ed. *A Perspective on English Avant Garde Film*, London, Arts Council of Great Britain, 1977.

Dwoskin, S. *Film Is . . . the International Free Cinema*, London, Peter Owen, 1975.

Field, S. 'Avant garde cinema: selective bibliography', *Edinburgh '76 magazine*, (1), 1976, pp. 91–4.

Film as Film: Formal Experiment in Film 1910–75, London, Arts Council of Great Britain/Hayward Gallery Publications, 1979.

Gidal, P. *Andy Warhol Films and Paintings*, London, Studio Vista, 1971.

— —. ed. *Structural Film Anthology*, London, British Film Institute, 1976.

— —. *Materialist Film*, London, Routledge, 1989.

Hanhardt, J. & Gartenberg, J. *The Films of Andy Warhol*, New York, Whitney Museum of American Art, 1988.

Koch, S. *Stargazer: Andy Warhol's Life, World and Films*, London, Marion Boyars, 3rd ed. 1991.

Kostelanetz, R. ed. *Moholy-Nagy*, New York, Praeger, 1970.

Kuenzli, R. ed. *Dada and Surrealist Film*, New York, Willis Locker & Owens, 1988.

Kurtz, R. *Expressionismus und Film*, Zurich, Rohr, 1965.

Lawder, S. *The Cubist Cinema*, New York, University Press, 1975.

Le Grice, M. *Abstract Film and Beyond*, London, Studio Vista, 1977.

Luginbuhl, S. ed. *Cinema Underground Oggi*, Padua, Mastrogiacomo Editore, 1975.

Manvell, R. ed. *Experiment in Film*, London, Grey Walls Press, 1949; New York, Arno Press reprint, 1970.

Mathews, J. *Surrealism and Film*, Ann Arbor, Michigan, University of Michigan, 1971.

Mekas, J. *Movie Journal: the Rise of a New American Cinema 1959–71*, New York, Collier Books, 1972.

Mellencamp, P. *Indiscretions: Avant Garde Film, Video and Feminism*, Bloomington, Indiana University Press, 1990.

Moholy-Nagy, L. *Painting, Photography, Film*, London, Lund Humphries, 1969.

— —. *Vision in Motion*, Chicago, Paul Theobald, 1947.

Moholy-Nagy, S. *Moholy-Nagy: Experiment in Totality*, New York, Harpers, 1950.

O'Pray, M. ed. *Andy Warhol: Film Factory*, London, British Film Institute, 1989.

Passuth, K. *Moholy-Nagy*, London, Thames & Hudson, 1985.

Renan, S. *The Underground Film: an Introduction to its Development in America*, London, Studio Vista, 1967.

Russett, R. & Starr, C. *Experimental Animation: Origins of a New Art*, New York, Da Capo, rev. ed. 1988.

Scheugl, H. & Schmidt, E. *Eine Subgeschichte des Films: Lexicon des Avantgarde – experimental – und underground films*, 2 vols., Frankfurt, Suhrkamp, 1975.

Sitney, P. ed. *Film Culture Reader*, New York, Praeger, 1970.

— —. *Visionary Film: the American Avant Garde 1943–78*, New York, Oxford University Press, 2nd ed. 1979.

Smith, P. *Andy Warhol's Art and Films*, Ann Arbor, Michigan, UMI Research Press, 1988.

Stauffacher, F. ed. *Art in Cinema*, San Francisco Museum of Art, 1947; New York, Arno Press reprint 1969.

Tyler, P. *Underground Film: a Critical History*, London, Secker & Warburg, 1971.

Youngblood, G. *Expanded Cinema*, New York, Dutton, 1970.

18. **Arts Documentaries**

Arts Council Film Library, *Documentaries on the Arts 1980–81*, London, Arts Council, 1980.
Besemer, S. & Crosman, C. eds. *From Museums, Galleries and Studios: a Guide to Artists on Film and Tape*, Westport, CT, Greenwood Press, 1985.
Breteau, G. ed. *Abécédaire des Films sur l'Art Moderne et Contemporain 1905–1984*, Paris, Centre Georges Pompidou/Centre National des Arts Plastiques, Musée National d'Art Moderne, 1985.
Chapman, W. *Films on Art 1952*, New York, American Federation of Arts, 1952.
Covert, N. & others. *Films on Art: Bibliography*, New York, Program for Art on Film, 1990.
Films on Art: a Specialised Study, an International Catalogue, Paris, Unesco, 1949.
French, P. 'A Bigger Splash', *Sight and Sound*, XLIV (2), Spring 1975, pp. 120–1.
Hayward, P. 'Introduction', *Picture This: Media Representations of Visual Art and Artists*, London, John Libbey, 1988, pp. 1–25.
'I didn't want to be a movie star', *Time Out*, 11–17 April, 1975 p. 9 (interview with David Hockney).
Klady, L. 'Return of the centaur', (Le Mystère Picasso), *Film Comment*, XXII (2), March-April 1986, pp. 20–2.
Landau, E. *Jackson Pollock*, New York, Abrams 1989.
Leenhardt, R. 'L'évolution du film d'art', *Gazette de Beaux Arts*, VI (102), July-August 1983, pp. 42–6.
MacPherson, D. ed. *Films on Art*, New York, Watson Guptill Publications; Ottawa, Canadian Film Institute, 1977, 2nd ed. of Chapman.
Micha, R. & others, *Films on Art*, Paris, Unesco, 1949.
Minas, G. *Bildende Kunst im Film der Bundesrepublik Deutschland Ergebnisse einer Bestandsaufnahme*, Berlin, Federal Republic of Germany, Instituts für Auslandsbziehungen, Stuttgart, in collaboration with Goethe Institut Munich and Inter Nationes, Bonn, 1986.
Naifeh, S. & Smith, G. W. *Jackson Pollock: an American Saga*, London, Barrie & Jenkins, 1990.
Namuth, H. *Pollock Painting*, ed. B. Rose, New York, Agrinde Publications, 1980.
Queval, J. 'Film and fine arts', *Sight and Sound*, February 1950.
Tuchmann, M. 'Nouns, gerunds and participial adjectives: Emile de Antonio's "Painters painting"', *Studio International*, CLXXXVI (957), July-August 1973, pp. 4–6.
Venturi, L. 'Films on art: an attempt at classification', *Quarterly of Film, Radio and Television*, Summer 1953, pp. 385–91.
Walker, J. A. 'Vincent', *Alba*, (11), Spring 1989, pp. 50–3 (review of a film by Paul Cox).
Webb, P. *Portrait of David Hockney*, London, Chatto & Windus, 1988.
Wechsler, J. 'The filming of art', *Daedalus*, Fall 1985.
Whittet, G. 'Picasso on film', *The Studio*, CLV (781), April 1958, pp. 116–17.

Index